D1299953

MODERNISM AND MASCULINITY

Modernism and Masculinity investigates the varied dimensions and manifestations of masculinity in the modernist period. Thirteen essays from leading scholars reframe critical trends in modernist studies by examining distinctive features of modernist literary and cultural work through the lens of masculinity and male privilege. The volume attends to masculinity as an unstable horizon of gendered ideologies, subjectivities and representational practices, allowing for fresh inter-disciplinary treatments of celebrated and lesser-known authors, artists and theorists such as D. H. Lawrence, Ezra Pound, Henry Roth, Theodor Adorno and Paul Robeson, as well as modernist avant-garde movements such as Vorticism, surrealism and Futurism. As diverse as the masculinities that were played out across the early twentieth century, the approaches and arguments featured in this collection will appeal especially to scholars and students of modernist literature and culture, gender studies and English literature more broadly.

Natalya Lusty is Associate Professor in the Department of Gender and Cultural Studies at the University of Sydney. She is the author of *Surrealism, Feminism, Psychoanalysis* and, with Helen Groth, *Dreams and Modernity: A Cultural History*. She is currently writing a book on feminist manifestos and the history of radical feminism.

Julian Murphet is Professor in Modern Film and Literature and Director of the Centre for Modernism Studies in Australia at the University of New South Wales. His publications include *Multimedia Modernism, Literature and Visual Technologies* and *Literature and Race in Los Angeles*. He has previously co-edited books on J. M. Coetzee and Cormac McCarthy. He is the editor of the new journal in modernist studies, *Affirmations: of the modern*.

MODERNISM AND MASCULINITY

EDITED BY

NATALYA LUSTY
University of Sydney

JULIAN MURPHET
University of New South Wales

CAMBRIDGE
UNIVERSITY PRESS

LIFE UNIVERSITY LIBRARY
1269 BARCLAY CIRCLE
MARIETTA, GA 30060
770-426-2688

WITHDRAWN
LIFE UNIVERSITY
LIBRARY

CAMBRIDGE
UNIVERSITY PRESS

University Printing House, Cambridge CB2 8BS, United Kingdom

Cambridge University Press is part of the University of Cambridge.

It furthers the University's mission by disseminating knowledge in the pursuit of education, learning and research at the highest international levels of excellence.

www.cambridge.org
Information on this title: www.cambridge.org/9781107020252

© Cambridge University Press 2014

This publication is in copyright. Subject to statutory exception and to the provisions of relevant collective licensing agreements, no reproduction of any part may take place without the written permission of Cambridge University Press.

First published 2014

A catalogue record for this publication is available from the British Library

Library of Congress Cataloguing in Publication data
Modernism and Masculinity / edited by Natalya Lusty, University of Sydney ;
Julian Murphet, University of New South Wales.
pages   cm
Includes bibliographical references and index.
ISBN 978-1-107-02025-2 (hardback)
1. Modernism (Literature)   2. Masculinity in literature.   3. Modernism (Art)
I. Lusty, Natalya, editor of compilation.   II. Murphet, Julian, editor of compilation.
PN56.M54M6126   2014
809´.9112–dc23   2013044144

ISBN 978-1-107-02025-2 Hardback

Cambridge University Press has no responsibility for the persistence or accuracy of URLs for external or third-party internet websites referred to in this publication, and does not guarantee that any content on such websites is, or will remain, accurate or appropriate.

Contents

vi

Contents

Notes on Contributors

CINZIA SARTINI BLUM, Professor of Italian, holds a Laurea in Lingue e Letterature Straniere from the Università degli Studi di Firenze and a Ph.D. in Romance Studies from Cornell University. She is author of *Rewriting the Journey in Italian Literature: Figures of Subjectivity in Progress* (University of Toronto Press, 2008, winner of the 2008 AAIS Book Award) and *The Other Modernism: F. T. Marinetti's Futurist Fiction of Power* (University of California Press, 1996). She edited *Futurism and the Avant-Garde* (special issue of the *South Central Review*, 1996).

JESSICA BURSTEIN is Associate Professor in the Department of English and the Department of Gender, Women, and Sexuality Studies at the University of Washington. Her *Cold Modernism: Literature, Fashion, Art* (Pennsylvania State University Press, 2012) argues on behalf of the aesthetics of surfaces in artists and writers including Mina Loy, Coco Chanel, Balthus, Hans Bellmer and Henry James. A recipient of fellowships from the American Council of Learned Societies and the Franke Institute for the Humanities at the University of Chicago, she is a member of the editorial committee for the journal *Modernism/modernity*.

JAMES DONALD is Dean of the Faculty of Arts and Social Sciences at the University of New South Wales and President of the Board of the Centre for Modernism Studies in Australia. He is author of *Imagining the Modern City* (University of Minnesota Press, 1999) and *Sentimental Education: Schooling, Popular Culture and the Regulation of Liberty* (Verso, 1992); co-author of the *Penguin Atlas of Media and Information* (Penguin, 2001); and editor or co-editor of more than a dozen volumes, including *Thresholds: Psychoanalysis and Cultural Theory*; *'Race', Culture and Difference* (Macmillan, 1991); *Close Up, 1927–1933: Cinema and Modernism* (Princeton University Press, 1998); and the *Handbook of Film Studies* (Sage, 2008). He edited the journal *Screen Education* and founded *New Formations*. He is currently completing a monograph on the international cultural significance of Josephine Baker and Paul Robeson between the World Wars. He was elected to the Australian Academy of the Humanities in 2006.

RACHEL BLAU DUPLESSIS is Professor Emerita of English at Temple University. Recent publications are *Purple Passages: Pound, Eliot, Zukofsky, Olson, Creeley and the Ends of Patriarchal Poetry* (University of Iowa Press, 2012) and *Surge: Drafts 96–114* (Salt Publishing, 2013). She has published critical books on modernism and gender analyses, edited several anthologies, and is also known for her multi-volume long poem, *Drafts*. She has been awarded a Pew Fellowship in the Arts and a residency for poetry at Bellagio, and she has held an appointment to the National Humanities Center.

MELISSA JANE HARDIE is Senior Lecturer in the Department of English at the University of Sydney. Her recent publications include essays on *Mad Men* and middlebrow literature, Lindsay Lohan, and Kitty Genovese.

MAREN LINETT is Associate Professor of English at Purdue University. She is the author of *Modernism, Feminism, and Jewishess* (Cambridge University Press, 2007) and the editor of *Virginia Woolf: An MFS Reader* (Johns Hopkins University Press, 2009) and *The Cambridge Companion to Modernist Women Writers* (Cambridge University Press, 2010). She has published articles on modernist writers such as James Joyce, Virginia Woolf, Dorothy Richardson, Jean Rhys, Elizabeth Bowen and Rebecca West, and she is currently working on a book-length study entitled *Modernism and Disability*.

NATALYA LUSTY is Associate Professor in the Department of Gender and Cultural Studies at the University of Sydney. She is the author of *Surrealism, Feminism, Psychoanalysis* (Ashgate, 2007) and, with Helen Groth, *Dreams and Modernity: A Cultural History* (Routledge, 2013). She is currently writing a book on feminist manifestos and the history of radical feminism.

DAVID MARRIOTT teaches in the Department of the History of Consciousness, University of California, Santa Cruz. His most recent books include *In Neuter* (Equipage, 2013) and *The Bloods* (Shearsman Books, 2011). He is currently writing a book on Frantz Fanon.

RÓNÁN MCDONALD is Australian Ireland Fund Chair in Modern Irish Studies and Director of the Global Irish Studies Centre at the University of New South Wales. He is the author of *The Death of the Critic* (Continuum, 2007), *The Cambridge Introduction to Samuel Beckett* (Cambridge University Press, 2006) and *Tragedy and Irish Literature: Synge, O'Casey, Beckett* (Palgrave, 2002).

TYRUS MILLER is Professor of Literature at the University of California at Santa Cruz. He is author of *Late Modernism: Politics, Fiction, and the Arts Between the World Wars* (University of California Press, 1999); *Singular Examples: Artistic Politics and the Neo-Avant-Garde* (Northwestern University Press, 2009); and *Time Images: Alternative Temporalities in Twentieth-Century Theory, Literature, and Art* (Cambridge Scholars Publishing, 2009). He has edited *Given World and Time: Temporalities in Context* (Central European University Press, 2008) and is editor and translator of György Lukács's post–World War II Hungarian essays in *The Culture of People's Democracy: Hungarian Essays on Literature, Art, and Democratic Transition, 1945–1948* (BRILL, 2013).

JULIAN MURPHET is Professor in Modern Film and Literature, and Director of the Centre for Modernism Studies in Australia, at the University of New South Wales, where he convenes the programs in English and Film Studies. His publications include *Multimedia Modernism* (Cambridge University Press, 2009) and *Literature and Race in Los Angeles* (Cambridge University Press, 2001). He has previously co-edited books on J. M. Coetzee and Cormac McCarthy, as well as the volume *Literature and Visual Technologies* (Palgrave, 2003). He is the editor of a new journal in modernist studies, *Affirmations: of the modern*.

PETER NICHOLLS is Professor of English at New York University. His publications include *Ezra Pound: Politics, Economics and Writing* (Macmillan, 1984); *Modernisms: A Literary Guide* (University of California Press, 1995); *George Oppen and the Fate of Modernism* (Oxford University Press, 2013) and many articles and essays on literature and theory. He is currently U.S. associate editor of *Textual Practice*.

THOMAS STRYCHACZ has published numerous articles and three books on modernist literature: *Modernism, Mass Culture, and Professionalism* (Cambridge University Press 1993); *Hemingway's Theaters of Masculinity* (Louisiana State University Press, 2003) and *Dangerous Masculinities: Conrad, Hemingway, and Lawrence* (University Press of Florida, 2007), the latter two focusing on the representation of masculinity in modernism. He teaches at Mills College, California.

Acknowledgements

This book was generously supported through a seed-funding grant from the Faculty of Arts at the University of Sydney. The editors would like to thank Viv McGregor and Damon Young for providing research assistance in the initial and late stages of the project. Thanks also to the anonymous readers for their thoughtful suggestions for improving the collection. Most of all, thanks must go to the contributors for their patience and dedication to the project.

Several of the introductory paragraphs of the DuPlessis essay contain material also in her *Purple Passages: Pound, Eliot, Zukofsky, Olson, Creeley and the Ends of Patriarchal Poetry* (Iowa City: University of Iowa Press, 2012).

Introduction
Modernism and Its Masculinities

Natalya Lusty

Modernism and Masculinity brings together a collection of essays concerned with the varied dimensions and manifestations of masculinity in the modernist period. The volume reframes the critical terrain of modernist studies by expanding the gendered portrait of modernity through the lens of masculinity. It offers a renewed opportunity to interrogate some of the distinctive features of modernist literary and cultural expression by attending to masculinity as an unstable horizon of gendered ideologies, subjectivities and representational practices. The focused perspectives that these essays bring to the gendered dimensions of modernist literary and cultural production has been made possible by the interdisciplinary field of masculinity studies, which has produced rich conceptual models for the critical analysis of men, masculinity and male privilege. The approaches and arguments of the essays in this collection are nevertheless as diverse as the masculinities that were played out across the early decades of the twentieth century.

Masculinity Studies

Academic and popular accounts of men and masculinity in the twentieth and twenty-first centuries have been routinely marked by a rhetoric of 'crisis' as a way to frame the threatened nature of masculinity, be they bourgeois or working class masculinities deemed 'at risk' from the encroachments of newly visible marginal groups – women, homosexuals, and ethnic, racial and other cultural minorities. This has led some scholars to question the adequacy of the term 'crisis' in light of the common assumption that masculinity in any given historical period will always be marked by instability and contestation.[1] This still begs the question, however, as to why the concept of crisis is rarely applied to femininity. What is it about masculinity and the masculine that recurrently assumes the rhetorical force of vulnerability, anxiety and even extinction? Given the history of male hegemony,

I

masculinity had largely (until recently) remained unmarked, a transparent and under-scrutinised category.[2] Subsequent attempts to examine the category of masculinity have precipitated a defensive response to a perceived questioning of authority (a reactionary crisis) *and* a constructive attention to the historical complexities and transformations of manhood, masculinity and male privilege. R. W. Connell's sociological analyses have been instructive in developing concepts of masculinity informed by empirical research based on the experiences of men and boys but also firmly rooted in the political goals of social justice. Connell's work was instrumental in defining the field of masculinity studies throughout the 1980s and 1990s, in part because she developed a series of critical concepts that analysed the systemic effects of male privilege and power even while exploring men's experiences of inadequacy and vulnerability.[3] Expanding the conceptual ground of the field through the identification of distinct formations of masculinity ('hegemonic', 'marginalized' and 'complicit'), Connell's work drew attention to the historically mutable nature of masculinity alongside the contemporary social forces that shape the heterogeneous experiences and practices of being a man.

The post-structuralist turn in feminist and queer scholarship sparked an important trans-disciplinary focus that expanded the critical terrain and the political goals of masculinity studies. Drawing on a range of critical tools, including deconstruction, psychoanalytic models, Althusser's theory of ideology, and Foucault's genealogical analysis of modern sexuality, feminist scholarship began to scrutinise more closely masculine forms of power ingrained within the sex/gender system. Eve Sedgwick's *Between Men: English Literature and Homosocial Desire* (1985) brought a valuable literary focus to the study of masculinity, defining literature as an important site for understanding the social and sexual bonds that inform the techniques of power and inequality. In a series of close readings of canonical eighteenth- and nineteenth-century literary works, Sedgwick examined 'the structure of men's relationships with other men'; the way male social bonds (rivalry, friendship, entitlement, mentorship and homosexuality) facilitated the exchange of women, real or imagined, in ways that empower men and regulate sexual desire and gendered identity.[4] The literature of Western modernity reveals, according to Sedgwick, 'a special relationship between male homosocial (including homosexual) desire and the structures for maintaining and transmitting patriarchal power.'[5] While the omnipresence of male homosocial desire rests on the prohibition of men choosing each other as sexual objects, the resulting alignment of homophobia and misogyny functions as a powerful oppressive of 'the feminine' in both men and women. The wider impact of Sedgwick's work for masculinity studies was to bring a fine-tuned literary eye to the analysis of the micro-rituals of power embedded in the social worlds of literary works, moving beyond Foucault's often-broad historical generalisations, which invariably occluded the gendered dimensions of disciplinary power.

With the work of Judith Butler, the idea of crisis or at least 'trouble' has assumed an altogether different turn, signalling the impossibility of a coherent gendered subject and its stable alignment with a sexed body. For Butler, the performative dimension of gendered behaviour allows us to see masculinity and femininity as constitutive effects of 'the regulatory practice of gender coherence' rather than as fixed forms of sexual difference.[6] As Butler argues, 'There is no gender identity behind the expressions of gender; that identity is performatively constituted by the very "expressions" that are said to be its results.'[7] According to Butler's argument, gender both constrains and enables particular expressions and practices that are always tied to the contingencies of time and place. The publication of *Gender Trouble* (1990) assisted in reconceptualising masculinity as tenuous and fragile, a 'stylized repetition of acts' rather than the expression of a core gendered ideal.[8] The provisional nature of gendered performance proffered the possibility of less oppressive and obligatory forms of masculinity, ones in which feminist and queer theorists might actively participate in shaping.[9] Butler's work prompted a renewed attention to the historical operations of masculinity and the dismantling of what Butler defined as the 'illusion of continuity between gender, sexuality and desire' that has served to define heterosexuality as the obligatory sexual orientation. Judith Halberstam's *Female Masculinity* (1998) offered an important corrective to that illusion by uncovering a barely visible history of female masculinities, from nineteenth-century invert practices to twentieth-century drag-king performances. In distancing masculinity from its immediate association with men, Halberstam uncovered the diversity of identifications, desires and practices that inform gendered identity. Kaja Silverman's *Male Subjectivity at the Margins* (1992) similarly turned to marginal and deviant masculine subjectivity in order to expose what she calls the 'dominant fiction' of conventional or phallic modes of masculinity. Investigating male subjectivities that 'eschew Oedipal normalization' in a range of literary and filmic texts, Silverman analysed the psychoanalytic vicissitudes (castration, alterity and specularity) that define a non-phallic openness to the domain of femininity. As Silverman argues, 'saying "no" to power necessarily implies achieving some kind of reconciliation with ...

femininity' (3). Providing an important *rapprochement* between psychoanalytic feminism and ideological critique, Silverman insisted on the importance of fantasy – unconscious desire and identification – alongside the role of ideology in the formation of subjectivity. Her analysis offered an illuminating account of conventional masculinity's fantasy of exemplarity, a 'murderous logic' that rests on a belief in 'the commensurability of penis and phallus, actual and symbolic father' (46). But as Silverman's rich case studies reveal, desire and identification also deviate from the expected paths and delineations that make up the 'dominant fiction' of phallic masculinity. Silverman therefore provided an important defence of feminist theory's increasing preoccupation with the analysis of masculinity, defining the book's motivations as steeped in the way 'masculinity impinges with such force on femininity'. Silverman thus contends that '[t]o effect a large-scale reconfiguration of male identification and desire would, at the very least, permit female subjectivity to be lived differently than it is at present' (2–3).

Although fully mapping the terrain of masculinity studies is beyond the scope of this introduction, the work described above illustrates the diversity of the field in overcoming the stifling dichotomies – constructivist and essentialist, historical and ideological – that have traditionally framed accounts of gender within the humanities and social sciences. While the essays in this collection do not always directly address the scholarship of masculinity studies, the volume as a whole is indebted to Sedgwick's call for 'a more historically discriminate mode of analysis' that pays close attention to the individual and structural conditions informing the nexus between modernity and masculinity.[10] The volume interrogates the idea of 'crisis' as it pertains to masculinity in the modernist period but remains open to the possibility of modernism's own self-diagnosis as a period in which men experienced radical transformation, often caught between new and obsolete models of masculinity. If the aesthetic and cultural practices of modernism defined masculinity in relation to cultural fragmentation *and* regeneration, this reflects the broader antinomies of progress and decline that shaped the cultural and discursive space of modernity.

Modernist Masculinities

World War One has long been defined as a collective historical wound gendering modernism as a site of masculine emotional trauma and corporeal fragmentation. The historical work on masculinity during this period has been exemplary in producing nuanced accounts of the protean experiences of war that both contested and conformed to the military and civilian expectations of men of the period.[11] Elaine Showalter's analysis of male hysteria has revealed the ambivalent psychiatric response to the epidemic of war neurosis, which by 1916 accounted for 40 per cent of British war causalities.[12] Often diagnosed as a lack of discipline or loyalty, military psychologists were reluctant to acknowledge the emotional and psychological vulnerability of men, which reflected a pervasive Victorian masculine ideal of courage, self-control and above all a manly ethos of not complaining. More recently Mark S. Micale has unearthed a more comprehensive, albeit barely visible history of the suppression of male nervous illness by Western scientific and medical discourses, which long upheld an image of male detachment, rationality and objectivity in the face of contrary evidence produced in clinical studies and on the battle-field. In suppressing the fragility of male mental and emotional experience, Micale suggests, Western medical knowledge is marked 'not by the steady, rational accumulation of knowledge, but by anxiety, ambivalence, and selective amnesia.'[13]

Sarah Cole and Santanu Das revise existing studies of First World War experience by examining a distinctive literary voice that captured the intensity, as well as the inexpressibility, of male wartime intimacy. Cole's *Modernism, Male Friendship and the First World War* (2003) turns to the familiar modernist themes of alienation, loss and fragmentation, but newly configures them as the 'excavated' remains of 'lost male comradeship'.[14] Examining the figure of the lost friend together with the beleaguered sense of male friendship in the work of Forster, Lawrence and the war poets, Cole traces the decline of the Victorian institutions (educational networks that fostered Hellenic ideals of male community and military ideals of comradeship and loyalty) that had provided protective and familiar forms of male friendship. Cole argues that the fracturing experience of war intensified the waning of traditional forms of male intimacy, giving rise to unstable and often incompatible forms of male community. Cole's study of the so-called threshold modernists revises the overriding portrait of modernism as an intensely collaborative male enterprise, providing an expanded narrative of how the war opened up a disjunction between private friendship and culturally sanctioned forms of comradeship, which both compelled and constrained male social bonds in the period. In *Touch and Intimacy in First World War Literature* (2005) Das, like Cole, is interested in reorienting our familiar sense of male forms of intimacy and the efforts of soldiers and nurses to capture the unrelenting physicality and emotional intimacy of life in the trenches and field hospitals. His optic, however, zooms in on the localised and transient forms of human contact that emerged from the eviscerating experience of what he terms the 'slimescapes' of the trenches: 'The experience of trench mud was one of the most powerful encounters of the human subject with the immensity and chaos of inert matter ... it brought the soldiers to the precipice of non-meaning in a world that was already ceasing to make sense.'[15] Das persuasively argues for the primacy of human 'touch' in a world stripped of the consoling myths of heroic masculinity, noting the irony of how 'the world's first industrial war, which brutalized the body on such an enormous scale, also nurtured the most intense of male bonds.' (136)

If World War One seemed to promise new forms of male-bonding that might ameliorate the Victorian ideal of masculine physical prowess and emotional self-discipline, the figure of the masculine fascist subject would soon haunt the landscape of nationalist masculinity. Klaus Theweleit's two-volume study, *Male Fantasies* has produced a confronting portrait of proto-fascist subjectivity and the psychic repressions of militarised forms of masculinity.[16] Reading the memoirs, letters and novels of the German *Freikorps*, mercenary soldiers employed to contain the spread of communism in Germany between the wars, Theweleit discovered the exaltation of a masculine militarised body in terms of hardness, impenetrability and self-discipline, a body defined as at risk of contamination by the soft, oceanic fluidity of the female body. The intense misogyny and violence directed towards women by the private *Freikorps* army disclose a psychic fragmentation that tied anxieties around the penetrability of the male body to the vulnerability of the nation state. Within this rigidly defined gendered imaginary, the masculine body and the nation state were thus rigidly bordered and protected from foreign contamination: Jews, communists, homosexuals or indeed any form of 'soft' masculinity. Theweleit's study has made a significant impression on recent theories of modern masculinity across a range of disciplines, in part because the thrust of his argument asserts, sometimes controversially, that the fantasies embedded within fascist masculinity are prototypical rather than extraordinary. Implicit in this argument is the idea that all embattled modes of masculinity depend on the pathologisation of those forms of femininity that pose a threat to men's desire for bodily and national control. Historically, Theweleit's study reveals how the fascist 'new man' of National Socialism was forged within a rigid gendered imaginary, the containment of which necessitated ruthless forms of persecution and violence.

The culturally regenerative space of modernism nevertheless provided an opportunity for the critical reappraisal of prevailing and emergent models of masculinity in Europe, the United States and elsewhere. The increasing fluidity of social and sexual roles made possible by industrialisation, commodification, the extension of the franchise, suffragism, sexology, psychology, urbanisation, and new forms of transport and communication meant that masculinity at the beginning of the twentieth century entered into a protracted period of cultural reflexivity and malleability. As the cultural influx from the colonised world was progressively absorbed into Western forms of social behaviour and self-consciousness, the very idea of 'being a man' came under renewed scrutiny and pressure. The effects of industrial warfare, as we have seen, disrupted long-established conventions of intimacy, honour and manly sacrifice. Conversely, as social mobility and migration became a fixture of everyday life, so 'the Jew' emerged as a distinctly feminised spectre of modernity, whose racial demonisation was to entail new forms of nationalist masculinity, fashioned through the violent protocols of pure bloodlines and fantasies of contamination. As national forms of hegemonic masculinity were being solidified in Germany and Italy, in Britain the visibly disruptive demonstrations of the Suffragists had already radically feminised the public sphere, even as their manifestos and political tracts often problematically tied women's political emancipation to sexual propriety.

The culture and artworks of modernism emerged from the flux of irreconcilable social energies. The 'new woman' and the 'new man' were salient figures in the cultural ideologies of art at the time, in response to the progressive erosion of gender norms in the system of commodity culture and in the ensuing rearrangement of public and private life. But while social, economic and political forces shifted gendered norms and the sexual ideologies that informed them, the ideologies of art reinvented them in unexpected and complicated ways. What emerges from the maelstrom of modernist cultural expression is a range of masculine subject positions, male practices and representations of masculinity, sometimes carrying with them the traces of the very femininity associated with tradition and mass culture (Joyce's Bloom), or the enervation of the emasculated modern man (Eliot's Prufrock). Leopold Bloom, the womanly man, is one prototype of the period: heroically defeating every challenge to his equanimity and humanism, yet lampooned mercilessly as an effeminate parasite and cosmopolitan liberal. Prufock is another model of modern masculinity: confounded by the impotence of his masculinity, his halting cry, 'That's not it at all, that's not what I meant at all', hints at sexual and emotional paralysis. The self-promotional hyper-masculinity of Futurism provides one response to the perceived feminisation of political culture, while the deconstructed libidos and emancipated emotions of surrealism strike out against the bourgeois values of post-war national reconstruction; between them, a vast array of provisional responses to the changing construction of contemporary masculinity cover the landscape of modernist practices.

But if the concept of masculinity is a contested site within the broader gendered system of modernity, modernism, as a historical, literary and cultural category, is equally under dispute. Rarely can critics agree on what modernism is or where it begins and ends, or what constitute its distinctive features, salient forms of expression or political motivations.[17] Under the banner of modernism, and its revisionist offspring, new modernist studies, sit a whole host of competing and heterogeneous cultural expressions: the formalist experiments of high modernism; the radical contestatory politics of the various avant-gardes; the politicised feminist consciousness in the writing of Woolf and West; the vernacular expressions of modernism emerging from movements such as Mass Observation in Britain; and the anti-colonial expressions of a global modernism, found in Fanon's psychoanalytic Marxism or Césaire's critique of European civilisation. The temporal locations, 'early', 'high' and 'late' modernism, while offering clear signposts to distinctive historical moments, inadvertently convey an historical teleology which cuts across what many critics have come to accept as the uneven development and experience of twentieth-century modernity and the multifarious political, cultural and literary expressions it inaugurated.[18] The modernist maxim, 'make it new' perhaps typifies the ambivalence and precariousness of modernist literary practice and its gendered claims to innovation. Here the verb 'to make' shifts the emphasis away from 'the new' in itself to the obstinate creative act of making something *appear* new. In gesturing towards the privileging of male creative practice as a 'making new' of traditionally feminine biological and reproductive powers, the maxim conveys a defensive reaction against the perceived effeminacy of male artistic labour and the perceived feminisation of the commercial public sphere. The rhetoric of the 'new', ambivalently staged through the precarious indeterminacy of 'appearance' also signals what Marianne DeKoven has defined as the '*sous-rature*' of modernism – its paradoxical conceptual status as 'an unresolved contradiction.'[19] This contradiction encodes modernist cultural expression as simultaneously radical and reactionary, as both old and new, as 'rich and strange'. According to DeKoven, this double movement produced a distinctly gendered reaction: 'male modernists generally feared the loss of hegemony the change they desired might entail, while female modernists feared punishment for that utter change.'[20] In spite of heightened anxieties about the perceived feminisation of literary culture and the public sphere, male privilege and power still dominated the cultural and political landscape of modernity. As a threshold effect, 'masculinity' thus becomes an exceedingly elastic category that might be mobilised in ways that are reactionary or innovative, rigid or adaptable – and sometimes both at the same time.

This collection absorbs the important wisdom of the increasingly elastic parameters of 'modernism' and the volatility of the 'masculine' in relation to other identity formations, but nevertheless surveys the complicated production and representation of masculinity in key sites of modernist literary and cultural practice across Europe and the United States. From a range of viewpoints and disciplinary positions, the collection addresses the tensions between the production of bodies, emotions, experiences, material practices and intellectual formulations that shaped and interrogated the epistemological certainties and artistic convictions of masculinity in the period. The collection builds on existing work in the field of modernist studies but also subtly contests the prevailing gendered portrait that conventional accounts of modernism presume. While masculinity studies has produced a formidable body of historical work on masculinity and important theoretical tools that have shaped and continue to shape our understanding of the power relations and cultural formations that inform the protean forms of masculine expression and representation, a more expansive analysis of modernist masculinity is long overdue.

Modernism and Masculinity is divided into four sections, each surveying the characteristic domains of modernist masculinity. 'Fields of Production' maps forms of masculine cultural practice that define a distinctive modernist awareness of the changing conditions and the resulting pressures of literary production, including editorial practice, the contested gendered space of literary and media production, new conceptions of authorship and the modernist promotion of literary culture. Rachel Blau DuPlessis opens with a comprehensive portrait of the discrete zones of masculine poetic forms and practices. Locating a tension between the rigid sexed and gendered binaries exhibited in modernist manifestos, essays and letters and a more ambivalent representation of masculinity in men's poetic expression, Blau DuPlessis finds 'multiple contradictions and imperial urgencies, gender ideas both progressive and defensive' in male modernist poetic culture. Without diminishing the often-misogynist inflection of modernist poetic practice, Blau DuPlessis contends that a fascination, sometimes bordering on identification, with 'the feminine' confounds the masculinist cast of male poetic expression. Melissa Hardie turns to male editorial practice in the complicated editing history and the post-publication life of

Djuna Barnes's iconoclastic modernist novel, *Nightwood*. In Hardie's analysis, T. S. Eliot's 'hygenic excisions' from Barnes's text are concerned with representations of sexual exchange that invoke a preoccupation with male bodily continence in ways that allegorically signal male editorial practice as 'forms of remnant and revenant tribute and trimming'. Turning to the intertextual citations and tributes generated by Barnes and her writing, in Peter Ackroyd's *Chatterton* (1987) and Ford and Tyler's *The Young and the Evil* (1933), Hardie extends her analysis of the pleasures and dangers of the supplementary life of the text and its author in ways that complicate 'the hetorosexual account of editorial exchange'. She argues that the fictionalised and anecdotal appearance of Barnes in two texts published more than fifty years apart 'allegorise the relationship between writer and text by making problematic the questions of chronology, sponsorship and the various nature of textual interventions.' Julian Murphet finds in the broader media ecology of modernism a gendered dynamic in which high modernist art asserts its masculinised 'uniqueness' against putative feminised 'entertainment'. Rehearsing the familiar gendered arguments around high modernism's defensive reaction towards mass forms of reproduction (the cinema, radio, photography, the phonograph), Murphet locates in the arch masculinity of modernist exceptionality 'both a reactive and self-misperceiving phenomenon' that drives its relentless campaign against the traditionally feminine dimensions of cultural production – 'sentimentality, spatiality, popularity' – which were increasingly associated with mechanical media. Concluding that masculine high culture aggressively asserts its claim to distinction as an 'ideological shelter' from the 'industrial deluge' of mechanical media, Murphet nevertheless alludes to the tactical fraternisation – which he allegorises as a scene of masculine seduction – that marked a tentative accord between old and new forms of media.

'Masculinity in Crisis' directly addresses a modernist anxiety enveloping masculine subjectivity and its self-protective expression in a range of literary and cultural sites. Whether perceived as in need of self-conscious reappraisal or subsumed by crippling uncertainty, a sense of crisis often pervaded reactionary and inventive forms of masculinity in the modernist period. Rónán McDonald finds in his account of Irish modernism modes of male inaction that sought to contest the ideology of industrious, active masculinity. Male inaction also informs a reaction against national and racial stereotypes of the Irish character, encompassing both the hyper-feminine image of 'the gentle, vulnerable "Hibernia"' and the hyper-masculine ideal of the violent '"bloodthirsty Fenian"'. As McDonald argues, the resulting contamination of available masculine roles produced 'a dilemma or a bind' rather than a crisis of masculinity as such. Locating a shift in male inaction from early to late Irish Modernism, from Yeats's concern with 'enchantment and self-sacrifice' to the 'conscious rhetoric of refusal and obduracy' in Joyce and Beckett, McDonald identifies a formal and stylistic disruption that create opportunities for new forms of masculine subjectivity. Within Irish literary modernism, male idleness thus becomes a political gesture that relieves the pressure of conforming to adulterated models of nationalist masculinity. Cinzia Blum, in her detailed analysis of the extravagant authorial persona of Marinetti and the exuberant rhetoric of his writing moves beyond the reductive image of futurist masculinity as simply misogynistic. Instead, Blum carefully positions Marinetti's (and Futurism's) dynamic programme of cultural renewal as a response to an 'embattled masculinity' emerging from fin-de-siècle theories of cultural decline – 'mediocrity, enfeeblement and powerlessness'. According to Blum the rhetorical and thematic violence staged in Futurism's manifestos and the celebration of the heroic, theatricality of men at war in Marinetti's later writing produces a paradoxical image of Futurist man, combining 'metallic hardness' with 'elasticity', 'romantic individualism' with 'anti-sentimental technicism.' In framing Marinetti's model of hyperbolic masculinity as a response to the logic of passéism, Blum highlights the unresolved contradictions driving his utopian futurist vision. In Natalya Lusty's examination of surrealist masculinity, she argues that surrealism's increasing interest in sexuality from the late 1920s hinged on its validation of 'experience' as a new form of cultural and political authority. Investigating the very different economies of experience informing the 'Recherches sur la sexualité' (Investigations into Sexuality) and Bataille's debut novel, *Story of the Eye*, Lusty traces an acute anxiety around the fragmentation and decline of masculine experience which precipitated surrealist efforts to reclaim the protean possibilities of marginal forms of experience. In privileging the emancipation of emotional states, deviant sexuality and the role of unconscious desire in mediating the everyday contours of experience, Lusty argues surrealism endeavoured to challenge post-war efforts to rehabilitate the masculine body and its experience of trauma though the institutions of 'family, religion, country' – the target of Breton's vehement opposition in the second manifesto.

'New Men' turns to the inventive refashioning of modernist masculinity as a way to contest obsolete modes of masculinity or to accommodate the tensions of sexuality, race and gender, which invariably split masculine subjectivity into competing identifications and identities. In her examination of Jewish masculinity and the 'new womanly *mensch*', Maren Linett notes the long history of the image of the feminised Jew, which took on new kinds of meaning within the modernist period. While Linett contends Joyce's representation of Bloom sanctioned femininity in men 'up to a point', her reading of Roth's *Call It Sleep,* through its binary representation of masculinity – the 'brutal father' versus the 'enforced gentleness' of the son – offers tentative possibilities for recognising the feminine in masculine identity. At the level of the plot, Linett nevertheless argues that the novel pushes femininity into the background by present- ing Roth's fictional alter ego as a 'feminised victim' who risks becoming a 'masculine victimiser'. In the final section of the novel, however, Linnet notes a stylistic experiment with form that 'refuses linear, authoritarian narration', allowing the possibility for femininity to become more than simply a 'temporary refuge' for masculinity. James Donald explores the figure of Paul Robeson through the agonistic tensions of the public and private masculine self. Drawing on the biographical reconstruction of Robeson by his wife, Donald presents Robeson as a man caught between his exhausting public reputation as 'a hero, a fighter and a free man' and as an exemplary New Negro, who was nevertheless vulnerable to the racial stereotype of the sexually voracious black man. Donald thus finds in Robeson a man very much haunted by the anxieties that split modern masculinity into an acting male Self and a judging male Self, and which constrained the promise of freedom and self-determination. Donald nevertheless defines Robeson's modernism in terms of his openness to 'the possibility of a cosmopolitan life', defined through a commitment to homelessness and non-identity. In David Marriott's critical reading of Caribbean modernism and its engagement with the politics of decoloni- sation, he argues that the search for a 'decolonial identity' in Carribean writing is often framed through a gendered discourse of 'asymmetry, sepa- ration, disavowal and ressentiment.' Within more recent critical work on black modernisms, Marriott suggests a new scrutiny of these 'masculine imaginaries' has begun to question the symbolic and rhetorical exclusion- ary power of anti-colonial nationalist representations of modernity and its 'low tolerance of sexual equivocation', which reproduce traditional gen- dered formulations of 'ethical and aesthetic liberation'. Turning to a close reading of Derek Walcott's 1965 lecture 'The Figure of Crusoe' as itself a paradoxical figuration of the 'character' of West Indian poetry, Marriott argues that Walcott's understanding of tradition and meaning through the 'masculine presence' of Crusoe defines the impossibility of any simple myth of origins: 'Crusoe's shadow looms large here to the extent that, in

Walcott's reading, it is he who defines blackness as abjection: and yet it is Crusoe's legacy that nonetheless comes to embody the black modernist attempt to move beyond the desire to abjure or surpass the abjected.' In his attention to the politics of masquerade and the critical reception of D. H. Lawrence's *The Fox*, Thomas Strychacz questions customary feminist responses that position the story's termination of masquerade at the end of the story through the 'anxiety hypothesis' – Lawrence's preservation of male authority through the re-assertion of 'normative sex and gender roles by writing women into their place'. Turning to the 'question mark' at the end of the narrative, Strychacz stresses the irresolution of the ending that unsettles the narrative logic and signifies instead 'Lawrence's narrative embrace of theatricalised gender roles and a rhetoric of performance that remain resistant to a sequence of disorder followed by reconstruction and then (natural) order.' The salutatory lesson of Strychacz's close reading is the final observation that the deployment of masquerade assumes a reversible figuration, 'adept at exploding gender categories or enforcing them'.

'Masculine Form' is concerned with the expression of the 'masculine' in the formal innovations of modernist artistic and intellectual culture. Tyrus Miller frames his analysis of Theodor Adorno's musicological writings through an emerging critical discussion that has drawn attention to the gendered elements and implications of Adorno's critical oeuvre, not least of which are the affinities and divergences between his 'negative dialectics' and feminist and queer theories of sexual difference. Indebted to that recent critical strain, Miller nevertheless confines his discussion to Adorno's aesthetics of radical modernism as it emerges through his exemplary canon of musical composers, from Wagner to Cage. Reading Adorno's use of the emblematic image of Homer's Odysseus, Miller argues that for Adorno this cunning hero served as 'a prism through which to consider the problem of the modern artist's appropriate comportment to modernity'. For Miller, the issue of comportment is expressed in the gendered characteristics of the male artists represented in Adorno's aesthetic canon, but crucially the critical canon that he defends is not merely 'a new way of making artworks; it is also, implicitly, a different way of being male.' Jessica Burstein, in her revisionist reading of Gaudier-Brzeska's artworks, argues for a reappraisal of the conventional critical history that has aligned 'abstraction with technophilia, with Vorticism, with masculinism'. Invoking Ezra Pound's curious description of Gaudier-Brzeska's animal sculptures as 'snuggly', Burstein suggests Gaudier's organicism, in combining abstraction with empathy, complicates the simple allocation of masculinism to modernism, Vorticism or even abstraction. Through the recurring image of Gaudier as animal ('fawn-like', 'a panther, crouching to the ground', 'a well-made young wolf'), drawn from the observations of his contemporaries, Burstein implies a morphing of artist and artwork that is 'sensual, queer, organic, and metonymic'. In reading Gaudier's sculpture, Burstein offers an alternative to the traditional gendered bifurcation of abstraction and organicism, thereby redefining the masculine inflections of modernist form. Peter Nicholls takes up the circular configurations that play out in Pound's masculine poetics, between the active formal defiance of 'bravura' and the threatened defensiveness of 'bravado'. In recognising Pound's 'crass misogyny' as indicative of his 'embarrassing bravado' in its display of an excessive masculine conceited display, Nicholls nevertheless draws attention to the secondary associations of 'bravado' as 'a cleaving to forms and values that for historical reasons have ceased to be tenable'. In teasing out the semantic circularity of these two terms as they inform the formal and conceptual features of Pound's *Cantos*, Nicholl's notes that for Pound the differently inflected but proximate meanings of the terms insist on 'a particular type of bravery that associated masculine drive with aesthetic constructivity'. Nicholls's reading of the *Cantos* thus makes clear that although Pound's bravado often hinges on 'an impotence masked by aggression ... exposing his rhetorical excesses as signs of merely personal frustration', this is countered by an admirable bravery that illuminates a formal 'brilliance of execution'.

Each of these four sections and the essays within describe discrete literary and cultural modes in which the analysis of masculinity provides a unique portrait of the gendered tensions that came to define the cultural field of modernism. The collection is neither the first nor final word on modernism and masculinity, and its obvious omissions include female masculinity, queer masculinity, working-class masculinity and a whole host of other masculinities that might be newly revived in the wake of this collection. Masculinity, like femininity, continually strains at the limits of its mythologisation: as such, modernist masculinity is not always or only about men, but the possibilities and impossibilities out of which its rhetorical and material capacities were formed and played out in the distinctive and vibrant cultural space of modernism.

Notes

1 See Christopher Forth, *Masculinity in the Modern West: Gender, Civilization and the Body*, Palgrave Macmillan, 2008.

2 Richard Dyer has made a similar critique in his examination of the universal, although racially invisible, nature of whiteness and its historical and cultural power in determining codes of Western aesthetics and representation. See *White: Essays on Race and Culture*, Routledge, 1997.

3 See R. W. Connell, *Masculinities*, Sydney: Allen and Unwin, 1995, and her earlier essay, 'Masculinity, Violence and War' in Paul Patton and Ross Poole, eds., *War/Masculinity*, Sydney: Intervention, 1985.

4 Eve Kosofsky Sedgwick, *Between Men: English Literature and Male Homosocial Desire* (Columbia University Press, 1985), p. 2.

5 Ibid., p. 5.

6 Judith Butler, *Gender Trouble: Feminism and the Subversion of Identity*, New York and London: Routledge, 1990.

7 *Gender Trouble*, p. 25

8 *Gender Trouble*, p.140

9 See *Constructing Masculinity*, ed. M. Berger, B. Wallis and S. Watson, New York and London: Routledge, 1995, and *Masculinity Studies and Feminist Theory: New Directions*, ed. J. Kegan Gardiner, New York: Columbia University Press, 2002.

10 *Between Men*, p.12.

11 See, for example, Paul Fussell, *The Great War and Modern Memory*, Oxford University Press, 1975, and Joanna Bourke, *Dismembering the Male: Men's Bodies, Britain and the Great War*, Chicago: University of Chicago Press, 1996.

12 Elaine Showalter, 'Male Hysteria' in *The Female Malady: Women, Madness and English Culture, 1830–1980* (London: Virago, 1985), p.168.

13 Mark S. Micale, *Hysterical Men: The Hidden History of Male Nervous Illness* (Harvard University Press, 2008), p. 7.

14 Sarah Cole, *Modernism, Male Friendship and the First World War* (Cambridge University Press, 2003), p. 122.

15 Santanu Das, *Touch and Intimacy in First World War Literature* (Cambridge University Press, 2005), p. 37.

16 See Klaus Theweleit, *Male Fantasies*, Vol. 1, *Women, Floods, Bodies, History*, trans. Stephen Conway, University of Minnesota Press, 1987, and *Male Fantasies*, Vol. 2, *Male Bodies: Psychoanalyzing the White Terror*, trans. Erica Carter and Chris Turner, University of Minnesota Press, 1989.

17 See, for example, Raymond Williams, *The Politics of Modernism*, London: Verso, 1989, and Susan Stanford Friedman, 'Definitional Excursions: The Meanings of Modern/Modernity/Modernism' in *Modernism/Modernity*, Vol.8, no. 3 (2001).

18 See, for example, Fredric Jameson, *A Singular Modernity: Essay on the Ontology of the Present*, Verso, 2002.

19 Marianne DeKoven, *Rich and Strange: Gender, History, Modernism* (Princeton: Princeton University Press, 1991), p. 4.

20 Ibid.

PART I

Fields of Production

CHAPTER I

'Virile Thought': Modernist Maleness, Poetic Forms and Practices

Rachel Blau DuPlessis

Many styles and modes of maleness are available at any given historical period, and these are often exaggerated and framed by representation.[1] Perhaps as fallout from the 'affective revolutions' of the late eighteenth and nineteenth centuries, poetry as an idea in long modernity manifests a liberatory, sublime, erotic, transgressive and pan-gendered aura.[2] Yet sometimes there is a *'rappel à l'ordre'* in this liberatory narrative, symptomatically in the sex-gender realm, and rigid masculinist claims compensate for the sense – out of romanticism and the decadent – that poetry and the poetic career are feminised or queered in some way.[3] These responses from 'virile thought' are contradictory: Are these zones dangerous and to be avoided? Or perhaps so tempting they must be warded off?[4] May they be cured/answered with the (physical? mystical? political?) energies of maleness reaffirmed? No surprise, then, that in Anglo-American and international twentieth-century poetries (modernist and just after), sex-gender metaphors and claims intermingled a good deal with questions of poetics, and then were remixed with major social changes within modernity.

The main claim, consistent from romanticisms through modernisms (as one historical 'unit' of modes of maleness), is a male-imperial potential for ranging across and deploying a variety of sex-gender stances: liberated sexuality, machine masculinity, homosociality, heterosexuality, hyper-masculinity, feminine-poeticalness, queerness of one sort or another, anti-bourgeois transgressive maleness and dandyish indifference – freely ranging among and appropriating from these conflicting stances, but not always interrogating them. One sees this in Ezra Pound's spectrum of personae: from poems of muscular Christianity ('Ballad of the Goody Fere'), hyper-masculine bombast ('Sestina: Altaforte'), sexy red-blooded maleness ('The Condolence'), sensitive troubadour ('Dance Figure'; 'The House of Splendour'; 'Apparuit'), modern sex-gender satirist ('Tenzone'; 'Salutation the Second'), decadent sympathiser ('Hugh Selwyn

Mauberley'), feminist male ('Commission') and urbane non-feminist male ('Portrait d'une Femme').[5] Using Gertrude Stein's cheerful if vague term, one might call this catholic and contradictory imperium of possibilities patriarchal poetry.

As Barbara Johnson reminds us with reference to Charles Baudelaire, the poetic career is constructed of 'male privilege', of which one part is 'the right to play femininity', separating the feminine from women – who, of course, may not particularly want it.[6] This privilege extends to male claims on any and all possible sex-gender positions in poetry. This does not mean that men necessarily support females in their literary careers or view females as having an equal possibility of deploying such multiple subject positions as the men command. Sometimes quite the opposite. This literary stance can go hand in hand with misogynist attitudes as well as with male-affirmative frankness: the imperative to 'dance the dance of the phallus' is not only joyously self-assertive but can also be a claim of political hegemony.[7]

At the heart of modernist maleness and poetic practices are, then, multiple contradictions and imperial urgencies, gender ideas both progressive and defensive. Gender relations and gender are 'both symptom and subject'; that is, the sex-gender system is a topic of debate, a source of multiple representations on its own and 'a stand in for other anxieties about cultural' and political life.[8] The eros of poesis – the ruthless and desirous bonds involved in poetry/art production as a social and cultural practice – is a powerful obliterator of fixed and normative gender ideas, and yet, at the same time, conventional sex-gender ideas and practices are hegemonic, emphatically policed and in continuous motion. In the complex interplay among these elements, many stances, many critiques and much cultural work have gotten accomplished. Deviance and errancy were (and are) legally, socially, economically and politically punished – if also tempting – subcultures.[9] Many male compensatory strategies in the artistic world result from this contradiction – aggressive macho behaviours, homosocial bonding in artistic groups, the claiming and hoarding of cultural power, powerful seductive behaviours towards other practitioners, and insistence on women as culturally weak, as static ideals or static degradations (both being historically immobile roles).[10] (There are also, of course, female compensatory strategies and post-binarist forays; these are not the topic here.) All these positions have implications for the nature of poetry and its practices; that 'real authentic [poetic] culture' remains the 'perogative of men' was an active if also actively contested claim in modernism.[11]

All modern writers lived within the steady pressure of historical changes in sex-gender regimes: female professional, intellectual, and political expectations; enactments of sexuality and pleasure removed from marital and doxological claims; and changes in the civic and ideological status of homosexuals, ethnic minorities, women and Jews, among others.[12] Marianne DeKoven proposes that 'male Modernism's self-imagination as a mode of masculine domination' occurs as a compensatory 'fear of women's new power' in the early years of the twentieth century.[13] One might better say 'distinct ambivalence to' this power. Further, 'masculinist misogyny' – one, and only one, among a set of attitudes – is connected to 'its dialectical twin: a fascination and strong identification with the empowered feminine', along with distinct caveats about empowered females.[14]

Poetry is the most marginal of modes 'in a society in which masculinity is identified with action, enterprise, and progress – within the realms of business, industry, science, and law'[15]; the professionalisation of writing and literary criticism in the twentieth century favoured fiction and journalistic popularising. The slow but inevitable opening of many professions to women evoked a craft-guild mentality on the part of some male writers – trying to limit access by titrating apprenticeships and also downgrading the 'masterworks' of those who did not learn in and from the exclusionary guild (a Catch-22, still visible in some poetic cohorts). The masculinity of modernist canonical poetry has the further need to struggle against the perceived 'femininity' of poetry as a mode of practice. Here is the modernist cliché par excellence: a certain kind of aesthetic elegance and investigative intelligence 'went with' heterosexual, homosocial maleness; a certain kind of middlebrow and mimetic, inadequate modernist-realism and/or sentimentalism 'went with' femaleness; an overreaching unbalanced exaggeration, exotic playfulness and decadent sensibility 'went with' gayness. This is, of course, ridiculous by any comprehensive overview of practitioners (and has been called out as an inaccurate view of the field by any number of critics), but such clichéd framing structures are always vital – and viral.

In early modernism, prescriptive and simplistically ethical positions about art, sexuality and gender abound. In *The New Laokoon* (1910) by Irving Babbitt, a harbinger of many modernist manifestos, any predominance of the feminine in art constituted 'a corruption' of sanity and balance.[16] Masculinist modernism is a form of concealed moralism in response to erosions of male hegemony, which are hardly attributable to females or to homosexuals (many economic, political and material forces overdetermine social change) but are nevertheless symptomatically focused upon them. Naming something 'feminine/ effeminate', like calling something 'primitive', was both a temptation and a warning that evoked gender and ethnic border patrols.

The first zone in which maleness, manhood and masculinity emerge in modernism is the continuous formation – or production – of poets, not as a biographical process, but as a cultural fact of gender claims made on poesis. This is exemplified by modern manifestos and essays in poetics taken as interventions in a career. The presentation of a poetics is a highly motivated act of power and proleptic historical entitlement. A poetics is a way of elevating literary and artistic acts to the highest seriousness, rejecting them as limited, decorative or genteel activities.[17] It is no surprise then that sex-gender materials (and sometimes class, national and ethnic materials) emerge in such documents.

Modernist manifestos arguably begin with F. T. Marinetti in 1909, with his apocalyptic – and sometimes mordantly comic – hyper-masculine declaration of militarism, patriotism and iconoclastic war on past culture. Although an Italian document, 'The Founding and Manifesto of Futurism' became notably influential in France and England. It is an early example of the strategic 'creative violence' towards hegemonic icons and assumptions that Michael Levenson attributes to modernism, and it included femaleness as a target.[18] As Peter Nicholls summarises, this manifesto, by attacking Woman, connected 'aesthetic radicalism with the struggle of the sexes'.[19]

In Marinetti, some men, already 'on the road', have a little automobile accident, casting the speaker into the 'nourishing sludge' of muddy water and industrial waste, instantly compared to 'the blessed black breast of my Sudanese nurse'.[20] The speaker and his pals are reborn as Futurists (with working-class men serving as midwives). This leads to a primal scene of both aesthetics and politics for male modernism, the invocation of an apocalyptic present.

Marinetti thereupon declares an inspiring series of binary terms with insistent new-time rhetorics. On one side are audacity, aggression, decisive action, speed, explosions, machinery, warfare and the staging of incendiary rage – an anti-humanist, vibrant totality of 'violence, cruelty, injustice' – as if one ever needed to instantiate these further. On the other side are passivity and tradition, the aristocracy and the Church, old art, tedious masterpieces and their dim champions, museums, chivalric ideologies around the female, 'moralism, feminism' and endless archeological layers of *patrimonia*, such as one might find burdensome in Italy (187–188). How 'feminism' gets mixed into this passéiste brew is instructive. As symbols of

this vapid past and possible enforcers of it, females are, for him, key figures. Hence 'scorn [contempt] for women' is Marinetti's theoretical/theat-
rical centrepiece (187).

It is just a tad ambiguous whether this famous slogan means that
the whole gender is to be despised or that the stereotyped passivity and
passéiste sentiments associated with women – such as romantic love, idealising the female, sexual parasitism, narcissism and sentimentality – are
to be rejected. Even if one splits the difference, this manifesto is a remarkable document of male ideology as cultural practice, a utopian gesture of
hyper-masculinity. In it, females are positioned both as outside of modernity and as the enemy of modernity.[21] Whether *disprezzo della donna*
meant exactly what we now see in it rather than a call for radical gender
newness, and whether or not it could have been attractive to a modern
female rejecting normative roles, nonetheless such propositions of misogyny, gender exclusion, racial sentimentality, cyborg machine-men and
cultural purgations by violence created souped-up masculinist affirmations in the guise of modernist poetics.[22]

Quite indebted to Marinetti's intervention, as Lawrence Rainey exactingly documents, Ezra Pound's imagist programme of circa 1914 continues
the manly stylisation of poetry suggested by this model.[23] He and the
other (young) 'men of 1914' (a phrase that is a claim of temporal power in
the Now made precisely by those men) wanted to professionalise poetry,
cleanse or purge poetic diction and return syntax (like sexuality) to its
natural order. Therefore a 'poetic' tone, as well as genteel (feminised)
amateurs, and the artful practitioners of belles-lettres are made endlessly
suspect.

But rather than an incendiary Marinetti-esque sweep in the name of a
militaristic transformation, Pound's 'A Retrospect' presents bluff, hearty
pragmatic advice to practitioners, suggestions all pointed towards austerity, precision, directness and 'the natural'. Practitioners become craftsmen-
technicians made, by his pedagogy, from 'candidates' or other aspirants;
most importantly, poets are experts, scientists, explorers in language.
Both the university model and the scientistic model of professionalism
exclude the casual versifier and loosely ignore women. In both Marinetti
and Pound, women cultural workers are generally positioned as the anti-
modern enemies of the new, something factually false, but persistent as
ideological slander.

'I believe in technique', Pound opines, 'as the test of a man's sincerity'; in this famous and useful credo, gender is unselfconscious yet palp-
able.[24] Gender continues to play a key role in a now famous passage about

adequate (Pound-approved) poetic language, which avers that it is 'harder and saner' than any prior language, austere, direct and forceful (1). This carefully constructed poetics of sincerity is masculine in implication. Clarity and precision, objectivity, impersonality and its apparently pure, truth-telling intentions stand up against subjectivity, the decadent, the ambiguous, 'rhetorical din, and luxurious riot', the decorative – all clearly feminine or effeminate in connotation. Swinburne was modernism's whipping boy (so to speak) of this kind of 'mushy' writing, and 'swishful Swinburniania' is Pound's homophobic dismissal of the effeminate.[25] Swinburne's 'lushness' (high proportion of shimmery sound, low proportion of discursive statement, overall syntactic and metrical intricacy) produces 'feminine' excess.

To underscore, Pound details what bad art is: 'sentimentalistic', 'blurry, messy', made of 'painted adjectives' and – the central gender trope – filled with 'emotional slither'.[26] Femaleness, effeminacy and metaphoric snakeiness are culturally reverberant – to be either corrected or rejected by men. 'Poppy-cock' (senseless talk) is another reviled category, with fatty, bodily and even (etymologically) scatological implications (12). The hygienic undertone to this masculinity encodes the feminine/effeminate as a despoiling/sullying/corrupting of culture.[27]

Modernism as a whole (along with critics and readers of modernism) are so saturated in these norms – so constructed by them – that it is difficult to see them precisely as assumptions: the propositions that excess is always bad for writing; that language can be reasonably transparent; that abstractions are always to be 'feared'; that the 'thing' whose 'direct treatment' is urged may not always be served by decontexualising and isolating it; that syntax needs to be so spare and pared as not to impose any relationships and meanings; that the sensuality of the signifier is untrustworthy.[28] To read the gender narratives of modernism, one must see these stylistic terms as signalling interests in play, not as eternal standards.

Pound's binary face-off between bad and good rhetorics clearly evokes the gendered zones of the feminine/effeminate versus the masculine – although these are not consistently mapped by him on female and male persons. This fact is notable. At the beginning of his career, Pound admired writers like Mina Loy and Marianne Moore, who were intellectual, unsentimental and experimental (using, therefore, 'masculine' rhetorics), and he even invented (in 1918) a special category of poetic diction, 'logopoeia', to account for their practice.[29] Pound was also unswervingly negative and ungenerous about female writers (like Amy Lowell), who, he averred, threatened his attempts at cultural consolidation and leadership. And their activities also threatened, in his view, his potential for income from his cultural products and interventions.

Female writers depict maleness and explore the androgynous and gender ambiguous with their own militant focus. Mina Loy's anatomy of a relationship occurs in part via anatomy itself; the 'skin-sac' of testicles sets a striking standard of frankness in 'Love Songs'. The casting of a cool eye on maleness and on femaleness is manifest in Marianne Moore's early poems, with their resistance to both the masculinist and the feminine (creating a feminist-inflected pox on all gender stereotypes). The heroes/heroines of H. D.'s early poetry are escapees from conventional gender binarisms, often found running across an erotically charged landscape as pursuers or pursued. The 'Greekness' of these materials encodes homosexuality, which receives equal billing with heterosexuality in early works by H. D.

When Pound and Eliot follow post-war aesthetic trends and declare a 'rappel à l'ordre' and agree to write in rhyming quatrains in 1919–1920, this interesting prosodic move is motivated among other things by rejecting the 'free love/free verse' association (e.g., in Loy) and the 'Lowellian lesbian' aura that some poetry had functionally accumulated (thus 'no vers is libre for the man who wants to do a good job').[30]

The anti-female fulminations voiced by the young male modernists, along with their resentment of professional women (as important editors and fellow writers), were an attempt by these men to position themselves in an already existing cultural field that included women with serious cultural power.[31] The accusation from Eliot and Pound of the 'feminization' of poetry was mustered to deflect attention from the salutary shock of female aesthetic and professional participation in modernity – their educational, economic and civic gains, their presence in cultural life as artistic producers, as contributors to foundational thought, as political activists, editors, publishers and supporters of literature.[32] Given Pound and Eliot's own considerable economic struggles at this time, both felt that too many productive and attention-getting females undermined their cultural ambitions. They itched to reduce or curtail the already existing and fast-increasing cultural power of women in their milieu, particularly seeking to guide, cooperate with, control and (if these did not work) to excoriate the female editors of many of the significant periodicals of modernism, crucial for dissemination and reception of their brand of the work of the New.

Arguments about standards, scientific principles and the systematisation of literary knowledge worked to separate literature and literary criticism from terms coded female (finishing-school accomplishments, dilettantism, genteel amateurism).[33] The coincidentally matching poems, 'Portrait of a Lady' (Eliot) and 'Portrait d'une Femme' (Pound), not only expressed young male rejection, but (at least in Pound's case) constructed the female figure as a know-nothing dilettante from a powerful feminist historical player with an original artistic practice.[34] The men of 1914 seriously (albeit sporadically) resisted female cultural coequality. Yet however influential and inflammatory, these attitudes did not sum up their (uneven, uneasy) sex-gender activities. Pound and Eliot's duplicities, double-messages and intellectual insecurity on the topic of female cultural producers are notable.

Pound is a useful avatar precisely because he veers so opportunistically among sex-gender opinions. The erotic freedoms, the New Woman élan, the slow but serious gains in female cultural and civic coequality brought about by the suffrage movement and educational reforms made males defensive and uneasy, at the same time giving them some satisfaction because of the exemplary modernity of women's political aggressiveness. This unstable mixture of pleasure and unease is visible in the arch, flirtatious tone of the 1914 *BLAST* manifesto (probably composed by Wyndham Lewis with Pound), which coat-tails on feminist militancy and is more than a little verbally seductive of the females accomplishing such bold, even shocking acts of political protest as the vandalism of the Velásquez Rokeby Venus in the National Gallery of London: 'We make you a present of our votes. Only leave works of art alone. ... Mais soyez bonnes filles! Nous vous aimons! We admire your energy. You and artists are the only things (you don't mind being called things?) left in England with a little life in them.'[35] This is all caps, and the use of French (the language of love) is a nice touch for men who may have felt upstaged (as Janet Lyon argues) by the actual – not fantasy – actions of a militant movement, including a window-smashing campaign against fashionable shops and bombs in public postboxes.[36]

There is a gradual increase of masculinist claims as Pound's career takes shape, but even then his more notorious messages of manly modernism are not the whole (contradictory) story. Pound's sex-radical analysis of the importance of sexual energy for both genders – certainly a useful dictum of modernist liberations – did, however, reserve a special place for penile leadership, in his scientist proposition of the brain-as-clot-of-seminal-fluid, and the narcissistic position of his 'charging, head on, the female chaos' in 'driving any new idea into the great passive vulva of London'.[37] While these are hardly Pound's final words on this topic, they are among his more luridly masculinist and self-aggrandising.

Among modernist manifestos, the gender fantasies in Andre Breton's 1924 'Manifesto of Surrealism' stand in contrast to Marinetti's passéiste females, for here the female figure is idealised as the avant-garde of surrealist concepts. Strangeness, the imagination as irrational, inspired madness, the liberations of oddity, the Marvellous, heterosexual desire as convulsive inspiration, dreamwork as research into the unconscious – all these concepts and more are magnetically linked to the iconic She. She is the 'native culture' that the poet-ethnographers of surrealism investigated and idealised. These primitives (Women) think differently, they are closer to nature, they are not as developed and they do not suffer the body-mind split because they have no highly developed mind. And there is blood involved, too … and fertility. This holistic fantasy that females live closer to an instinctual realm offered women a poetics (at a price) and allowed for the very familiar position of females in Western civilisation (woman as ideal; woman as Other) to reappear once more amid the denizens of the Very New.

Hence, in surrealism, Females and some Others (sprinkled with the ersatz glitter of romantic primitivism) are particularly gifted, but – does this surprise anyone? – their special status does not lead to any ease of historical coequality or status as subjects. Rather, in surrealism, women in male ideology hold a remarkable double position as Muse of Surreal-beauty, transgression and the Marvellous, along with some hard-won participation and distinctive agency as productive artists. Accordingly, sometimes in surrealism some women act from and beyond their iconic position. A visual text of Man Ray is a useful place to see this double status, in his famous photo of Marquise Casati (1922). As a result of a double exposure, she is blurred, yet with one set of wide-open eyes bubbling up over another. This encapsulates both the grotesque strangeness of women and their potential for hyper-alertness in this milieu. Few historical women throve in this double regime, although some did (Meret Oppenheim is one), since the terms under which they were idealised were erotically and intellectually liberating even when, as female figures, they served as endless metaphor for the poetics of this generally masculine cohort.

Breton rabidly detested and excluded active homosexuals from this otherwise homosocial formation. The 'transgressive' and the 'feminine' had to stay located in actual women; sexually transgressive maleness had to be heterosexual; and the erotic pulse of males in this cohort could not make the 'wrong' object choice, or explicit excommunication from the group would result. For a liberatory 'revolution', surrealism was symptomatically normative, even churchly, in its sex-gender rules.

In fact, a good deal of the poetics of early modernism was wedded to the 'two-sex model' of extreme gender difference, and insisted on males as artistic leaders – no matter the actual evidence. It has taken contemporary feminist intervention (which itself was sometimes based on unbendingly binarist notions of female difference) to undo this hegemonic view of modernism as formed solely by magisterial males. A key structure of maleness in modernism deployed the feminine, the effeminate and masculinity in various ways, yet tried to narrow and obliterate female claims to similar and parallel materials.

If many male poets of modernism produced programmes and manifestos that are very rigid in their sex-gender binarism, in their actual poems, they often produced far more complex and flexible works. The contrast and contradictions between the poetic texts and the programmatic statements make the terrain of 'virile thought' interestingly uneven. In some of his exclusionary statements, Pound sounds like a market protectionist – wanting an all male journal, for instance[38] – but when he is invited to edit T. S. Eliot's 'The Waste Land', he creates a wavering, gender-anguished and sexually-fraught text.

'The Waste Land' (1922) is a poem constructed with a suffusing cross-gendered 'voice', whom Eliot claimed as the central figure. Tireseas is, at root, a figure of sex-gender ambiguity – hermaphrodite? androgyne? bisexual? – sufferer of sexual pain and inchoate prophecy. These terms mean rather different things but amalgamate both/all genders, both/all sexes.[39] The work treats a haunted, unsatisfying, errant and embittered set of sexual dilemmas (homosexual propositions and yearning, hysterical resistance to heterosexual expression), including the ethical issues of instrumental sexual intercourse, tepid acquiescence to and performance of rape, and a decided, if oblique, discussion of abortion. The sorrow and confusion around contemporary sexual relations, post-war anomie and a sense of the loss of meaning are all treated with a complex intensity that does not reduce to easy statements about modernist masculinity.

Despite his every sexist remark, Pound did not cut 'The Waste Land' to emphasise either its masculinist elements or the 'journalistic sex-squabble' that are overt in some of the draft materials.[40] Given the fulminations about female writers in Pound and in Eliot, the excision of Fresca, the vulgar female writer, from the final poem is a datum of unusual richness. This character is, after all, the zone in which their anxieties about female professionalism and autonomy, as well as manipulativeness, sentimentality and bad writing could have been broadcast, the allegorical apogee of their 'feminization of poetry' grumbling and their masculinist claims. By the redactions, Pound saved Eliot from sex-gender oversimplifications. This despite Pound's own similar simplifications. The programmatic masculinism of their essays, manifestos, or letters was not uniformly sustained in the poetry of either poet, although it was not altogether absent either.

In short, male poetic activity in modernism takes any number of varying and contradictory forms. There might be a satiric anguish and bitterness, as in Eliot's poems before 'Ash Wednesday', featuring bachelor characters intermingling prissy sorrow, fears of engulfment (by threatening/sordid females and threatening/sordid disorder) and existential liminality.[41] There might be fascination with strong, erotic, idealised females and a deploring of female professionalism, political analysis and coequal social participation (as sometimes in W. B. Yeats). There might be affirmations of the importance for both genders of orgasmic sexual vitalism (as in D. H. Lawrence, but only for certain styles of heterosexual intercourse). There might be a good deal of male empathy for the frustrations and rage of female professionals – even when (in the case of William Carlos Williams) he had helped to cause those frustrations in the first place (with Marcia Nardi, or 'Cress' in *Paterson*).

William Carlos Williams's poetics of receptivity and attentiveness in 'The Practice', his fascination with births (which he often witnessed as a physician) led him to a stance of empathy with all human sorts and conditions that did not differentiate aggressively by gender hierarchy, although it retained significant traces of idealising and debasing attitudes (as in his lusty excitement for both 'virgin' and 'whore'). He also maintained a seriocomic sense of sexualities and erotic prowess – for both genders. Indeed Linda Kinnahan has proposed that Williams absorbed fraternally the gender-critical poetics of modernist women and eroded, although without erasing, some of the masculinist ideology of modernism.[42] His female figures, like his classed figures, are often depicted with a disruptive resistance and 'attitude', which he both respects and cheers. Among his many poems about sexuality and gender, 'Dance Russe' both affirms and questions his male 'happy genius' status, as 'genie' and tutelary spirit of place, naked, dancing and alone when his family is sleeping.[43] This is as much a portrait of vulnerability as of assertion. It is of a piece with the fond 'astonishment' about the real that Williams often produces, an even-handed reportage of all sorts of moments, including those rife with sexual desire and portraits of the genders in action.

D. H. Lawrence's poems, particularly the 1929 book *Pansies*, features male vitalism; the title pun on 'pensées' offers a definite corrective, via phallic naturalism and verbal frankness, to any other meaning of the word *pansy* – that is, gay man or sissy. Lawrence argues from nature – even touching on anality, the 'black of the corrosive humus' that sustains the sweet flower – about the natural curative qualities of phallic heterosexuality.[44] He has many unpleasant words for bourgeois manhood ('stale'; 'soggy like a wet meringue' [524, 431]); for those who neither manifest sexual energy nor respect that 'spark' (446); for the entertainment industry and its manipulations of the erotic; for any anti-sex social or ideological position, from bourgeois ideology to belief in sin (463–465). His libertarian sexual ethics condemns homosexuals, intersexuals (of the Edward Carpenter variety – weak men, strong women 'of indeterminate sex' [522]), and 'energetic' (politicised or modern) women (537). And he downright hates lesbians (475). But finally he blames men-not-being-men for these social-sexual ills. 'Willy-wet-legs' is his graphic image of the dribblers (559, also 533). Men should be powerful because centred, not cerebral but haptic, pleasure-oriented because vitalist, dominant by the force of their existential sexuality, socially calming and not grasping because instinctually satisfied, sexually responsive but contemptuously ironic about those who would attempt to control 'The Little Wowser' of phallic manhood (493).

This mythos of 'true maleness' did have its female critics (535). In 1923, journalist and novelist Alyse Gregory discussed gender freedom and sexual liberation; her female hero is 'the modern, investigatory, subtly alive, defiantly free woman'.[45] She is therefore incensed with the contemporaneous critique of independent women that came repeatedly from 'anti-feminist' complainers – like de Gourmont and Lawrence (151). She sees that Lawrence's 'women must accept a new kind of mystical subjugation … perpetually receptive, held in a pliant "sub-life"' (151). In a similar 1924 article, Gregory is enchanted that Lawrence talks so openly of sexuality, but finds derisory his increasing dogmatism about male dominance and his relentless exhortations for control of women.[46] For her, Lawrence's male-oriented picture of heterosexual intimacy attacks female independence.

The transgressive, polymorphous evocation of bliss, the urge to dissolve consciousness and boundaries, the strong hedonism and 'drift' – discussed outright in Pound's 'Hugh Selwyn Mauberley' and remaining an exquisite temptation in this portrait of poets and their careers – are all renderings of the endless textual arousal without completion theorised by Roland Barthes (albeit for narrative) in *The Pleasure of the Text*. This decadent mode, the flirtation with transgressive masculinities and the verbal temptations of stylistic elegance all suggested a queered maleness with voluntary and pleasurable links to the feminine; this position is a continuing subtext to the kinds of 'virile thoughts' already delineated here.

Indeed, a new poetic genre, invented or propelled during early modernism, emerged with a counter-hegemonic sex-gender narrative. In origins and many of its manifestations, the prose poem is variously antinormative, ethically errant and at times erotically effervescent to the point of being anti-masculinist or anti-virile (as well as anti-bourgeois and sardonic, framing socially suspect gestures). Jonathan Monroe and Margueritte Murphy both view the prose poem as invested in a genre binary (prose/poetry) mapped on a gender binary (male/female). The nineteenth-century stylisation of realistic prose as masculine and picturesque, and of poetry as beauty-seeking and feminine, suggests a synthesis: the prose poem, between the two, an odd, androgynous mixture.[47]

This sex-gender evocation applied to a genre occurs by virtue of its 'subversive' or 'disruptive' goals, wayward development, exquisite style, descriptive flair or impudent themes.[48] Murphy argues from the Wilde trial that his letters, dubbed 'prosepoems' (to try to excuse their sexual overtones and seductive panache), linked this genre to decadence, gayness and taboo sexuality (47). Thus in England, the prose poem acquired a suggestive status: 'A "third" genre, like a "third sex" may well be suspect' (51).

In France, the genre's history differed, but the transgressive quality remained. Given Stephane Mallarmé's gleeful announcement 'Poetry has been under attack' with a delegitimation of the exactingly legalistic rules of French prosody – the genre 'prose poetry' emerges from a deliberate transgression of rigid literary norms.[49] In Charles Baudelaire's 1862/1869 *Spleen de Paris*, a scandalous anti-bourgeois perversity prevails – male behaviour is impulsive, destructive, spiteful, cowardly, indecent, narcissistic, bragging, nasty, beleaguered by an imp of the perverse. The 'hero' is a splenetic, non-conformist male, who desires the kind of salvation that one might supposedly receive from religion (consolation, transcendence, transformation) – but he gets it instead from an exaggerated fixation on taboo erotic (if heterosexual) objects, and through exotic evocations, narcotic obsession and masturbatory frissons.

In the English prose poem, the amoral fables of Oscar Wilde (*Poems in Prose*, 1894) were transgressive in another way. Wilde's remake of New Testament parables provide a blandly ironic *détournement* of Christianity: Christ's sacrifice is judged as based in His masochist desires; His healing skills are busybody meddling and provoke further pain and suffering; the unintended consequences of the most sacred stories derail their apparently noble goals and deturn their sanctified conventionalised morals. Christ himself is quasi-erotic (even languidly Caravaggesque). Normative values need not apply when beauty is at stake.

This neo-decadent acceptance of bejewelled diction and secular amuse-
ment is audible in such sonically scintillating poetries as the work of
Wallace Stevens, with his claims about 'the essential gaudiness of poetry'.[50]
Harmonium (1923) is a work of bliss, aural excess, and dazzling verbal
charm and elegance. Yet his poetry is almost exclusively gender neutral, and this is particularly striking in contrast to both the more satiric
moments in Pound and Eliot and the humane vignettes of both genders
in Williams.

However, in the 1940s, Stevens plays a good deal with manhood as a
metaphor not for sexual binarism, but for the investigative mind: the phrase
'plus gaudiest vir' combines the stylistic scintillation of his poetic practice
with the stabilising word 'man'.[51] In a late essay, he insists on 'The Figure
of the Youth as Virile Poet' (1944). But these 'virile thoughts' differ consid-
erably from masculine assertion. Using the Latin root, *vir*: 'Virtue in the
midst of indulgence and order in disorder that is involved in the idea of
virility' are his benchmarks (685). This manliness or 'virility' has to do with
the quality of meditation on his 'imagination of life'. Meditation is inextric-
ably involved with a complicated figure who makes sporadic appearances in
this essay: 'Inexplicable sister of the Minotaur' – an austere muse related to
a mythical bull-headed male and a double of the virile poet: for 'your words
are mine, mine yours' (685). This is neither easily parsed nor reducible, but
seems certainly to acknowledge an androgynous companionship in such
'virility', which is not potency but rather a quality of focus, austerity, care
for the pursuit of illumination that draws on a sense of the real 'delineating with accurate speech the complications of which it is composed' (675).
Binarist or differentialist gender thinking is only part of this mix.

The evenness of his apprehensions is visible in 'of Modern Poetry' – a
signature work from 1942, in which 'the poem' or 'the poem of the mind'
or 'the poem of the mind in the act of finding / what will suffice' has to
go beyond prior 'scripts' in this new theatre of modernity. To investigate
what it should be, 'the poem' 'has to face the men of the time and to
meet / The women of the time' with an even-handed curiosity similar to
that of Williams (218–219). Questions of sufficiency and 'insatiability' of
'satisfaction' in his poetry occur between the real and the imagination,
between the actor and the audience, in some mutually constructed dialectic. Poetic authority is not aggressively masculinist. When (in 'Life on
a Battleship') 'the men / Returned on board *The Masculine*', something
far beyond social conflicts should motivate their devotion to the life of
thought, rather than to war, for in meditation 'There's the true masculine' (200). Of course while claiming to be gender-blind, his terms mean,

generally, male-humanist, but in an under-emphatic way. Gender binarist representations are, however, more febrile where Africanist representations are concerned, for Stevens maintains an identificatory interest in the natural, warm masculinity he imagines for black male figures and a suspicion of the sexuality of the black female figures whom he sometimes depicts.[52]

Modernist manhood has a somewhat different implication in the works of African-American and African-diaspora writers such as Langston Hughes, Countee Cullen, Claude McKay and Melvin B. Tolson, given that their full personhood (that is, manhood) was always under siege from racist social restrictions. The use of manhood as a term and concept was often affirmative and socially critical for blacks, who had a differential investment in the word and its meaning, given that reaching full black citizenship in the United States was threatened, and often besieged. 'They told me that Black is an isle with a ban / Beyond the pilgrims' Continent of Man' is Melvin Tolson's dry epigram, fighting ignorance with irony.[53]

Langston Hughes's affirmation of raced (not neutral) manhood in poetry is also involved with class and gender. In 'The Negro Artist and the Racial Mountain' (1926), Hughes claims that a bourgeois life is linked to loss of affirmative blackness, and (in his extended discussion of African-American women's social-uplift clubs) also linked to gender. Such white-oriented respectability and desire for 'healthy' literature policed down-to-earth realist depictions of African-American slang and dialect, rejected the representation of 'low-down' folks, allusions to jazz, and socially frank situations. For Hughes, manhood is a claim of social honesty and independence of mind, not sweetening social reality in poetry (although Hughes did sometimes become picturesque). Cullen's poem in response to Hughes's insinuations that Cullen's aesthetic was white-identified ('To Certain Critics') uses the word 'man' largely in the sense of human. Cullen thereby refuses what he antiseptically calls any 'racial option', a principled choice for him but also an anguished one: 'For never shall the clan / Confine my singing to its ways / Beyond the ways of man'.[54] The encrypted pun on clan/Klan is telling and mean-spirited; the race consciousness of the groups, the self-conscious black and the white racist, was not at par either in implication or in power. In this Cullen reveals the limits of pure humanism, but also its situational nobility. By 'the ways of man' is meant, of course, generally human and not specifically raced.

In Claude McKay's militant sonnet, 'If We Must Die', written in 1919, in the era of lynchings and the heyday of Ku Klux Klan terrorism in the South of the United States and other regions, the enemies of manhood are those who would deny human rights to blacks. These are described as animals – 'dogs' and 'monsters'. 'Man' becomes simultaneously the sign of black (or other brave) maleness affirmed in being fully human. To be a 'man' is to be a person willing to confront injustice boldly even when injustice has overwhelming power. McKay's affirmation has poethical power (to use Joan Retallack's term[55]) and functions as an exhortation: 'Like men we'll face the murderous, cowardly pack / Pressed to the wall, dying, but fighting back!'[56] The interesting ambiguity of the term manhood (male personhood, black humanity and general humankind) along with the humanist-inflected form of the sonnet are used here to exquisite political and poetic effect.

'The centuries have a way of being male' is a striking aphorism from 'The Figure of the Youth as Virile Poet'.[57] This seems neither a proud masculinist statement nor an untrue finding – and it insinuates that the 'centuries' are somewhat creepily aware of the inadequacy of that proposition. Certainly as Stevens sweeps through intellectual history in his account of the interrelation of poetry and philosophy, male thinkers are the people he cites; they are canonical for him, as for any number of readers in 1944. Therefore one reason for an intervention such as this, written in 2012, is to induce 'the centuries' of the future (as well as those of the past) to stop being only male. Because they are not and they never actually were.

Notes

1 The phrase 'virile thought' in my title is from T. E. Hulme, *Further Speculations*, ed. Samuel Hynes (Minneapolis: University of Minnesota Press, 1955), p. 69.
2 See Adriana Craicun, 'Romantic Poetry, Sexuality, Gender', in James Chandler and Maureen N. McLane, eds., *The Cambridge Companion to British Romantic Poetry* (Cambridge: Cambridge University Press, 2008), pp. 155–156.
3 Ezra Pound, *Guide to Kulchur*, c.1938 (London: Peter Owen Limited, 1966), p. 95.
4 This may not be a historical fact, but it is certainly a datum of ideology. A recent U.S. children's book offers contemporary evidence that 'boys/ don't write poetry. // Girls do'; see Sharon Creech, *Love That Dog* (New York: Harper Collins, 2001), p. 1. The boy character is converted to poetry in this insistent pedagogic narrative.
5 The ventriloquism and mastery of positions that 'personae' involve are, Peter Nicholls argues, chosen in opposition to passive/receptive reveries on the indefinable, the form in which inspiration was depicted in the 1890s. See Peter Nicholls 'The poetics of modernism', in Alex Davis and Lee M. Jenkins, eds., *The Cambridge Companion to Modernist Poetry* (Cambridge: Cambridge University Press, 2007), p. 54.

6 Barbara Johnson, *A World of Difference* (Baltimore: Johns Hopkins University Press, 1987), p. 127; vide Andreas Huyssen, *After the Great Divide: Modernism, Mass Culture, Postmodernism* (Bloomington: Indiana University Press, 1986), p. 45.

7 Ezra Pound, *Personae: The Collected Shorter Poems of Ezra Pound* (New York: New Directions, 1950 [c.1926]), p. 86.

8 Cary Nelson, 'The Fate of Gender in Modern American Poetry', in Kevin J. H. Dettmar and Stephen Watt, eds., *Marketing Modernisms: Self-Promotion, Canonization, Rereading* (Ann Arbor: The University of Michigan Press, 1996), p. 325.

9 'Errancy' is Colleen Lamos's useful catch-all term for the effeminate, hysterical, sadomasochistic, homosexual, homoerotic, voyeuristic or matrisexual in male writers. See Lamos, *Deviant Modernism: Sexual and Textual Errancy in T. S. Eliot, James Joyce, and Marcel Proust* (Cambridge: Cambridge University Press, 1998).

10 Michael Davidson, *Guys Like Us: Citing Masculinity in Cold War Poetics* (Chicago: University of Chicago Press, 2004).

11 See Huyssen, *After the Great Divide*, p. 47.

12 A reminder: one result of this kind of article is to make it seem as if its writer is mono-ocular, caring only about critical gender studies at the expense of all other features in culture. This is simply a reading effect.

13 Marianne DeKoven, 'Modernism and Gender', in Michael Levenson, ed., *The Cambridge Companion to Modernism* (Cambridge: Cambridge University Press, 1999), p. 174.

14 Ibid.

15 Huyssen, *After the Great Divide*, p. 45.

16 Babbitt was T. S. Eliot's professor at Harvard and a noted traditionalist about whom Eliot wrote approvingly on several occasions (see Gail McDonald, *Learning to be Modern: Pound, Eliot, and the American University* [Oxford: Oxford University Press, 1993], pp. 123–133). A climactic anti-romantic passage: 'To set color above design, illusion above informing purpose, suggestiveness above symmetry, is to encourage that predominance of the feminine over the masculine virtues that has been the main cause of the corruption of literature and the arts during the past century'; Irving Babbitt, *The New Laokoon: An Essay on the Confusion of the Arts* (Boston: Houghton Mifflin Company, 1910), p. 249.

17 McDonald, *Learning to Be Modern*, p. 77.

18 Michael Levenson, *The Cambridge Companion to Modernism* (Cambridge: Cambridge University Press, 1999), p. 2.

19 Peter Nicholls, *Modernisms: A Literary Guide* (Berkeley: University of California Press, 1995), p. 88.

20 Filippo Tommaso Marinetti, 'The Founding and Manifesto of Futurism', in Mary Ann Caws, ed., *Manifesto: A Century of isms* (Lincoln: University of Nebraska Press, 2001), p. 189.

21 See Janet Lyon, *Manifestoes: Provocations of the Modern* (Ithaca: Cornell University Press, 1999), pp. 99–102; and Carolyn Burke, 'Mina Loy

(1882–1966)', in Bonnie Kime Scott, ed., *The Gender of Modernism: A Critical Anthology* (Bloomington: Indiana University Press, 1990), pp. 232–233.

22 Nicholls, *Modernisms*, pp. 88–90.

23 Lawrence Rainey, 'The Cultural Economy of Modernism', in Levenson, ed., *Cambridge Companion to Modernism*, pp. 35–45.

24 Ezra Pound, *Literary Essays of Ezra Pound*, ed. T. S. Eliot (London: Faber & Faber, 1954), p. 9.

25 Ezra Pound, *Instigations* [1920] (Freeport, NY: Books for Libraries Press, Inc., 1967), p. 239.

26 Pound, *Literary Essays*, pp. 11–12.

27 Janet Lyon, *Manifestoes*, pp. 137–138.

28 Pound, *Literary Essays*, pp. 5, 3; see Nicholls, *Modernisms*, pp. 196–197.

29 Pound, 'Others', in Bonnie Kime Scott, ed., *The Gender of Modernism: A Critical Anthology* (Bloomington: Indiana University Press, 1990), p. 366; see Rachel Blau DuPlessis, *Genders, Races, and Religious Cultures in Modern American Poetry, 1908–1934* (Cambridge: Cambridge University Press, 2001), pp. 38, 43.

30 Carolyn Burke, 'The New Poetry and the New Woman: Mina Loy', in Diane Middlebrook and Marilyn Yalom, eds., *Coming to Light: American Women Poets in the Twentieth Century* (Ann Arbor: University of Michigan Press, 1985), pp. 37–57; Ezra Pound citing T. S. Eliot in *Literary Essays*, p. 12; James Longenbach, 'Modern Poetry' in Levenson, ed., *Cambridge Companion to Modernism*, p. 119.

31 Sandra Gilbert and Susan Gubar, *No Man's Land: The Place of the Woman Writer in the Twentieth Century, Volume 1. The War of the Words* (New Haven: Yale University Press, 1988); Gail McDonald, *Learning to Be Modern*, pp. 78–79.

32 Cristanne Miller, 'Gender, Sexuality and the Modernist Poem', in Alex Davis and Lee M. Jenkins, eds., *The Cambridge Companion to Modernist Poetry* (Cambridge: Cambridge University Press, 2007), p. 69. When Eliot writes his father in 1917 that he is taking over the editorship of *The Egoist*, he says the 'struggle' is to 'keep the writing as much as possible in Male hands, as I distrust the Feminine in literature' (31 October 1917, *The Letters of T. S. Eliot, Volume I, 1898–1922* ed. Valerie Eliot [New York: Harcourt Brace Jovanovich, 1988], p. 204). The efficient crossing between two binaries (male-female; masculine-feminine) is notable.

33 Gail McDonald, *Learning to Be Modern*, pp. 77–79.

34 Rachel Blau DuPlessis, *Blue Studios: Poetry and Its Cultural Work* (Tuscaloosa: University of Alabama Press, 2006), pp. 122–136.

35 *Blast* #1, ed. Wyndham Lewis (June 20, 1914): 151.

36 Lyon, *Manifestoes*, pp. 102–113.

37 Ezra Pound, 'Postscript to *The Natural Philosophy of Love* by Rémy de Gourmont' [1921], *Pavannes and Divigations* (New York: New Directions, 1958), pp. 203–207; and in Scott, *Gender of Modernism*, p. 357.

38 Pound, c.1915, *The Selected Letters of Ezra Pound to John Quinn, 1915–1924*, ed. Timothy Materer (Durham: Duke University Press, 1991), p. 41.

39 Wayne Koestenbaum, *Double Talk: The Erotics of Male Literary Collaboration* (New York: Routledge, 1989); Lamos, *Deviant Modernism*; Tim Dean, 'T. S. Eliot: Famous Clairvoyante', in Cassandra Laity and Nancy K. Gish, eds., *Gender, Desire, and Sexuality in T. S. Eliot*, (Cambridge: Cambridge University Press, 2004), pp. 43–65; Suzanne W. Churchill, 'Outing T. S. Eliot', *Criticism* 47.1 (Winter 2005): 7–30.

40 Pound, 'Postscript', p. 205.

41 Cf. the 'bachelor' in Eve Kosofsky Sedgwick, *Epistemology of the Closet* (Berkeley: University of California Press, 1990), pp. 182–195; Maud Ellmann, *The Poetics of Impersonality: T. S. Eliot and Ezra Pound* (Cambridge, MA: Harvard University Press, 1987).

42 Linda A. Kinnahan, *Poetics of the Feminine. Authority and Literary Tradition in William Carlos Williams, Mina Loy, Denise Levertov, and Kathleen Fraser* (Cambridge: Cambridge University Press, 1994).

43 William Carlos Williams, *The Collected Poems of William Carlos Williams, 1909–1939*, vol. I, ed. A. Walton Litz and Christopher MacGowan (New York: New Directions, 1986), pp. 86–87.

44 D. H. Lawrence, *The Complete Poems of D. H. Lawrence* ed. Vivian de Sola Pinto and F. Warre Roberts (New York: The Viking Press, 1971), p. 418.

45 Alyse Gregory, 'The Dilemma of Marriage', *The New Republic* 35.448 (July 4, 1923): 151.

46 Alyse Gregory, 'Artist Turned Prophet' [a review of D.H. Lawrence], *The Dial* 76 (Jan. 1924): 66–72.

47 NB: this also indicates the instability of this kind of attribution; remember that realist middlebrow fiction was also gendered female in other of these discussions of gender and genre.

48 Margueritte S. Murphy, *A Tradition of Subversion: The Prose Poem in English from Wilde to Ashbery* (Amherst: University of Massachusetts Press, 1992), p. 82.

49 Stéphane Mallarmé, c.1894, *Mallarmé in Prose*, ed. Mary Ann Caws (New York: New Directions, 2001), pp. 32, 33.

50 Wallace Stevens, *Collected Poetry and Prose*, ed. Frank Kermode and Joan Richardson (New York: The Library of America, 1997), p. 768.

51 Ibid., p. 236.

52 DuPlessis, *Genders, Races*, pp. 118–123.

53 Melvin B. Tolson, *'Harlem Gallery' and Other Poems*, ed. Raymond Nelson (Charlottesville: University of Virginia Press, 1999), p. 25.

54 Countee Cullen, 'To Certain Critics', *My Soul's High Song: The Collected Writings of Countee Cullen, Voice of the Harlem Renaissance*, ed. Gerald Early (New York: Doubleday, 1989), p. 206.

55 Joan Retallack, *The Poethical Wager* (Berkeley: University of California Press, 2003).

56 Claude McKay, 'If We Must Die', in Cary Nelson, ed., *Anthology of Modern American Poetry* (New York: Oxford University Press, 2000), pp. 315–316.

57 Wallace Stevens, *Collected Poetry and Prose*, p. 675.

CHAPTER 2

'That Man in My Mouth': Editing, Masculinity and Modernism

Melissa Jane Hardie

Ever since its 1936 publication, Djuna Barnes's novel *Nightwood* has been associated with acts of editorial tact and custodial pressure. The novel's publication by Faber & Faber was vouchsafed by the presence of T. S. Eliot's editorial hand, and this particular relationship has dominated consideration of the novel's editing history, even though the editorial acts to which it was subject came from several hands. Concern with the novel's fitness during the negotiations over its publication has found its post-publication echo in adjudications that find the novel difficult to reconcile with Barnes's other work. Within the critical account of her writing, *Nightwood* has received far greater attention than any other text, and while this tendency has been addressed in the last decade both through a spread of critical activity across her ouevre and the consolidation of her work in new editions, *Nightwood* remains centre stage.

In the critical consolidation of Barnes's place in modernist studies that took place through the 1980s and 1990s Andrew Field, Jane Marcus, and Shari Benstock all discussed the editing of *Nightwood*, concentrating on the part played by T. S. Eliot in the preparation of the manuscript for publication. Field asserted that Eliot named the text; Benstock that Eliot was responsible for paring down the manuscript 'more than two-thirds' and that he was persuaded by Edwin Muir to publish the text in 1935.[1] In 1989 Marcus offered a preliminary, concise, detailed account of the excisions Eliot made as editor:

> He corrected her French and German and marked out many passages on Jews, one on King Ludwig, and a scene with the doctor in jail, as well as passages that might be considered obscene. He crossed out, 'You can lay a hundred bricks and not be called a bricklayer, but lay one boy and you are a bugger' (202). He told her to think over whether she wanted to say of Jenny, 'when she fell in love it was with a perfect fury of accumulated dishonesty', and he told her to take out Matthew calling himself a faggot, a fairy and a queen in the scene in the carriage. He crossed out

'and the finger of our own right hand placed where it best pleases' and the McClusky passages on a girlish boy in the war. In the description of the 'Tuppenny Upright' he crossed out 'letting you do it', but she restored it in 1949. He wanted to change 'obscene' to 'unclean' on the last page and said he couldn't understand why Robin had candles in the chapel at night. Barnes's penciled note says, 'Sample of T.S.E.'s 'lack of imagination' (as he said)'. Also cut is a homosexual courtroom joke in which the judge asks, 'What do I give a man of this sort?' and the clerk replies, 'A dollar, a dollar and a half, two dollars'. The whole of Matthew's circumcising the regiment scene is cut.[2]

Marcus drew her examples from both the typescript copies of *Nightwood* and miscellaneous folders of excised material deposited by Barnes at the McKeldin Library, University of Maryland. Her useful summary suggested that Eliot's particular anxieties over the manuscript of *Nightwood* centred upon its representation of male homosexuality. In particular, her summary indicates Eliot excised representations of homosexual exchange: economic exchange, judicial exchange, the exchange value of labour and corporeal exchange – ritual circumcision.

This period of conjecture culminated in Cheryl J. Plumb's edition of a revised *Nightwood*, which detailed all the available typescript materials held in the Djuna Barnes collection, reanimating the life of a text whose editing has been considered fundamental to its understanding, without there existing a substantial examination of precisely how those processes were initiated, by whom and to what ends. If the phantom text of an 'original' *Nightwood* has served as a reference point in much of the writing about the novel, the exposition of the material that actually remains and a useful documentation of the skeleton *of* that early text leaves curiously unsatisfied the narrative of violence over textual materials, which had been a feature of Barnes criticism. If Barnes's opus has been editorially pared down to one significant text – *Nightwood* – in a complementary move, that text has been understood to coexist with a larger, penumbrous, more exact 'whole', both more and less 'finished' than the published novel.

Plumb's new edition clarified many aspects of the editing of *Nightwood*, a form of revision metonymically signalled by the restoration of the title to Barnes; early in her introduction she notes that Barnes was contemplating the title in 1935 and Eliot gave it his imprimatur. Even though he did not invent it, Eliot showed a positive inclination towards the title Plumb describes as a form of 'concurrence' at odds with the preferences of a third party she decisively reintroduces to this scene of editorial labour, Barnes's friend and fellow writer, Emily Coleman.[3] Plumb's revision of the story of *Nightwood*'s editing, which concords (or 'concurs') in large part with Herring's extensive biographical telling of that story, triangulates a scene of exchange and excision that has previously been characterised as an agonism between author and publisher. A tendency to describe the editing of this text through such an agonism produces a model of the life of the text rather simpler than that indicated by the extant evidence. Field's assertion that Eliot named the text was symptomatic of the claims made on behalf of Eliot, which appear to draw from his 'Introduction' the suggestion of a collaborative labour on the text. In the list Marcus gives of Eliot's editorial interventions, her examples of Eliot's editorial hand at work demonstrate his particular attention to textual representations of sexual exchange. Those exchanges may also be read as allegories of editorial practice. As allegories of exchange they operate antithetically to the practice of prophylaxis Eliot performs in removing these passages from the text. This double reading of editing, as an exchange subtended by a practice of hygienic excision, is a preoccupation of this chapter, which moves through tableaux of editing as forms of excision that are preoccupied with figures for masculine bodily continence. It revisits this symptomatic preoccupation with two post-publication retellings of the coming-to-being of the published volume as meta-textual engagements with an anxiety over continence, forms of remnant and revenant tribute, and trimming.

For one strand of criticism, Eliot figured as a significant secondary author of the text, and while feminist-inflected Barnes studies lacked a compelling, factual account of the editing of *Nightwood*, its critical reflex was to understand Eliot's role as censorious rather than facilitating. It seems indisputable that Eliot made the publication possible and was a minor player in the significant editorial changes to the manuscript delivered to press. Recent work has produced a burgeoning discourse around the editing of *Nightwood*, where two recent monographs in particular have drawn similar conclusions disparately nuanced. For Daniela Caselli, Barnes wrote an 'improper modernism' in her 'bewildering corpus', a thesis unassimilable either to a reading of *Nightwood* as an exceptional text among her output or to a reading of the editing of *Nightwood* as an act of disciplinary excision. Caselli's reading of Barnes's work permits the assimilation of *Nightwood*'s instability as a textual object, consonant with her other texts: 'Nightwood is too written, too emotional, too obscure, too abstract, too stylized: it refuses to be contained, to occupy a position of unadulterated modernist resistance.'[4] Monika Faltejskova ventilates the minutiae of detail to concur with Marcus's characterisation of Eliot's activity as censorious: '[a]ll passages Eliot cut dealt with sexuality and religion, and either significantly softened or in places eliminated the homosexual and lesbian tone of the book.'[5]

An agonistic model of the relationship between editor and writer results in the creation of a privileged domain in which the edited scraps of the text offer privileged access to the text, a back-door opportunity to try out an intentionalist reading. Whereas the published version of the text is produced as a closed system, the existence of extra material undoes its integrity. Edited material problematises the status of the finished text, as a 'dangerous supplement', as gratuitous material which, once edited out, will always be out of place.[6] Once they have become extrinsic to the life of the book, that is, the published version of the text exchanged in the market place, editorial excisions offer themselves as a pleasure supplementary to the orthodox one of conjugal exchange between writer and reader. To read them becomes a private and intimate over-acquaintance with the 'text'.

The status of a text and its edited portions thus promise a number of potential pleasures and problems. Offering a pleasure supplementary to the heterogeneous exchange between text and reader, excisions metonymically figure a masturbatory, private pleasure, analogous to the theoretical status of the 'dangerous supplement' that serves to undermine the integrity of the 'whole' text. As matter out of place, however, editorial excisions stand to the published text as filth, in Mary Douglas's formulation, and their investigation may be troped as anality: the editor as the deject experiencing the abject wholeness of the text.[7] If editorial excision is troped as castrative, feminising the published text as a body marked with corporeal lack, editorial practice is normalised as a mark of sociality – what makes the text 'fit and proper' for the public domain – and the original, uncut version of the text may be read merely as a fantasy of an integrated body. Such an account necessarily offers the edited portions of the text as metonyms for the phallus, an appropriate figuration for the intentionalist reading of edited material as a signifier of a transcendent textual 'meaning'.

A more finessed account of this model might align editorial practice not with castration but with circumcision. Lingis describes male circumcision as the removal of a labial foreskin from the penis.[8] Circumcision removes the mark of the natural and offers a representation of excision as incision, as cultural initiation, an appropriate analogy for the edited text, which then assumes the status of denaturalised phallus. One of Eliot's excisions from the manuscript of *Nightwood* – the scene in which O'Connor 'circumcises a regiment' – may be read as his own erasure from the scene of editing. Circumcision as metaphorical editing occurs in one

of Eliot's letters to Ezra Pound during the editing of *The Waste Land* in
a homoerotic and sadistic tableau that shares more with Dr O'Connor's
surgery than Bloom's fantasy.[9] O'Connor's work with the knife may have
been uncomfortably close for Eliot, given his own implementation of this
metaphor. His excision of this scene may also be read as a repression of
the identification of his editorial pencil with O'Connor's scalpel, a metonymic correlation of Eliot and O'Connor for which Baxter argues in 'A
Self Consuming Light'. In reading this tableau as an editorial fantasy, its
figuration on the penis is itself supplemented by an account of the editorial encounter as tribute.

Masturbation becomes solicitude, becomes tribute; the figurative legacy
of Bloom's masturbation is editorial exchange as gift. The poetics of the
editing of *Nightwood* may similarly be analysed through the intertextual
functions of citation and tribute, in texts which draw attention to Barnes's
writing through deictic and rhetorical position: Ford and Tyler's *The Young
and the Evil* (1933) and Ackroyd's *Chatterton* (1988). What are the implications of reversing a tendency to read from editorial intervention to tribute, and reading instead textual tribute for its editorialising implications?

These instances of citation and praise – or disparagement – suggest ways
in which the historical location of these texts, before and after *Nightwood*,
figures the complexity of a proxemic account of editing through historical
and sexual allegory. Both texts employ an epideictic structure, praising
and blaming, in their incorporation of a narrationally out-of-place commentary on Djuna Barnes, and both demonstrate the functioning of epideixis as adjudication and tabulation, a structure of assessment not unlike
the editorial intervention. Both, in their borrowing of the name of Djuna
Barnes, demonstrate a structure of textual appropriation at work in editing
and epideixis alike, one whose complications rest in a proxemic relation
to the body of the text and writer. Significantly, in both *The Young and
the Evil* and *Chatterton*, the heterosexual account of editorial exchange is
complicated by figures of proliferation; the multiplicity of authorial and
editorial positions offers one further instance of the narrative interpella-
tion of a figurative superfluity coextensive with the text.

'Never Again!': Ackroyd's Barnes

An extended allusion to editorial transgression in Peter Ackroyd's 1987
novel *Chatterton* conjures the figure of Harriet Scrope, a plagiarising
modernist who figuratively and literally steals men's plots to enable her
own writing. In this figure Ackroyd recapitulates in Bloomian anxious

fragments exchanges over a series of modernist manuscripts, and in particular T. S. Eliot's work on the manuscript of *Nightwood*. Ackroyd, whose biography of Eliot was published three years before *Chatterton*, creates a mock-biographical frame for the editorial labour that took place over the *Nightwood* manuscript. Ackroyd's account does not correspond to the textual evidence: it shows Eliot's role as both less productive and less anxious than his allegory suggests, but it does concord with (and even implicitly endorse) common wisdom on the subject.

Harriet Scrope is a minor figure in *Chatterton* who plagiarises plots to enable her own writing: '[s]he picked out at random *The Last Testament* by Harrison Bentley and, even as she began to read it, she realised that here was the answer to her problem. ... The experience of employing a plot, even though it was the invention of some other writer, had liberated her imagination.'[10] Her memoirs, haphazardly dictated first to a female Oxford graduate and then to the protagonist, poet Charles Wychwood, are scandalous borrowings of the main plot in a narrative that examines the twin tributes of elegy and plagiarism. Their deceiving account of modernism parodies the Bloomian fictionalising of Chatterton's career given by Ackroyd, as they also parody Ackroyd's labour as the biographer of T. S. Eliot. It is appropriate they are delivered orally, as the mouth works as a figure for femininity and female sexuality in the novel's representation of Harriet. Djuna Barnes appears through anecdote in the seventh chapter, which opens with Harriet Scrope examining her gums, 'leering at her reflection', able to see 'nothing'. 'Never again!' she said out loud. 'I'll never have that man in my mouth again!'[11] The text suggests fellatio but instead tells us that the intruder was a dentist, and at that moment Harriet's erstwhile amanuensis, Charles, enters. Oral sex, displaced within a discourse of hygiene, reappears as a figure for textual history. Wychwood's offer of a secret prompts another version of this figure, mouth as metonym for sexual disclosure and arousal: '[s]he always assumed that the secrets of the young concerned sex, and she ran her tongue across her upper lip.'[12]

But the literary secrets of the old are what make the mouth water in this novel, and it is Harriet, not Charles, who reports an oral indiscretion:

> 'Now Eliot was a sweetie. He published my first two novels. ... Not that he knew anything about fiction, of course. Are you taking this down, dear?' Charles had been doodling on the paper – dead faces, with no eyes – but now he began to write as she talked. 'It was Djuna Barnes who recommended me. She was a dreadful woman, really'. Harriet sighed. 'She was a lesbo, you know. And an American'. She shook herself, as if her old-fashioned Chanel dress had suddenly grown too tight for her. 'She tried

to tongue me once. I don't mind a few kisses and cuddles from my own
sex – you know Sara Tilt, don't you? – but I draw the line at tongue. It's the
roughness I can't stand. It makes me vomit'.
    Charles wrote down 'tongue' and then stopped. 'Do you want me to
mention this?'
    'Well, I hope she's dead by now'. Harriet had another moment of anx-
iety. 'She is dead, isn't she?'
    'I'll look her up'.[13]

T. S. Eliot is the man in Harriet's mouth, filling up the 'nothing' as she
fabricates (we learn) an acquaintance with the writer. Djuna Barnes is
offered as the interceding advocate, confusing her role as go-between with
the real thing, and producing a simile of nostalgic female tumescence: 'as
if her old-fashioned Chanel dress had suddenly grown too tight for her'.
Simile, as a figure of resemblance (rather than identity), operates here on
a meta-figurative level as a figure for female tumescence as simulacrum of
the phallus, an 'as if' phallus.[14] In the same way, a literal Barnes is figured
in a fictional text to stand for a simulated literary intercession. In this case
the figurative work signals the material production of an 'as if', phony
author in one of various moments in *Chatterton*, where the real is a simulacrum of fiction. Barnes's oral intercession is as outmoded as the tight
dress, its phoniness marked by its being out-of-date (literary history is the
locus of the phony in *Chatterton*) and proleptically signalled by Charles's
doodle of dead faces.
    In fact, the fictionalised trio of *Chatterton* offers the number of those
who worked on *Nightwood* as it was being prepared for publication, if
not their relative places. Ackroyd's narrative of plagiaristic plotting gives a
skeletal account of the kinds of textual work done by Barnes, and others,
in constructing a literary modernism, 'modernising' tradition.
    We are told of Harriet Scrope's first novel that 'kind words from Djuna
Barnes and Henry Green were printed on the back of the American edition.'[15] There is no indication that Barnes made any similar literary rec-
ommendations to Eliot; for instance, Barnes refuted George Wickes's
suggestion that she had performed a comparable service for Natalie
Barney over the publication of *A.D.: The One Who is Legion*.[16] Ackroyd,
however, is well aware of Eliot's advocacy of *Nightwood* and, of course,
these 'kind words' attributed to Barnes are a displaced rendition of
Eliot's endorsement, which, as Ackroyd notes in his biography of Eliot,
was indeed reproduced for the American edition.[17] Ackroyd twists literary history, eroticising the relations between female writer and male editor through the fanciful introduction of a female accomplice. This erotic

triangulation, fraudulent and abject, is a misprision of literary history, a version of the history of Eliot and 'his' writer which marks a deliberate historical 'error' with a sexual mistake and misdemeanour. The word-of-mouth recommendation becomes a slip of the tongue, or parapraxis. Orality is cathected in the discourses of sexuality and textual editing: a masculine oral intrusion serves the functions of hygiene and prophylaxis (editing as dentistry); female oral indiscretion is produced through the misprision of the relations of editor, writer and intermediary. Feminine orality, threatening sexual impropriety and requiring an hygienic prophylactic intercession, marks the private sphere work of plagiarism and confession, which is in contestation with the public sphere work of biography and editing as writing tasks.

The anecdote of the French kiss is related in place of the 'true' anecdote of textual engendering, the furtive plagiarism of the plot of *The Last Testament*. Harriet Scrope bears false witness as she produces an account of lesbian appropriation, which nonetheless symptomatically reinscribes the kind of plot hijacking that produces the lesbian's 'masculinity complex' and is reproduced by it. In the cause of ironising the propriety of the female writer as a less noble plagiarist than the young Chatterton, Ackroyd adulterates the historical record to reproduce a historicised lesbianism, whose Francophile relic is the timelessly chic Chanel dress. Perhaps because his true interest is in male homosocial contestations, Ackroyd introduces such a familiar topos of modernism to sidestep a consideration of a *heterosexual* relation of writer and editor.

'Pages in Waiting': Ford and Tyler's Barnes

Chatterton offers an account of the relationship between text, writer and editor through recourse to a structure of masculinised citation and intercession subtending exchanges between women. Barnes, having become irrelevant to an account of contemporary interest, is turned to figure archaic and repressed deviance. In 1933, however, Ford and Tyler's *The Young and the Evil* made use of the name of Djuna Barnes for its cult and prestige status:

> Julian said I think I like Djuna Barnes which is a good way to think.
>
> Karel crossed his legs and forearms with the glass in his left hand. Yes and if Miss Barnes were to come past my gate I'd say come into my yard Miss Barnes and sit upon my porch and I will serve you tea and if you will recite one of your poems I will be glad to learn it backwards.
>
> Julian said all things of course are going backwards past her ear.[18]

The different prose styles of *Chatterton* and *The Young And The Evil* may be aligned with their different representations of textual exchange. Julian and Karel's discussion of Djuna Barnes marks her incorporation as privileged text into the lives of gay bohemia in Greenwich Village in the late 1920s and 1930s, an assimilation proposed through quaint sociality on an impossible porch. A conversation between men becomes the site for a form of textual finesse through inversion, one whose tropes may be read as figures for editorial intervention. It offers the porch-side recitation of Barnes's text in an encounter framed both by the conversation in which it occurs and by the text's opening pages. Chapter One describes an encounter between 'mythical creatures', troping the text's interest in its own characters as mythological: 'Well said the wolf to Little Red Riding Hood no sooner was Karel seated in the Round Table than the impossible happened. There before him stood a fairy prince and one of those mythological creatures known as Lesbians. Won't you join our table? they said in sweet chorus' (11).

Karel's invitation to shift from the 'Round Table', an enticement to remove himself from the place of dynastic succession and rivalrous co-mingling, is made more attractive by the offer of the position of the 'fairy prince', a perverse Lancelot, as an alternative position within masculine genealogies. His offer is embedded within another conversational impossibility, the anecdotal exchange between the wolf and Red Riding Hood, in which the wolf and Red Riding Hood, as characters in a tale, tell tales of the fictional Karel. This introduction offers an allegory of competing genealogies through conversational exchange and tribute, in a hypotactic structure of conversational embedding, a structure reproduced in the Barnes tribute. Stories are sourced in other stories no less fictional; by implication Barnes's work as text finds its source in the exchange between Julian and Karel. Barnes repays the compliment twice: through her sponsoring of *The Young and the Evil* in a blurb, and through her citation of its opening description of this encounter, in one of *Nightwood*'s most memorable asides: Nora's realisation that 'children know something they can't tell, they like Red Riding Hood and the wolf in bed!'[19] Ford and Tyler's 'fairy prince' appears in *Nightwood* as well, in the fabulous account of an epicene character, the 'prince-princess'.[20]

Ford and Tyler's opening paragraph describes the proper noun 'Lesbian' as 'mythological' in a transferred epithet, offering an urbane normalising of the unreal 'Little Red Riding Hood' and a complementary mythologising of the sexually marginal. Barnes's reworking also figures cross-generational and inter-species desire. The male collaborative text honours Barnes in an invitation whose perversity is comparable to the unsolicited sight of the wolf and Red Riding Hood, an encounter in which the tea party becomes the locus for a tribute perversely rendered: 'I will be glad to learn it backwards.' Karel is enticed from the 'Round Table' by the sight of 'the most delightful little tea-pot'.[21] The authors' own encounter with the *text* of Djuna Barnes is analogous to this encounter between the insouciant characters of mythology and folklore, becoming a mythologised encounter.

Julian's contribution, '*all* things of course are going backwards past her ear' [my emphasis], describes Barnes as magnetic, a recording machine capturing the text as it moves behind her. It figures tribute as retrospective, in the same way that anecdote, in the opening, is figured as a chronological regression. It depends on the sexualization of the ear as an organ of reception, conception and reproduction (a sexualization also performed in Barnes's *Ryder*, published several years earlier). This figure offers Karel's backward recitation as an inverted source of text: a backwards 'fathering' is worked into this tribute: Barnes's forward recitation, reworked as seduction, is complemented by its return to her ear – backwards. Whereas *Ryder* offers the social nexus of an aggregation of women – plural marriage – to allegorise a model of masculine homosocial textual creation, in *The Young and the Evil* the tea party à *deux* becomes a threesome à *tergo*. The creation of the text is fantasised as a fathering by two men, a collaborative effort that mimes the status of 'Ford and Tyler' as a double signature.[22]

Barnes's *actual* 'kind words' on the back of Ford and Tyler's *The Young and The Evil* suggest that any such tribute would be at best a double-edged sword. Her endorsement of the authors of *The Young and the Evil* allies the function of authorship with homosexuality:

> Never, to my knowledge, has a certain type of homosexual been so 'fixed' on paper. Their utter lack of emotional values – so entire that it is frightening; their loss of all Victorian victories: manners, custom, remorse, taste, dignity; their unresolved acceptance of any happening, is both evil and 'pure' in the sense that it is unconscious. No one but a genius, or Mr. Ford and Mr. Tyler could have written it.[23]

Barnes suggests the text offers generational change, marked by the rejection of 'Victorian victories', a phrase which plays on the metaphorised name of Victoria as tautological and also, as it turns out, transitory.

Ford and Tyler's text offers an emblematic representation – static, 'fixed', photographic – in contrast to the novel's encomium to Barnes, in which they represent her work in a dynamic process of exchange. [A comparison of Ford and Tyler's representation of a moving text and Barnes's representation of photographic 'fixing' suggests a contrast between the technologies of photography and cinema. Such a plotting also points to generational difference and is biographically implicated in Tyler's more famous career as early and influential film critic.[24] These contrasting figurations of authorial function scheme a chiasmus, where the single author produces a text metaphorised by the collaborative pair as dynamic, whilst the multi-authored text is metaphorised by the single (or singular) author as a static product. This chiasmus suggests an attempt to insinuate the structural position of the actual author(s) in and as the praise of the author(s) being described.]

Barnes's note is epideictic, calling to account a generation now '"fixed" on paper' for its lacks and irresolutions. *The Young and The Evil* as emblematic 'fixture' facilitates this blaming. Her last sentence aligns the function of authorship with genius, but also with the collaboratory pair of Ford and Tyler, grammatically singular and thus reduced to a single referent (and thus a referent of sameness). As that which eludes definition, the 'certain type' is a category of the exceptional other, exceptional for its ability to mimetically transcribe or 'fix'. Their exceptional skills are distinct from 'genius' though, and offered as symptoms of a category somewhere between genius and non-genius; they belong to an 'intermediate' category which metonymically suggests the category of the authorial 'third sex'.

The fictionalised and anecdotal appearances of Djuna Barnes in both Ackroyd's and Ford and Tyler's texts, more than fifty years apart, allegorise the relationship between writer and text by making problematic the questions of chronology, sponsorship and the various nature of textual interventions. From Scrope's plagiarism, which textually instantiates Ackroyd-as-writer's 'plagiaristic' borrowing from Ackroyd-as-biographer's access to the publishing and editorial life of *Nightwood* (the 'plot'), to Karel's backwards authorship of the Barnes poem, texts are figured as pliable tokens of exchange, and their exchange is figured through elaborate sexual codings.

Coda: Run Girls, Run!

Barnes's relationship with Charles Henri Ford, one of the collaborative pair of 'Ford and Tyler', extended to his involvement in the transcription of portions of *Nightwood* as it was being written in Tangier and elsewhere during the 1930s.[25] Ford's move from co-authorial collaboration with Tyler to amanuensis took place even as *The Young and the Evil* went to press. *The Young and the Evil* offers a complicating metaphor of textual transcription – recitation – through refiguring inter alia the position of 'author' as that of the instrument of transcription. Barnes's incorporation into *Nightwood* of the figurative material of the opening of *The Young and the Evil* in turn serves to animate the typist-collaborator as a possible interpersonal referent allegorised within this intertextual transplantation. It reintroduces as the source of figuration the function of Ford-as-author within Barnes's text. Ford becomes the pretender or 'fairy prince', heir apparent to the textual genealogy of which *Nightwood* is a part by virtue of the citation of his earlier work, an ironising hysteron proteron whose structure is proleptically instantiated in the earlier text as a backwards tribute.[26]

A remnant of excised writing offers ground for the contemplation of Ford's typing hand which is most clearly evident in the early draft of a section of *Nightwood* called 'Run Girls, Run!'[27] Expunged from the published version of the text, it is clearly typed on a different instrument from those that produced the later typescripts, and written in a style that more closely resembles *Ryder*. This portion of excised script materially instantiates an archaic early life for the novel, offering an evolutionary reading of the progression of the novel's composition from Tangier to Britain, from Ford as typist to Eliot as publisher, from 1920s pastiche to 1930s gothic. My reading hinges upon the sheer unlocatability of this drafted section, which cannot be aligned within the published text, thematically or through plot. This unlocatability finds tropological confirmation in the identification of Barnes's interlocutor with the function of typist (Ford). The unlocatability of 'Run Girls, Run!' as an edited portion of the text of *Nightwood* indicates some of the difficulty inherent in an historical account of textual composition; 'Run Girls, Run!' becomes a material instantiation as well as a metaphor of the impenetrability of textual origins. The metaphorics of such a reading, however, may reproduce precisely those tropes of male intervention and feminine impenetrability, a reading which depends upon rehearsing its very dislocation from the narrative of *Nightwood*'s composition.

The chapter canvasses violent heterosexual initiation, metaphorised as the entrance into a text: 'he pushed down upon her, to encompass a smother, a great bolster from Stratford, saying: "Sink back in to folk-lore, make of your flesh the venison thinkers toughen their wits on, for the sooner I[']m done with you, girl, that much sooner you will be sung of!"'[28] Figuring the rape as a form of textual initiation, 'Run Girls, Run!' initiates an account of rape as the failure of prophylactic editing. Such a claim is offered by the rapist, who figures it on a genealogical family tree: Barnes writes 'The faggots shall thicken in the branch for lack of your dust to sweep.'[29] This form of sexualized textual initiation eliminates cleansing. The broom, as the metaphoric instrument of textual cleansing, is figured through its prior, unedited life, as a faggot – halfway between a branch and a broom. The instrument itself becomes the 'matter out of place'; out of place in the tree, Barnes offers the 'faggot' as a pun for those sexual positions similarly out of place in genealogy. The 'thickened' faggots figure both tumescence and the seizure of the family tree in a state of suspense. The tree is 'fixed', to use Barnes's description of Ford and Tyler in her note on *The Young and The Evil*. Rather than finding in 'Run Girls, Run!' a topos of impenetrability which offers orientation, I read it through a structure analogous to the backwards tribute of *The Young and the Evil*, as a disorientation of authorial and editorial functions, which requires us to read backwards to it, rather than to read from it an account of the text's early days. 'Run Girls, Run!', as early and edited draft, remains to be read. Composed in the future tense, and opening with an account of forestalled sexual violence, it digresses instead upon its own status as 'pages in waiting'.[30] Barnes's pun collects an allegory of editorial and textual inheritance through service, and a reversal of the temporal precedence of the early life of the text.

Notes

1 Andrew Field, *Djuna: the Life and Times of Djuna Barnes* (New York: G.P. Putnam's, 1983), p. 212; Shari Benstock, *Women Of the Left Bank: Paris, 1900–1940* (London: Virago, 1987), p. 428.

2 Jane Marcus, 'Laughing at Leviticus: *Nightwood* as Woman's Circus Epic', in Mary Lynn Broe, ed., *Silence and Power: A Reevaluation of Djuna Barnes* (Carbondale and Edwardsville: Southern Illinois University Press, 1991), pp. 399–400 n.29.

3 Cheryl J. Plumb, 'Introduction', Djuna Barnes, *Nightwood: The Original Version and Related Drafts* (Normal: Dalkey Archive Press, 1995), p. viii.

4 Daniela Caselli, *Improper Modernism: Djuna Barnes' Bewildering Corpus* (Surrey: Ashgate, 2009), p. 156.

5 Monika Faltejskova, *Djuna Barnes, T. S. Eliot and the Gender Dynamics of Modernism: Tracing Nightwood* (New York and Oxford: Routledge, 2010), p. 92.

6 The phrase 'That dangerous supplement' comes from Derrida's analysis of Rousseau and masturbation as a figure of writing-as-supplement which offers 'the restoration, by a certain absence and by a sort of calculated efface-ment, of presence disappointed of itself in speech'. See Jacques Derrida, *Of Grammatology*, trans. Gayatri Chakravorty Spivak (Baltimore: Johns Hopkins University Press, 1984), p.142. Here, by associating editorial practice with sup-plementarity, I am both signalling masturbation as the supplement for which, '[a]s substitute ... its place is assigned on the structure by the mark of an emp-tiness' (*Of Grammatology* 145), and anticipating my discussion of Ford and Tyler's encomium to Barnes, in which they precisely restore to Barnes's text 'presence disappointed of itself in speech'.

7　Mary Douglas writes, 'if uncleanness is matter out of place, we must approach it through order. Uncleanness or dirt is that which must not be included if a pattern is to be maintained.' *Purity and Danger: An Analysis of Concepts of Pollution and Taboo* (London: Routledge and Kegan Paul, 1978), p. 40.

8　Elizabeth Grosz quotes Lingis's observation in *Excesses* that 'circumcision castrates the male of the labia about his penis, as the clitoridectomy castrates the female of her penis'. Elizabeth Grosz, 'Inscriptions and Body-maps: Representations and the Corporeal', in Terry Threadgold and Anne Cranny-Francis, eds., *Feminine Masculine and Representation* (Sydney: Allen and Unwin, 1990), p. 71.

9　Koestenbaum details the numerous references to circumcision and foreskin in Eliot and Pound's letters over the editing of *The Waste Land*, including Eliot's poem 'Blue-eyed Claude the Cabin Boy': a clever little nipper who filled his ass with broken glass and circumcised the skipper. See Wayne Koestenbaum, *Double Talk: The Erotics of Male Literary Collaboration*, (New York: Routledge, 1989), p. 123.

10　Peter Ackroyd, *Chatterton* (London: Sphere Books, 1988), p. 102–103.

11　Ibid., 96.

12　Ibid., 97.

13　Ibid., 100.

14　Sara Tilt's name reintroduces the figure of a female phallus through a metaphor of the phallus as a signifier of inclination or tropism through the proper name 'Tilt'/trope. This can be read as another version of a 'repulsive' woman (see Melissa Jane Hardie, 'Repulsive Modernism: Djuna Barnes' "The Book of Repulsive Women"', *Journal of Modern Literature*, 29:1 (2005): 118–132.)

15　Ackroyd, *Chatterton*, p. 101.

16　George Wickes, *The Amazon of Letters: The Life and Loves of Natalie Barney* (New York: G.P. Putnam's Sons, 1976), p. 179.

17　Peter Ackroyd, *T.S. Eliot* (London: Abacus, 1985), p. 223.

18　Charles Henri Ford and Parker Tyler, *The Young and the Evil* (New York: Gay Presses of New York, 1988), p. 18.

19　Barnes, *Nightwood*, 117.

20　Ibid., 194–195.

21　Ford and Tyler, *The Young and the Evil*, 11.

22　In *Double Talk*, Koestenbaum offers a series of case studies of such structures of male collaborative fathering.

23　From the back cover of *The Young and the Evil*.

24　Parker Tyler, *Magic and Myth of the Movies* (New York: Henry Holt, 1947); a seminal publication in film criticism.

25　Gillian Hanscombe and Virginia L. Smyers, *Writing for their Lives: The Modernist Women, 1910–1940* (London: The Women's Press, 1987), p. 102; Field, *Djuna*, pp. 165–167.

26　Parker Tyler is the 'silent partner' of this exchange.

27　A version of this typescript was published in *Caravel* 2 (March 1936): n.p., and reprinted in *Vagaries Malicieux: Two Stories by Djuna Barnes* (New York:

Frank Hallman, 1974), pp. 30–41. For this analysis I am working from the typescript, which Barnes headed with the handwritten note: 'From something published, I think in New Orleans or was it Majorca', a topographical slide which informs my reading.

28 Barnes, 'Run Girls, Run!', in *Nightwood*, 244.

29 Ibid.

30 Ibid.

CHAPTER 3

Towards a Gendered Media Ecology

Julian Murphet

Theodor Adorno once remarked of Nietzsche that 'He fell for the fraud of saying "the feminine" when talking of women.'[1] Adorno's point was that the system of gender has nothing essential to do with biology and ought instead to be conceived of as something like the privileged lens through which we habitually think difference on the model of a hierarchy. When Nietzsche wanted to approve of a given term in a binary pair, he feminised its other and masculinised the valourised term. 'Hence the perfidious advice not to forget the whip', noted Adorno; even though 'femininity itself is already the effect of the whip'. 'The feminine character is a negative imprint of domination' (102). But this dialectic never stands still, and in what follows I want to explore the perverse retroactivity of that 'negative imprint' at a moment when, as a result of the rapid industrialisation of Western culture, it was itself to have become dominant. For what a gendered account of the media ecology of the modern period reveals is that Nietzsche's misogynist gesture became symptomatic of an 'embattled' minority (artists) at the very time that 'the feminine' was perceived, under the auspices of 'mass culture' and its various media, to have assumed an insuperable hegemony in the capitalist world. These men fell for the fraud of saying 'the feminine' when talking of culture. The result, *in nuce*, was modernism.

I

In the heyday of modernist ideology – as it congealed in the 1950s – it was Clement Greenberg who canonised the doxa of medial purification, according to which what the arts had to demonstrate in modernity was that 'the kind of experience they provided was valuable in its own right'; otherwise 'they were going to be assimilated to entertainment pure and simple.'[2]

Each art, it turned out, had to effect this demonstration on its own account.
What had to be exhibited and made explicit was that which was unique
and irreducible not only in art in general, but also in each particular art.
Each art had to determine, through the operations peculiar to itself, the
effects peculiar and exclusive to itself. (5)

'Peculiar', 'particular', 'each its own': Greenberg urged the specificity of
mediality. It was only through the assertive performance and construal of
each medium's innermost 'operations' that art itself was going to survive
the ceaseless commercial equivalences of 'entertainment'.

It quickly emerged that the unique and proper area of competence of each
art coincided with all that was unique to the nature of its medium. The task
of self-criticism became to eliminate from the effects of each art any and
every effect that might conceivably be borrowed from or by the medium of
any other art. Thereby each art would be rendered 'pure', and in it purity
find the guarantee of its standards of quality as well as its independence.
'Purity' meant self-definition, and the enterprise of self-criticism in the arts
became one of self-definition with a vengeance. (5–6)

The latency of a gender proper to this 'enterprise' is perfectly clear: insofar
as the project of medial purity was related to virtues of 'independence',
'vengeance', and 'self-definition', it was always and already a masculine
one. The negative term, 'entertainment', which as Greenberg noted was
already giving way under its own tendencies to therapy, was a soup of
uncritical assimilation: a feminine morass.

  The principle of individuation outlined by Greenberg – that, threatened
by the indifferent sameness of the culture industry, art had to discover
what was unique to itself; and that it could only do so through activities
internal to the various media that made it what it was – is carried over in
modernist aesthetics to the works themselves; nowhere so programmatically as in Adorno's *Aesthetic Theory*. 'Immersion in the individual work,
which is contrary to genres, leads to an awareness of the work's immanent
lawfulness.'[3] For Adorno, the logic of differentiation in modernity affects
the work by necessitating its withdrawal into monadological immanence;
only thus can it address the whole. Further, it would be accurate to say
that the 'immanent lawfulness' specific to modernist works itself devolves
frequently into a radical particularisation, as expressed in the phenomenon of the 'relative autonomy' of the parts themselves: the chapters of
Ulysses, the sections of *The Cantos*, the 'attractions' in an Eisenstein film,
or the local 'fanatically labored passages of painting' on a Picasso canvas.[4]
At every level, from the most abstract one of 'Art', to the minutest col-
ourations of brushstroke and tone, the principle is one of self-definition

according to a masculine dynamic of opposition, repellence and vanquishment. The shudder that passes through 'the arts' in their recoil from feminine subsumption in mass culture is one of erectile autonomisation: a hardening of the tissues, a stiffening abstraction of the medial muscles and a self-glorying salience of form.

These phallic figures of speech are advised. In an account of the remarkable popularity of Otto Weininger's book *Sex and Character* among the European intelligentsia, John Edward Toews writes:

> In Weininger's universe, the realm of high culture was a product of higher beings who incarnated the highest in everyone, who educated their fellows in the moral task of repudiating their sensual being (femininity and Jewishness), and who interrupted the causal and functional networks of material/historical existence with epiphanies of timeless spiritual form. Such activities had been corrupted, become decadent, in those fin-de-siècle artistic and philosophical movements that surrendered to the seductive pull of the sensually contingent. Drawing heavily on artistic heroes such as Wagner and Ibsen, Weininger called for a more purified and autonomous art, an art that mirrored, articulated, and thus helped to achieve the redemptive goal of spiritual transcendence, of purified masculinity.[5]

What Greenberg canonised as a gendered law of form, Weininger had already lionised as a heroic project of cultural cleansing. Needless to say, the media through which such cleansing would take place were archaic: word, tone and bodily gesture. At the same time, Wilhelm Worringer's account of the heroic 'life-denying inorganic' crystalline hardness of a whole field of neglected abstract aesthetics, withstanding that 'gratification in the beauty of the organic' and its feminine tendency towards empathy and sensuous immersion characteristic of traditional aesthetics, set the tone for a generation's gendered meditations on the arts.[6] Empathic activity, 'in which I experience an expenditure of energy', is what the hard course of masculine abstraction precisely 'seeks to suppress' (160). Worringer gets to the heart of his gendered understanding of the masculine wellsprings of all art in his account of 'the civilized people of the East', whose dread of the 'unfathomable entanglement of all the phenomena of life' led them to 'press back' against that chaos with the dawning rationality of abstract art (161). Consider the sexual implications of the following:

> Tormented by the entangled inter-relationship and flux of the phenomena of the outer world, such peoples were dominated by an immense need for tranquillity. The happiness they sought from art did not consist in the

possibility of projecting themselves into the things of the outer world, of enjoying themselves in them, but in the possibility of taking the individual thing of the external world out of its arbitrariness ... of eternalising it by approximation to abstract forms and, in this manner, of finding a point of tranquillity and a refuge from appearances. Their most powerful urge was, so to speak, to wrest the object of the external world out of its natural context, out of the unending flux of being, to purify it of all its dependence upon life ... to render it necessary and irrefragable, to approximate it to its absolute value. (161)

The allegorical lessons of this fable were clear to Worringer's contemporaries, not least Wassily Kandinsky and T. E. Hulme. Kandinsky liked to write of the creative 'spirit' that, behind and within matter, occasionally breaks forth in apocalyptic intensity: '*The white fertilizing ray*' cutting through '*The black, fatal hand*' of feminine phenomenality.[7] Hulme's 'virile self-assertion' and amply testified misogyny carried over to his aesthetics in such a way as to colour the London avant-garde's sense of its own mission and purpose.[8] He took the gendered opposition directly into art-critical analysis, as in his review of Epstein's *Venus* (1913), a pregnant nude, of which he wrote, 'The tendency to abstraction, the desire to turn the organic into something hard and durable, is here at work. ... Abstraction is much greater ... because generation, which is the very essence of all the qualities which we have here called organic, has been turned into something as hard and durable as a geometrical figure itself.'[9] The 'rigidly dehumanised stylisation' of Epstein's marble nude as a purification of the feminine 'flux' of mere contingency[10] is a process we can see continued in the extraordinary *Rock Drill* (1913–1915), where the little homunculus-fetus peers out grotesquely from the abdomen of the male cyborg-soldier.

Abstraction was thus enshrined as a masculinisation of femininity, and rendered internal to each art, each medium, as a moralising prophylactic against the levelling and enervating tendencies of empathic 'entertainment'. Indeed, as far as Wyndham Lewis was concerned, what this amounted to was (as per the instance of *Rock Drill*, with its re-internalisation of the organic as a parthenogenic modality of the inorganic), a 'mating' of the 'direct and hot impressions of life' with 'Abstraction, or the combinations of the Will'.[11] This copulation was perforce a subjugation, a subjection of 'hot' impressionism to the cold manipulations of the geometric Will; not an aversion, but a reconquest of territories lost to the rot and slither of nineteenth-century sentimentalism. Modernist aesthetics, at least in their most 'advanced' avant-garde formations, turned often enough upon a violent overthrow of Victorian passivity and prostration before the onrush of sensory data. Pound was to put it this way:

> You may think of man as that toward which perception moves. You may think of him as the TOY of circumstance, as the plastic substance RECEIVING impressions. OR you may think of him as DIRECTING a certain fluid force against circumstance, as CONCEIVING instead of merely observing and reflecting.[12]

This is the simplest expression of what had rapidly become an orthodox gendered division of labour at the level of sense perception in modernist aesthetics: on the one hand, a 'plastic substance RECEIVING impressions', and on the other, a 'CONCEIVING' power, 'DIRECTING a certain fluid force against circumstance'. The thrust of modern aesthetics lay in a vigilant discrimination between the impressionistic 'sensually contingent', and this mystical seminal projection; and a logic of separation of one from the other, which in practice led precisely to the medial autonomy that for Greenberg was to have characterised all modernisms. In the process of guarding each medium against the lassitude of feminine reflectionism, each attained to its own pitch of masculine purity.

Behind this will to division and the separation of duties among the arts lay a fertile force indeed, epitomised in Pound's estimation of Lewis's own 'vortex': 'Every kind of geyser of jism bursting up white as ivory, to hate or a storm at sea. Spermatozoon, enough to repopulate the island with active and vigorous animals'.[13] Such ejaculatory adulation took its cue from the intensities peculiar to Lewis's discrete aesthetic series: poetic, pictorial, typographic, propagandistic. The 'jism' in question found fruit not only in the commonality of Lewis's project, but moreover in its forcible division into medial proprieties. It was in each particular art that the genius manifested itself: 'The thought of genius ... is a sudden outspurt of mind' in the medium before it; 'the individual genius ... the man in whom the new access, the new superfluity of spermatozoic pressure (quantitative and qualitative) up-shoots into the brain, alluvial Nile-flood, bringing new crops, new invention',[14] is one who can canalise that bank-bursting torrent into given medial flood-plains.

This vulgar seminal embodiment of the traditional concept of genius (which as Tim Armstrong notes was far more widespread than Pound's ebullient rhetorical apotheoses[15]) is peculiar to the modern period and notably displaces the Goethean conception of genius as stemming from the mouth of the mother.[16] To relate the work of genius to the literal phallic processes of erection and insemination is to tie pen- and brush-strokes, along with chisel-taps and musical composition, to male biological functions in a manner that skates dangerously close to the very feminised/sexualised 'body' of culture from which this reactive ideological formation was recoiling. Whereas the Goethean voice was abstract and metaphysical enough to sustain an entire Hegelian hierarchy of artistic valuations, this newly concocted genital *Ursprung* of genius located the source of conception too close to mortal processes to allow for any actual 'purification'. In Tim Armstrong's account of the resultant paradox in Yeats, 'Wisdom is ideally self-sufficient, unmediated. But in order to enter art, it must "spend" itself, abandoning its unity of being to the downwards pathway of incarnation and time' (140). Moreover, this very abandonment is carried over to the domain of aesthetics itself, where the great abstraction of 'Art', in order to be realised, has to be materialised in concretely embodied media, each with its own laws and dynamics of 'abstraction'. So it is that the recourse to seminal metaphorics in the defence of 'art' against the predations of an engulfing mechanical media system exposes itself, at the level of its logic, to the very thing it most wants to resist: an indiscriminate sexual mediation. Paradoxically, to masculinise is simultaneously to render oneself deliriously effeminate. As Armstrong writes, 'One response to [the] paradox is to actively seek an alliance with the feminine; to shift the self, as it were, onto the ground on which it is mediated' (140).

II

The reasons behind the widespread artistic will to subjugate impressionism at all costs lay arguably less in the cultural lag of a certain Victorianism in the arts than in coeval developments elsewhere in contemporary culture; most especially in the rise of the mechanical media and of an entirely new field of technological culture associated with the second machine age. 'Impressionism' itself, as a code-word for a languid nineteenth-century aesthetic passivity, could be applied equally to the most electrifying medium of the age: cinema. As early as 1896, Maxim Gorky was waxing wroth over the deluge of impressionism unleashed by the flickers:

> Say what you will, but this [the cinematograph] is a strain on the nerves. ... Our nerves are getting weaker and weaker, are growing more and more unstrung, are reacting less and less forcefully to the simple 'impressions of daily life' and thirst more and more eagerly for new, strong, unusual, burning and strange impressions. The cinematograph gives you them – and the nerves will grow cultivated on the one hand, and dulled on the other! The thirst for such strange, fantastic impressions as it gives will grow ever

greater, and we will be increasingly less able and less desirous of grasping the everyday impressions of ordinary life. (99)

The very opposite of a cool fluid abstract force directed against the flux of phenomena, the cinema had loosed a new torrent of 'fantastic impressions' that alienated the masses still further from any adequate mastery over their 'ordinary life'. Pound was to have rehearsed the always-already cinematographic nature of alienated urban life a little later: 'In a city the visual impressions succeed each other, overlap, over-cross, they are "cinematographic", but they are not a simple linear sequence. They are often a flood of nouns without verbal relations.'[17] The trouble with Marinetti's Futurism, in that case, was precisely that it had failed to engage *critically* with this river of nominal impressions, to erect any kind of abstract barrier between us and 'it' (the city as lure and siren); instead capitulating with the worst kind of 'accelerated impressionism', whose logical consequence was (completing the circle) 'the cinematograph. The state of mind of the impressionist tends to become cinematographical. Or, to put it another way, the cinematograph does away with the need of a lot of impressionist art. ... Futurism is descended from impressionism. It is, in so far as it is an art movement, a kind of accelerated impressionism. It is a spreading, or surface art, as opposed to vorticism, which is intensive' (90).

This curious accreditation of the cinema as having 'done away with' the need for Victorian impressionism lends a serious contemporary critical force to the modernist campaign against feminine 'spreading, or surface' culture, since it shifts the burden of guilt away from the 'creampuff' residuals of Tennyson and Rossetti, and towards a seductive new industrial power. To be sure, the former remains a potent threat: 'The "nineties" have chiefly gone out because of their muzziness, because of a softness derived, I think, not from books but from impressionist painting. They riot with half decayed fruit.'[18] But the real front has moved. To that extent, the cinema conveniently stood in for what was being widely understood as the 'feminine' nature of the mechanical media per se, which were reframing and remediating the traditional media and *système des beaux-arts* in the first two decades of the twentieth century. To adopt Mary Ann Doane's convenient opposition, whereas the older arts concerned themselves with the 'necessary' and inevitable aspects of modernity – its structures, codes, residues and totality – the newer media were 'descriptive' (in Lukács's sense) and thereby capitulated 'to the vast and uncontrollable, and ultimately meaningless, realm of the contingent'.[19] The opposition is, again, a gendered one: the contingent's femininity is capricious, changeable and unequal to meaning. So too are the media that specialise in its recording: gramophones, tracing 'the waste or residue that neither the mirror of the imaginary nor the grid of the symbolic can catch: the physiological accidents and stochastic disorder of bodies'[20] ; photographs, tracing 'mere surface coherence ... photography merely stockpiles the evidence'[21]; and so forth.

Fernand Léger, painter and (thanks to *Ballet mécanique*) filmmaker, observed in 1913 that 'modern mechanical achievements such as color photography, the motion-picture camera, the profusion or more or less popular novels ... have effectively replaced and henceforth rendered superfluous the development of visual, sentimental, representational, and popular subject matter in pictorial art.'[22] The law of displacement and superfluity was a Darwinian one; as he put it, 'This will have killed that' (199). The traditionally feminine dimension of old-fashioned cultural production – sentimentality, spatiality, popularity – has devolved to the mechanical media. Reactively, in the domain of the 'proper' arts, the end result was just as Greenberg would later summarise: '*Each art is isolating itself and limiting itself to its own domain*' (199; italics in original). If the 'spreading, or surface' arts of modern technology had now monopolised the terrain of the sentimental and representation – if they had absorbed Victorian culture into their own law of multimedia advancement – then this left 'Art' the sole remaining task of turning in upon itself severally, in 'strategies of inwardness', [23] *noli me tangere* gestures of absolute withdrawal, dismissals of the very 'lure and threat of contingency' in the feminine.[24]

Ibram Lassaw, a member of the American Abstract Artists Group, summarised the gendered law of technological privation in 1938:

> Until the invention of printing on a mass scale, and the development of photography, painting and sculpture were the only means of conveying ideas (outside of speech) to the millions of people who were completely illiterate. Now photography and cinema have been brought to such a high state of perfection that painting cannot hope to compete with them in either description or story telling. Stripped of these superimposed tasks, the underlying structure of art becomes clear. Colors and forms alone have a greater power to move man emotionally and psychologically. It becomes more and more apparent that art has something more and something much greater to offer.[25]

Description here morphs irresistibly into prescription, as the simple 'stripping' away of now supernumerary impressionist tasks by technology frees 'art' for 'something much greater', which turns out to be 'a new form of magic'. 'The artist no longer feels that he is "representing reality"', writes Lassaw, 'he is actually making reality' (379). Once again the gendered trope of a cultural landscape littered with shopworn signs rears its head. 'Direct sensual experience is more real than living in the midst of symbols, slogans, worn-out plots, clichés. ... Reality is something stranger and greater than merely photographic rendering can show' (380). As James Joyce was to comment in his 1903 Paris notebook, 'A photograph is a disposition of sensible matter and may be so disposed for an aesthetic end but it is not a human disposition of sensible matter. Therefore it is not a work of art.'[26] Photography, feminine by nature, merely disposes sensible matter as evidence; what it lacks is that manly 'white fertilizing ray', the 'greater' magic of 'making' via artistic Will.

The familiar association in Eliot's 'The Waste Land' of the gramophone and the feminine 'typist home at teatime' has a notable history. Edward Bellamy's 'With the Eyes Shut' (1889) indulges the whimsical fantasy of a near-future time in which printers have been destroyed by phonography. All printed matter, including the great works of literature, are now readily available through the ubiquitous technology of the 'indispensables', sound-reproductive machines with playback, whose voices are almost always feminine: 'What then shall be said of the delight of sitting at one's ease, with closed eyes, listening to the same story poured into one's ears in the strong, sweet, musical tones of a perfect mistress of the art of storytelling, and of the expression and excitation by means of the voice of every emotion?'[27] This seductive mechanised femininity extends to the clocks of this world, tolling through the night in 'low, rich, thrilling contralto tones [which] appeared fairly to coruscate with previously latent suggestions of romance and poetry' (737–738). Adorno wrote of the phonograph that its success depended upon its deliberate feminisation as a machine. 'The transformation of the piano from a musical instrument into a piece of furniture ... is recurring in the case of the gramophone but in an extraordinarily more rapid fashion. The fate of the gramophone horn marks this development in a striking manner. In their brassiness, they initially projected the mechanical being of the machines onto the surface. In better social circles, however, they were quickly muffled into the colored masses or wood chalices.'[28] The commercial rationale for this feminisation of the machine was transparent; as a marketing director of Victor put it in the early 1920s, 'it was my opinion that ladies did not like the mechanical-looking things in their parlors.'[29]

Radio, meanwhile, was nothing other than the tolling death-knell of the very concept of male authenticity and originality in the domain of culture: 'In radio the authentic original has ceased to exist and, as a category, it has fallen behind the actual state of technological development.'[30] The strange temporalities and aural qualities of the radio voice (light-speed transmission;

the 'hear stripe' of white noise; the disembodied liveness) led to what Adorno
called 'a touch of unreality and witchcraft ... one of the essentials of [the
radio] voice'.[31] (74) Feminised from within by the curious powers of electro-
magnetic propagation, the radio voice emanated stranger signals still. The
1922 story 'Out of the Air' contains an image of the 'sensitive' girl, Eileen;
an image that forever identifies the medium with her gender:

> Some riddle seemed to beset her, filled the air about her – some inar-
> ticulate cry, you might say, elusive, impalpable, afloat in the ether. And
> with her arms flung wide, it was as if she were resolved to tear that riddle
> from the air by some occult process ... her sensitive fingers spread out,
> attuned to things beyond mortal comprehension. Like antennae – was my
> odd thought at that moment, suggested doubtless by the stricken wireless
> tower just beyond her – stark against the leaden sky like her own palpitant,
> expectant figure. ... [E]nergized by some mysterious power outside of her-
> self, attuned to harmonies of the ether that we mortals never hear.[32]

Of course, this was also the period during which, thanks to the invention and industrial spread of the typewriter and Dictaphone, the functions of writing per se were distributed anew along an unparalleled gender
divide. As Friedrich Kittler, among many, has observed, the 'fact that "the
female clerk could all-too easily degrade into a mere typewriter" made her
an asset. From the working class, the middle class, and the bourgeoisie,
out of ambition, economic hardship, or the pure desire for emancipation
emerged millions of secretaries. It was precisely their marginal position
in the power system of script that forced women to develop their manual
dexterity, which surpassed the prideful handwriting aesthetics of male secretaries in the media system.'[33]

It was also the moment, distended in time, during which not only were
the 'Tiller Girls' the emblematic face of mass production as entertainment,
but more affirmatively, for Miriam Hansen, the women of modernity
were actively engaged in creating a counter-public sphere in the darkened
houses of the world's multiplying cinemas. It is not simply that, as Larry
May quotes William Harrison Hays, 'More and more is the motion picture industry being recognized as a stimulant to trade. No longer does
the girl in Sullivan, Indiana, guess what the styles are going to be in three
months. She knows because she sees them on the screen' (236); nor that,
in Kracauer's estimation, Kittler's typewriter-girls were themselves already
in a delirious feedback loop with the flickering screens they flocked to:
'Sensational film hits and life usually correspond to each other because
the Little Miss Typists model themselves after the examples they see on
the screen.'[34] It is that the public sphere, being constituted through the

mechanisms of the newer media, was itself being irresistibly feminised. Hansen's account is succinct: 'If modern advertising and the department store had mobilized the female gaze in the service of consumption, the cinema seemed to have institutionalized women's scopophilic consumption as an end in itself, thus posing a commercially fostered threat to the male monopoly of the gaze.'[35] This unnerving autonomisation of female scopophilia by the cinematic apparatus in its rapid maturation during the silent period was complicated by its participation in a broader process: 'If, in the fissures and detours of this process, the cinema assumed the function of an alternative horizon of experience for a large number of women, it was enabled by the same conditions that were working in favour of working-class and immigrant audiences: the instability of the cinema as an industrial-commercial public sphere, conflicts between short-term economic and long-range ideological interests, and the uneven development of modes of production, representation, and exhibition' (123). It was these very contradictions and inconsistencies that provided the conditions in which a veritable counter-public sphere could emerge, in which women were in many senses the governing majority. This was that horizon in which the screen and publicity image of Rudolph Valentino could flare up as a specifically female desiring inflection of the potent masculine image, unthinkable in any previous media constellation.

In all, the newer mechanical media were invariably addressed in feminine terms, and, although they enriched mainly male executives and patent-holders, engendered a newly female counter-public sphere. Unleashing a female gaze, a feminine voice, a women's work-force and a new phase of commodity fetishism propagated by the image and the song, these media brought 'women' (or the cultural representation of an entire sex) into conceptual close-contact with machinery, automatism and seriality. It was against precisely this matrix of assumptions and stereotypy that the masculine rigidities and purities of abstraction and autonomy reacted. So it was that, in one of the most curious of cultural chiasmuses, modern technology and mass production (dependent in essence on science, the ratio, and factory production) were coded feminine, in order that the non-machinic media of paint, sculpture, music and verse could attain to a masculine quality of independence and autonomy.

III

The now-traditional 'great divide' between 'mass culture as feminine and inferior' and the 'masculinist mystique' of 'high culture' can thus be pushed a small step forward[36]: these powers are nothing other than the media that constitute them, or in other words, two distinct media systems undergoing a process of conversion and differentiation (elsewhere I call this the hypothesis of 'convergent differentiation'[37]). To the extent that industrial and economic history was forcing a convergence between a long-established media system or 'discourse network' centred around the written page, and a nascent media system defined by mechanical reproduction, so too was that process resisted internally by the older system, which then aggressively differentiated itself from the newer one and differentiated itself internally according to a pervasive gesture of purification and abstraction. The logic of this differentiation was ritually gendered as masculine: as we have seen, while a cluster of tropes of femininity dictated the terms through which the mechanical media would be understood, the older arts and crafts could pursue lines of flight into their own essence via masculine figures and tactics of disavowal, purity and (ironically) prosthesis, or what J. G. Ballard called 'the castration complex raised to the level of the art-form'.[38]

The virtue of this move, it seems to me, is that we shift the emphasis away from both the sex of any given practitioner and the represented 'contents' of any given work of art, to focus on the underlying means of representation themselves as always and already gendered – a shift that permits us to understand gender not as simply connected to any specific body or theme, but as foundational to the ways in which modernism was conceived as a rear-guard defensive action on behalf of media technologies (paint-and-easel, bronze and stone, chamber orchestras, the stage, etc.) rendered to some extent redundant or effortlessly remediated by newer ones. The assertive masculinity of this helpless defensive posture – 'fortifying its boundaries ... maintaining its purity and autonomy'[39] – was (a) doomed in advance as any kind of breakwater or protective membrane against the industrial deluge of mechanical media; and (b) almost ridiculously comical in the context of the declining relevance and authority of the arts in the age of mass production (i.e., against the rigorous logic of Ford's assembly line or the brutal accumulation of Pierpont Morgan, the aesthetic posturing of Wyndham Lewis and Ezra Pound looks deliciously effeminate). The 'masculinity' of the various modernisms, then, is both a reactive and a self-misperceiving phenomenon, devised as a prosthetic suit of organic armour with which to withstand the resistless blows of mechanical reproduction. To that extent, it has to be stipulated that this masculinity is a *performative* one, assumed with a knowing self-consciousness that no more exculpates it of its misogynist excesses than it does condemn it in advance for every strategic essentialism with which it flirts. For if there is no way of evading the conquest by the newer mechanical media of almost all cultural space, a tactical masculinisation of the older media will at least offer a provisional ideological shelter and base of operations from which to conduct raids and begin fraternisation with the 'enemy' which, as feminine, may even be available for seduction.

Notes

1 T. W. Adorno, *Minima Moralia: Reflections from Damaged Life*, trans. E. F. N. Jephcott (London & New York: Verso, 2005), p. 103.
2 Clement Greenberg, 'Modernist Painting', in Francis Frascina and Charles Harrison, eds., *Modern Art and Modernism: A Critical Anthology*, (London: Harper and Row, 1982), p. 5.
3 Theodor Adorno, *Aesthetic Theory*, trans. Robert Hullot-Kentor (New York: Continuum, 2004), p. 266.
4 T. J. Clark, *Farewell to an Idea: Episodes from a History of Modernism* (New Haven: Yale University Press, 1999), p. 190.
5 John E. Toews, 'Refashioning the Masculine Subject in Early Modernism: Narratives of Self-Dissolution and Self-Construction in Psychoanalysis and Literature, 1900–1914', *Modernism/Modernity* 4.1 (1997): 33–34. [31–67]
6 Wilhelm Worringer, from 'Abstraction and Empathy', in Frascini and Harrison, eds., *Modern Art and Modernism*, p. 159.
7 Wassily Kandinsky, 'On the Question of Form', in Kandinsky and Franz Marc, eds., *The Blaue Reiter Almanac*, Documentary Edition, ed. Klaus Lankheit, trans. Henning Falkenstein (London, Tate Publishing, 2006), pp. 147, 148.
8 Miriam Hansen, 'T. E. Hulme, Mercenary of Modernism', *ELH*, Vol. 47, No. 2 (Summer, 1980): 363–365.
9 T. E. Hulme, Quest Society lecture on Epstein, *Speculations: Essays on Humanism and the Philosophy of Art*, ed. Herbert Read (London: Routledge and Kegan Paul, 1924), p. 107.
10 Richard Cork, 'Vorticism and Sculpture', in *Blast: Vorticism 1914–1918*, ed. Paul Edwards (Aldershot: Ashgate, 2000), p. 52.
11 Wyndham Lewis, 'The London Group', *Blast* 2 (July 1915), p. 78.
12 Ezra Pound, 'Vortex', c.1914, in *Ezra Pound and the Visual Arts*, ed. Harriet Zinnes (New York: New Directions, 1980), p. 151.
13 Ezra Pound, letter to John Quinn, 10 March 1916, in Timothy Materer, ed., *Selected Letters of Ezra Pound to John Quinn 1915–1920* (Durham: Duke University Press, 1991), p. 66.
14 Ezra Pound, 'Postscript to *The Natural Philosophy of Love* by Rémy de Gourmont' (1921), in *Pavannes and Divagations* (New York: New Directions, 1958), pp. 203–214.

15 See Armstrong, *Modernism, Technology and the Body* (Cambridge: Cambridge University Press, 1998), pp. 133–158.

16 See Friedrich Kittler, *Discourse Networks 1800/1900*, esp. Ch. 2 'The Mother's Mouth', trans. Michael Metteer with Chris Cullens (Stanford: Stanford University Press, 1990), pp. 25–69.

17 Ezra Pound, Review of Jean Cocteau, *Poésies 1917–1920* (Editions de la Sirène, Paris), *The Dial*, Volume 70 (January 1921): 110.

18 Pound, *Literary Essays*, ed. T. S. Eliot (London: Faber, 1960), p. 363.

19 Mary Ann Doane, *The Emergence of Cinematic Time: Modernity, Contingency, The Archive* (Cambridge, MA: Harvard University Press, 2002), p. 12.

20 Kittler, *Gramophone, Film, Typewriter*, p. 16.

21 Siegfired Kracauer, *The Mass Ornament: Weimar Essays*, trans and ed. Thomas Y. Levin (Cambridge, MA: Harvard University Press, 1995), p. 52.

22 Léger, 'The Origins of Painting and its Representational Value' in Charles Harrison and Paul Wood, eds., *Art in Theory 1900–1990* (Oxford: Blackwell, 1992), pp. 198–199.

23 Fredric Jameson, *Fables of Aggression: Wyndham Lewis, the Modernist as Fascist* (Berkeley: University of California Press, 1979), p. 2.

24 Doane, *Emergence*, p. 19.

25 Ibram Lassaw, 'On Inventing Our Own Art' (1938), in Harrison and Wood, eds., *Art in Theory*, p. 379.

26 James Joyce, 'Aesthetics', *Occasional, Critical, and Political Writing*, ed. Kevin Barry (Oxford: Oxford University Press, 2000), p. 104.

27 Bellamy, 'With the Eyes Shut', *Harper's New Monthly Magazine* 79.473 (Oct 1889): 737.

28 Adorno, 'The Curves of the Needle', in *Essays on Music*, ed. Richard Leppert, trans. Susan Gillespie (Berkeley: University of California Press, 2002), p. 273.

29 Leon Douglass, quoted in Tim Gracyk, 'Leon F. Douglass, Inventor and Victor's First Vice President', *Victrola and 78 Journal* 8 (Spring 1996), available at www.gracyk.com/leon.shtml.

30 Theodor Adorno, *Current of Music*, ed. and trans. Robert Hullot-Kentor (Cambridge: Polity, 2009), p. 90.

31 Adorno, *Current of Music*, p. 74.

32 Lee Foster Hartmann, 'Out of the Air', *Harper's* (September 1922): 499.

33 Friedrich Kittler, *Gramophone, Film, Typewriter*, p. 194.

34 Siegfried Kracauer, *The Mass Ornament*, p. 292.

35 Hansen, *Babel and Babylon*, p. 122.

36 Andreas Huyssen, *After the Great Divide: Modernism, Mass Culture, Postmodernism* (Bloomington and Indianapolis: University of Indiana Press, 1986), p. 55.

37 See Murphet, *Multimedia Modernism: Literature and the Anglo-American Avant-Garde* (Cambridge: Cambridge University Press, 2009), pp. 21–25.

38 J. G. Ballard, 'Project for a Glossary of the Twentieth Century', in Jonathan Crary and Sanford Kwinter, eds., *Incorporations* (New York: Zone Books, 1991),

p. 271. See also Tim Armstrong, *Modernism, Technology*; Hal Foster, *Prosthetic Gods* (Cambridge, MA: MIT Press, 2004), pp. 109–150; and Jessica Burstein, 'Waspish Segments: Lewis, Prosthesis, Fascism', *Modernism/Modernity* Vol. 4, No. 2 (1997), pp. 139–164.

39 Andreas Huyssen, *After the Great Divide*, p. 54.

PART II

Masculinity in Crisis

CHAPTER 4

Nothing to Be Done: Masculinity and the Emergence of Irish Modernism

Rónán McDonald

ESTRAGON: *Nothing to be done*

Samuel Beckett, *Waiting for Godot*

The most famous Irishman in modernism, Leopold Bloom, spends 16 June 1904 cooking inner organs, running errands, helping the Dignam family and attending to his job as an advertising copyeditor. But this 'womanly man' is atypical, and not just compared to the other major male protagonist of *Ulysses*, the unwashed ruminant, Stephen Dedalus. From the languid aristocrats of Oscar Wilde to the shiftless student in Flann O'Brien's *At Swim Two Birds*, via the lyrical tramps of Synge and the urban poets of O'Casey, men in the Irish modernist canon spend a lot of time doing nothing, even if they can talk a good talk. In this they are far from unique in modernist literature, from the decadents onwards. But there are particular cultural formations in Ireland that make male passivity a notable strain.[1] The preponderance of enchanted, idle, paralysed, lethargic, sacrificial, overly-cerebral or obstinate men can be traced to the Irish Revival, and the gendered discourses of nationality with which it struggled.

This essay unravels modes of male inaction in Irish modernism, tracing some of the impasses of masculinity to the historical and cultural conditions of the Revival. For much of the twentieth century, critical orthodoxy regarded the major Irish modernists such as Joyce and Beckett as 'modern' precisely to the degree that they transcended national questions, focusing on universal interests rather than the supposedly provincial concerns of the Irish Revival. But thinking on the relationship between nationality and the modern has been overhauled in recent years and the importance of peripheral and postcolonial modernisms has been widely recognised, while the Irish background of Wilde, Joyce, Beckett and Bowen is greatly feeding into the critical reception of their work.[2] A category such as 'Irish modernism', which would once have seemed incurably oxymoronic, has become ubiquitous in recent years. Relatedly, the rise of the new modernist studies and corresponding shifts in Irish studies has meant that borders between the Irish Revival and modernism are now recognised as much more porous.[3]

The resistance to an ideology of productive, active masculinity exerts pressure on literary form, slowing the teleological momentum of realism and thereby sequestering part from whole. This is one reason why the decadence movement was an incubator for more outré modernist experimentalism. Passivity leads to a local heaviness that makes the totalising impetus of holistic forms sag. Inaction in literary terms tends towards devolution of literary power, such as we find in the formal entropies of Beckett or the comic 'democratization' of character in *At Swim Two Birds*, both of which, in different ways, confound the sclerotic ideologies of postcolonial Ireland. This essay argues that deliberate idleness, or insolent indolence, emerges from a history of withdrawal from useful masculine citizenry that can be traced to the literary Revival, despite the contradictory emphasis in that movement on the necessarily muscular project of nation building. My argument, broadly put, is that male inaction shifts from early to late Irish modernism, from modes of enchantment and self-sacrifice in Yeats to the more conscious rhetoric of refusal and obduracy in Joyce and Beckett. The orientation of inaction tends towards what we might call modernist form because it slows down narrative propulsion and disrupts dramatic totalities and teleologies. In the resulting thickened textures, gaps, distensions and absences new possibilities for subjectivity can be glimpsed.

Semi-colonial Masculinity

As many commentators and cultural theorists have noted, the Irish nation and the Irish character have long been figured as feminine.[4] This association cleaves persistently to the cognate, gendered discursive binaries around which the Irish-English opposition is structured – Saxon versus Celt, civilisation versus barbarism, urban versus rural, progress versus tradition, faith versus superstition, modernism versus revival.[5] This gendered association had a long pedigree, both within Ireland itself and in English attitudes to Ireland. On the one hand, Ireland had long been figured in myth, song and legend as a woman with many names – the *Sean Bhean Bhoct* (Poor Old Woman), *Róisín Dubh* (Dark Rosaleen), *Cathleen ní Houlihan* or just 'Mother Ireland'. At the same time, British ethnology often imagined the Irish as possessing childish or feminine characteristics. Typically, this 'Celticism' was wedded to a gendered discourse in which the

'Saxon' embodied the protoypically 'masculine' qualities of pragmatism, stolidity, reliability, rationality, while the 'Celt' manifested the necessary counterpoint: emotional, undisciplined, contrary, unstable, imaginative. These Celticist taxonomies, theorised by Ernst Renan and elaborated by Matthew Arnold, served a key function in Victorian England where Celts were an exotic 'fringe' foil to normative Saxon self-identification.

Irish nationalists sometimes deployed Arnoldian ideas of the Celt, rewiring them to justify independence rather than union. If the 'effeminate' Irish character – emotional and irrational – seemed to render it unfit for self-government in English eyes, these qualities could be recast as spiritual and idealistic, demonstrating Irish distinctiveness not just from Britain, but from a debased and materialistic modern world. At the same time, however, Irish 'fitness for freedom' demanded the normative manliness extolled in Britain. The Irish needed to show themselves to be strong, ordered, enterprising and pragmatic. So Irish nationalist ideology and by extension the literary Revival needed to embrace contradictory values, establishing themselves as both feminine enough to be a distinctly Celtic nation and manly enough for self-government. The Irish revivalists spurned imported mass culture, but they could not figure it as dangerously feminine in the manner of other modernist elites, because the alternative they were offering – authentic Irish tradition – was itself tied to discourses of womanhood.[6]

There were other quandaries. That *manly* self-mastery needed to demonstrate Ireland's fitness for freedom was dialectically opposed to an idea of *maleness* with which the Irish were also often associated: brutishness, violence, savagery. The Victorian virtue of 'manliness' defined itself precisely by discipline and control over the bestial appetites of 'maleness'. But if the fighting Irish lacked manly virtue and self-control, they had an abundance of what Ashis Nandy has identified as colonial 'hyper-masculinity'.[7] Ireland was alternately soft, childlike, effeminate and incapable of self-government and wild, obstreperous, brutish and ungovernable. The ethnological typology is heavily wedded to a class as well as a national or a racial politics.[8] But nonetheless that English projections of the Irish character can double back from the hyper-feminine image of the gentle, vulnerable 'Hibernia' into the savage male, the bloodthirsty Fenian, indicates something of the dilemma from which Irish discourses of masculinity emerged.

Images of the Irish male in Britain – feminine, buffoonish, savage – along with the figure of the stage Irishman – wheedling, loquacious, witty, entertaining, lazy, garrulous – were images Irish writers variously internalised and resisted. These gendered dynamics are familiar to any student of Irish culture. Less familiar, however, is the effect it may have had on masculine formations. [9] This is not so much a 'crisis' of gender ideology, as it is a dilemma or a bind. There was a need to assert a reactive masculinity, but the available roles were occupied or contaminated. Perceived threats to manhood in the metropolitan centre, from emancipated women, Jews, the working class, were answered by vigorous assertions of masculinity. But this response was more problematic in Ireland, so that even overt performances of masculinity – such as the Easter Rising of 1916 – simultaneously resisted and reflected hegemonic militarism.

The colonial context may seem to invite comparison with India and other British colonial dominions. But the comparisons are perforce limited and the applicability of colonial models to Ireland has been fiercely contested in Irish studies.[10] Ireland was part of the union during the nineteenth century, proximate to the rest of the United Kingdom and strongly represented in the British army and in British imperial administrations. The anomalous and liminal position of Ireland might lead us to follow the example of Derek Attridge and Marjorie Howes and borrow from *Finnegans Wake* Joyce's neologism 'semicolonial' to describe its cultural condition.[11] It resembles a colony from one stance and an imperial power from another. This status affects the circulation of and resistance to English ideas of the Irish and, thence, constructions of Irish masculinity.

Moreover, in semi-colonial Ireland the relationship between 'settler' and 'native' is more blurred than in colonies where racial or linguistic divisions obtain. Many of the originators of what came to be known as the Irish Renaissance or Revival were Protestant, Anglo-Irish and identified with London as their capital. The so-called Father of the Revival, Standish O'Grady (1846–1928), responsible for bringing images of the Irish hero Cuchulain out of the archive, held strongly unionist convictions.[12] Frequently, in these cases, ethnologies of the Irish are mobilised within Ireland along class lines, or from metropolitan East to rural West. In other words, Anglo-Irish writers project onto the Irish peasantry versions of femininity or savagery recognisable from English constructions of 'Irishness'. Take as an instance, *Hurrish* (1886), by the Anglo-Irish novelist Emily Lawless. Its eponymous hero has

> the genuine Celtic temperament – poetic, excitable, emotionable [sic], unreasoning. Of the more brutal and cruel elements, which too often, alas! streak and disfigure that strain, he had hardly a trace. He was kindly to softness, and tender-hearted almost to womanliness.[13]

Offsetting Hurrish is the less desirable version of Irish masculinity, in the form of the drunken, lecherous Mat Brady, 'unwieldy, red-faced, heavy-jawed, brutal – a sort human orangutang or Caliban' (20), an embodiment of the bestial, lazy, simian Irish male that owe so much to pseudo-Darwinian typologies. This stereotype of the red-faced, often red-haired, bulky, inebriate, quasi-troglodytic Irishman endures well into the twentieth century and is widely parodied in the work of high Irish modernists. One might point at the bestial associations of the Citizen, in the 'Cyclops' episode of *Ulysses*, or the comic depiction of Mr Nackybal (a rearrangement of Caliban), in Beckett's *Watt*.[14]

If the Irish internalised colonial images of themselves, then they also took on Victorian and Edwardian ideas of masculine virtue. Despite the calls by Douglas Hyde and others on the necessity of 'deanglicising Ireland', codes of muscular Christianity that underpinned Empire also infused nationalist rhetoric, precisely at the moments when autonomy and separatism was being most vigorously asserted, such as the build-up to the Easter Rising in 1916.[15] This was so in literary as well as political circles. In seeking to establish the value and dignity of Irish manhood, the revivalists held up the figure of Cuchulain, the Irish mythic hero whose legendary athleticism in Gaelic sports and prowess on the battlefield seemed to provide Ireland with its own Achilles. Oliver Sheppard's 1911 sculpture of the dead hero still stands in the General Post Office in Dublin, where the Irish Republic was proclaimed at the start of the Rising. While Cuchulain may have provided 'a symbol of masculinity for Celts, who had been written off as feminine by their masters', he was as Declan Kiberd pithily puts it, 'a British public-schoolboy in drag'.[16] Some later Irish modernists and counter-revivalists had a strong impulse to demythologise this cult of militant masculinity. Samuel Becket delivers his mordant judgement in *Murphy*, when his character Neary creates a scene in the GPO by banging his head against the buttocks of the legendary hero.[17]

As is so often the case, Yeats bridges the revivalist and modernist impulses and his depictions of Cuchulain show a more tormented and modernist figure than that of Patrick Pearse's militaristic cult (St Enda's, Pearse's school, carried Cuchulain's motto – 'I care not though I were to live but one day and one night, if only my fame and my deeds live after me').[18] There is a notable clash between the man-of-action rhetoric of Cuchulain and his performative instantiation, especially in Yeats's verse drama, where he is often strikingly non-militant or militant in tragically counter-effective ways. Yeats's plays *On Baile's Strand* (1903), *At the Hawk's Well* (1916), *The Only Jealousy of Emer* (1922) and *The Death of Cuchulain* (1939) see him hungering for passivity or versions of permanence and immortality. In *On Baile's Strand* the hero is having a midlife crisis. He is torn between his wild individualism and a yearning for the security of established society and, with it, progeny. This is a play that dramatises conflicted versions of manhood, where the male subject seeks to reconcile autonomy with coherence, the self with the nation. It stages a deeply troubled masculinity in which identity is tragically arrested and the Oedipal paradigm inverted, as Cuchulain unwittingly kills his only son. By the end of the play, Cuchulain's 'actions' are an exercise in insanity and futility. Stricken with grief, trauma and guilt, he battles with the breaking waves. His action is pointless, misdirected, unhinged. It is significant that here and in Yeats's earlier poem 'Cuchulain's Fight With the Sea' (1892) he engages in mock battles with the sea, so mythically associated with the feminine. It surely indicates an urge to escape the boundaries of the nation and his gendered role in its imaginary.

Cuchulain is a cultural icon revived in order to enchant, but as a dramatised figure he hinges between enchantment and disenchantment. Many of his legends end in his frustration and disillusionment. This not only makes him a signally modernist totem but also decelerates his capacity for male action, for potency.[19] His inert body is freighted, even fetishised, and becomes appropriated, as in Sheppard's sculpture, by a web of sacrificial, often Christian associations. In the later Yeats, Cuchulain is often an atrophied and acquiescent figure. He is entirely stripped of his heroic distinctiveness in the great poem 'Cuchulain Comforted' (1939), but this seems a relief or a release. His battle armour becomes a shroud that he must sew for himself, alongside the ghosts of cowards. Even this most distinctive figure of manly action here connects to a wider trope of an androgynised Irish masculinity that is explicit in other major modernist texts such as *Playboy of the Western World* (1907) or *Ulysses* (1922).

Enchanted to a Stone

These images of Cuchulain also connect to a deep structure within the imagining of Irish masculinity, which sees successful agency emerging only from within the frames of failure. This mode of thinking feeds into the 1916 Rising and the cult of sacrifice and Christian martyrology that inspired it. As the hero of Patrick Pearse's play *The Singer* says, 'One man can free a people as one man redeemed the world. I will take no pike. I will go into battle with bare hands. I will stand up before the Gall as Christ hung naked before men on a tree.'[20] Motherhood is a recurrent invocation of the myth of Irish male sacrifice, partly because of the mythic tradition of Mother Ireland, calling on her brave sons to recover her lost fields. In Yeats's and Lady Gregory's play *Cathleen Ni Houlihan* (1902), the *locus classicus* of this myth in modern Irish literature, there is a double-image of the female Ireland as mother and lover who lures young men to submit their lives in her service, affirming the logic of male sacrifice as an act of consummating the nation. In this play, which draws consciously on the *aisling* tradition in Irish poetry, Irish nationalist masculinity finds its expression in modes of *enchantment*. It therefore denies agency, and comes perilously close to an idea of male valour as precisely the seduction of self rather than its willing sacrifice. It is an ambivalent endorsement, but Yeats deploys the story in the service of his own anti-middle class politics and the logic of the play vouchsafes an idealism, patriotic and self-abnegating, implicitly nobler than the pinched mercantilism of bourgeois marriage. This opposition is reflected in the play through the Hiberno-English of the characters and the verse spoken by Cathleen Ni Houlihan. The play splices dichotomous linguistic and dramatic registers, its realism seems secure then thwarted, like the expectation of marriage at the start of the play. It is an example of how a sort of passivity can, like violence, register in a formal rupture.

When nationalist violence does erupt in Ireland from 1916–1922, ending in bloody civil war, the myth of enchantment is ripe for deflation. Sean O'Casey's Dublin plays seeks to indict nationalist armed action as blind zealotry destructive of what really matters – hearth and home security – and in *The Shadow of a Gunman* (1923) Catheen Ni Houlihan is mentioned only sardonically. More subtly in Joyce's *Ulysses*, the image of 'Mother Ireland' is not refused so much as revealed as a shadowy, incomplete project. Joyce, unlike O'Casey, does not 'debunk' myth with the alternate presentation of humanist 'reality', but rather exposes the subjective and colonial wounds underlying the symbolic relation. When Stephen Dedalus refuses to pray by his dying mother's bedside he is acting on an ethic not only against fake piety, but also against the national mythologising of the mother trope. But it is a guilt-ridden abnegation that haunts him during the day. Shortly after being goaded by Buck Mulligan for refusing his mother's request, Stephen associates the old milk-woman with a series of symbolic figures, including the 'sean bhean bhoct', the allegorical embodiment of Ireland. But this old woman, ironically, does not recognise the Irish language that Haines the Englishman speaks, mistaking it for French. She is figured as abject, colonially humiliated, and Stephen's relentless brooding seems an unpromising version of the 'enchanted' son of Ireland. The nationalist heroism is radically deflated here, the possibility of redemptive action denied. It is hard to see how Stephen can act effectively, in cahoots as he is with 'her conquerer [Haines] and her gay betrayer [Mulligan].'[21]

The linkage of male 'enchantment' with political sacrifice that compresses nationalism and masculinity occurs elsewhere in Yeats, most famously in 'Easter 1916' (1921). But there are manifold representations of manly virtue in his work. One is the austere, lone figure of the Anglo-Irish hero, brought down by the middle-class vulgarians. Charles Stewart Parnell (1846–1891) filled that role for Yeats at times, a totemic figure of betrayed Irish masculinity, for him as for James Joyce. Yeats projects onto the declining Ascendancy class a doomed sort of stoic virtue of which Parnell is the exemplar. Because this group eludes the developing national imaginary, its representative is figured in individualistic mode, as a solitary hero. Perhaps the most celebrated instance is 'An Irish Airman Foresees his Death' (1919), where the speaker (never named, but based on Lady Gregory's son) elects for the 'lonely impulse of delight' that leads him to the self-annihilating 'tumult in the clouds'. Yeats could not support the British imperialist war, but embracing an ethos of aristocratic transcendence allows him to avoid the political cause for which Robert Gregory died, while also elegising the Ascendancy class to which he belongs. The hauteur of Yeats's ideal Anglo-Irishman adopts the bravery and valour of the English soldier, while shedding it of any pro-Allied feeling. Instead he embraces *sprezzatura* and an aristocratic scorn of life. Even as his country is 'Kiltartan cross', his countrymen 'Kiltartan's poor', the figure in the sky is one of inviolate solitude, his decision motivated by indifference to the puny concerns of mere survival. It is an exercise in literary authority that hinges on metaphors of deftness, balance, poise and supreme grace, formally achieved in the prosody, particularly through the use of chiasmus:

> Nor law, nor duty bade me fight,
> Nor public men, nor cheering crowds,
> A lonely impulse of delight
> Drove to this tumult in the clouds;
> I balanced all, brought all to mind,
> The years to come seemed waste of breath,
> A waste of breath the years behind
> In balance with this life, this death.[22]

The pleasing formal poise and balance coils around a bleak decision. It is a poem that makes a virtue of suicide. But the airman does not make his choice for anything as prosaic as martyrdom or sacrifice. Rather he elects the 'tumult in the clouds' because of a 'lonely impulse of delight' and because of a perception of pointlessness in life, decreed a 'waste of breath'. Yet he comes to and acts upon this conclusion through recognisable codes of masculine adventurousness, level-headedness and bravery. The poem performs in its prosody, as the airman performs in his mental balance, a lucid, rational, panoptic judgement, yet at the same time, in an unlikely marriage of Kipling and Kafka, he asserts modern alienation and meaninglessness. However, despite the reactionary class politics of this poem, it exposes a key contradiction in normative masculinity. If 'manliness' is the control that a gentleman has over his own 'male' appetites, then the Irish airman exposes the implicit contradiction in this dialectic. So masterly is his 'manliness' that it overwhelms not only the antisocial appetites of his natural condition but the very survival instinct itself. He is civilised into oblivion.

The airman is, in many senses, a singular figure. Yet comparison between him and other men in Yeats's work and Irish modernist texts is instructive. He strikes a note of refusal, the *non serviam* of Stephen Dedalus. Yet he does so through self-abnegation, even a mode of submission, that again makes him seem a most *passive* actor who meets his 'fate' and chooses it. An equally famous poem from Yeats's canon that also brings masculine virtue and military self-sacrifice into alignment is 'Easter 1916'. Here it is the third-person poet who brings scrutiny to bear on the rebels' motivations, through a series of unanswered questions. There is a sectarian distinction here. The Catholic, middle-class rebels have not weighed their decisions, have not arrived at the lofty judgement of the Anglo-Irish aristocrat. They are certain, but their certainty emerges as zealotry rather than conviction. It emerges from the fanatical heart, not the judicious head: 'Hearts with one purpose alone / Through summer and winter seem / Enchanted to a stone / To trouble the living stream'; 'Too long a sacrifice / Can make a stone of the heart.'[23]

Both poems use alternating ABAB rhyming scheme embedded in a quatrain structure but, crucially, the trimetrical line of 'Easter 1916' gives a far more propulsive quality than the tetrameter deployed in 'An Irish Airman Foresees his Death', where the prosody seems as detached and balanced as the speaker. The rebels, on the other hand are dreaming and 'enchanted'. Yet, even though the poet seems ambivalent about their sacrifice, he asserts its tragic dignity. Significantly, the trope of motherhood emerges in the concluding lines. The hitherto anonymous men are elegiacally named, as an act of public tribute. But the tribute is figured in strongly private terms: 'To murmur name upon name, / As a mother names her child / When sleep at last has come / On limbs that had run wild.' The rebels may have left the living stream and become monumental, but the poetic inscription is, with a powerful counterpoint, rendered in intimate terms, as a mother comforting her child.

Yeats has been accused of 'infantilizing' the rebels here. By rendering them as 'wild' children, he reduces their agency and reproduces colonialist typologies.[24] But reducing their agency is of a piece with the way Yeats often constructs manliness, even in the case of the supremely controlled Irish airman or the archetypal Cuchulain. One might note that the crucial verb 'to change' is always passive except, in the third, 'nature'-based stanza: the rebels *are* 'changed', they never *do* the changing themselves. The masculine subjects are caught within networks of association and signifying webs that are historically discursive and performative, moving from comedy to tragedy, and finally the ascription of their own names. The rebels' individual agency is circumscribed by their enchantment, bewilderment and 'excess of love' and this is formally reflected in the poet's own bewildered questioning.

More Talk, Less Action

Of all the art forms enlisted to nation building by the Irish revivalists, drama was the most central. The connection between nationality and gender, which I have been arguing confounded Irish constructions of 'masculinity', emerges with all its contradictory force on the stage. But what of its depictions of male inaction? 'Action', according to Aristotelian norms, was regarded as essential to effective drama. But Samuel Beckett demonstrated that one could also make theatre of inaction, launching himself into global fame with *Waiting for Godot* (1955), in which 'nothing happens, twice'.[25] Beckett's play was revolutionary, but the dramatic possibilities of waiting and inaction had been much explored on the Irish stage in works such as Synge's *Riders to the Sea* (1904) and Lady Gregory's *The Workhouse Ward* (1909). So too had 'distraction', by which characters compensate for their inefficacy through pointless blather. On the Irish stage, talk often has an inverted relationship with action and this is strongly coincident with gender. The men in Irish drama are often great talkers, but strikingly ineffective when it comes to pragmatic matters. The garrulous, charming, sometimes poetic, often roguish Irishman goes deep into the history of theatre in Ireland and Britain – as the history of the 'Stage Irishman' attests. One of the strongest associations of Irishness is a capacity for 'blarney'. If the founders of the Irish national theatre sought to demolish the stage Irish slur, the idea of verbosity endured strongly. One of the possibilities it affords is to allow Irish theatre to stage oppositions between what is said and what is done, between the richness of speech and the paucity of material transformation. Men on the Irish stage are, we find, often the inverse of that most recognisable trope of modern masculinity, the 'strong silent type'.

Captain Jack Boyle, the delusional braggart of O'Casey's *Juno and the Paycock* (1924), belongs to a recognisable male comic archetype, down to his ingratiating sidekick, Joxer. This comic pairing is the bane of poor, overworked Juno, striving to keep the family together. But Irish drama is not unique in this depiction, and braggadocio is often key to the performance of homosocial manliness. What may be more distinctive about the Irish case, however, is the frequency with which on the Irish stage, the good talker garners a sort of poetic capital, the way proficiency of language stands for masculine virtue. Despite his terminal idleness, the strutting garrulity of the paycock gives him dramatic stature, even poignancy. In the plays of John Millington Synge, eloquent and poetic tramps accrue an imaginative prowess that elevates them above the debased world of labour in which they are forced to exist. And this prowess is often taken for an alternative male virtue that is emancipatory from dull social conformity. We can discern this paradigm in *The Shadow of the Glen* (1903), *The Well of the Saints* (1905) and *The Playboy of the Western World* (1907). In each of these plays, the 'outsider' evokes a romantic and ideal life away from the drudgeries of social life that is powerfully seductive to a woman. Manliness is practised verbally. 'Poetry talk' is identified with virility, sometimes explicitly ('I've heard all times it's the poets are your like – fine, fiery fellows with great rages when their temper's roused').[26]

But these poet-tramps cannot integrate into society. They can talk but not function with social efficacy. The plays set up an opposition between material success and cultural capital. Masculinity belongs to surplus value, not productive activity. The rich Hiberno-English language contrasts with the material scarcity of the stage. This engenders a severance between action and talk, between aesthetic and reality, between value and fact, between gallous stories and dirty deeds that leads to a distinctly modernist aporia. But it is precisely the failure to 'do' that brings the social lack into relief, both for the emotionally starved characters and for the audience. In other words, that society cannot accommodate the poetic men, and they cannot accommodate society, reveals something of a general enervation and dysfunction. It is another instance whereby male inaction acts as subversive refusal.

The most extensive exposition and critique of these oppositions occurs in *Playboy of the Western World*, a play which, as the title suggests, is heavily invested in modes of meta-masculinity. The community's normative masculinity is one of poetic or mythic violence, and when the border between the story and the actuality is rent, the hope of salvation and emancipation is destroyed. The villagers, having been seduced by the stories of violence, are appalled by its reality: 'there's a great gap between a gallous story and a dirty deed' (169). The play thus subverts the connection between manliness and violence, while at the same time critiquing that mode in Irish discourse, including Irish drama that replaces *action* with *talk*. Pegeen and the rest of the community were assuaged in their anomie and boredom by the 'gallous story' that afforded the delusion of energetic, rebellious resource. When violence actually erupts, they transform into biddable colonial subjects, fearful of the authorities and eager to hand over the perpetrator. Christy himself is liberated by his own performance of manliness, which allows him to pass through the Oedipal blockage and (to his twice-resurrected father's delight) go 'romancing through a romping lifetime' (173). But the comic note is offset by Pegeen's plaintive final cry – 'Oh my grief I've lost him surely. I've lost the only playboy of the western world' (173) – which seems to affirm an incompatibility between the realised subject and society, the part and the whole. In this, for all its investment in vital and primitive energies, the play connects with the Parisian decadence that is more overt in Synge's early work. The rich language of Synge's drama weighs not just against the possibilities of narrative action, but also against the formal totality of the play, creating fugitive, dislocated moments of possibility outside the governing structure. These dislocated moments are enabled, again, by an inactive or ineffectual masculinity (twice Christy tries and fails to kill his father), played off comically against a community that conflates masculine virtue with anti-authoritarian violence.

Refusing the Copy

One of the aspects of Christy that make him an epitome of male modernist crisis is the precariousness of his manliness. His effeminacy is signalled in many ways, and reinforced by his father's scorn, by, for instance, his admiring himself in a mirror at the beginning of Act 2: 'Didn't I know rightly I was handsome, though it was the divil's own mirror we had beyond, would twist a squint across an angel's brow' (95). This surfeit of self-consciousness is something that weighs heavily on the Irish modernist male. The cracked mirror indicates a subjectivity that is both split and imitative. Joyce's Stephen Dedalus, who perhaps more that any other embodies the role of Irish Hamlet, decries the 'cracked looking-glass of a servant' as 'a symbol of Irish art'.[27] One of the struggles of the modernist male is how to signify differently within inherited frames. This is a colonial impasse in Ireland and, in many cases, is answered by a gesture of refusal of what is deemed in normative terms as desirable or legitimate. There cannot be a perfect reflection, only a copy of an alien norm or received role. When action is conforming, agency is best exercised through negation. This is a note that is struck through a range of modernisms. In Ireland it underpins the pervasiveness of obstinately inactive males. It is an obstinacy that goes beyond mere idleness and is often simultaneously a symptom of circumscribed agency and a reaction to it.

We find both symptom and resistance in Joyce's short story 'Counterparts'. The story uses the idea of replication simultaneously as plot device and metaphor. The work-shy Farrington, who works as a scrivener, strains against the tedium and confinement of his job. He is a violent and explosive man, and his refusal to conform to his working role is also indicative of resistance and restlessness that, as so often in *Dubliners*, reveals unrealised potential. If we take as the archetypal scrivener Bob Cratchit from Dickens's *A Christmas Carol* (1843), then Farrington, his Celtic counterpart, differs in almost every respect, not least his tall, bulky physique. It is as if he is too big not just for the job but for the story in which he appears. There are not enough words and too many are clichéd and 'copied', just as Farrington's performed masculinity with his friends is derivative, shallow and defeated. He goes from one mode of imitation – copying handwriting – to another – combative, homosocial one-upmanship. The final imitation of the story is that of the terrified son, who, facing a beating from the drunken Farrington, throws out overheard pieties – 'I'll say a *Hail Mary* for you, pa, if you don't beat me. ... I'll say a *Hail Mary*'.[28]

Mr Alleyne, Farrington's boss, ascribes his incompetence at his job to insubordination and idleness. He is right, but only partly so. Farrington's troubled laziness is part of being trapped in a cycle of replication: copying the contracts, buying the rounds of drinks, imitating Mr Alleyne's Northern accent to his friends. He is caught in a system of 'copying' that denies any possibility of his own self-realisation and any authentic action. Farrington's self-esteem and status outside his office come from his 'strong man' role, but this too is merely imitative masculinity, performed better by the visiting 'acrobat and knock-about *artiste*', Weathers, who twice beats him at arm wrestling.

Cuchulain in *On Baile's Strand* is also much concerned by the inadequate replica, disdaining the idea of a son who might mar him in the 'copying'.[29] The play's tragic momentum obtains from Cuchulain striving to fit into a society despite his contrapuntal yearning for unfettered freedom. Both Farrington and Cuchulain respond to prescribed roles with a mixture of passivity and explosive, misdirected violence. That both end by visiting violence on their sons attests to the untenable contradictions. As Irish modernism develops, some of the binds of masculinity are loosened through a more overtly androgynous identity, like that of Leopold Bloom, or met more by self-conscious gestures of denial and withdrawal, such as those of Stephen Dedalus or Beckett's Murphy. If so, it is an idleness that can be understood as a political gesture, a refusal to be locked into the remorseless labour economy and its alienations. Gregory Dobbins argues that idleness comes to the fore in Irish modernism precisely in reaction to the Revival, when, Joyce and others seek to spurn the teleological orientation of the Revival with its busy institutional structures of 'nation-building'.[30] But for all the ostensible oppositions between the Revival and later Irish modernism, for all the critical positions that cast Yeats and Joyce into oppositional relation, the dilemmas of masculinity that are confronted in late Irish modernism were incubated in the work of Yeats and Synge and, in particular, the need for Irish culture to negotiate its gendered, semi-colonial position.

Notes

1 Greg Dobbins notes that 'within Irish modernism the lazy, idle schemer is specifically gendered as male'. *Lazy Idle Schemers: Irish Modernism and the Cultural Politics of Idleness* (Dublin: Field Day Publications, 2010), p. 28.

2 Laura Doyle and Laura Winkel, eds., *Geomodernisms: Race, Modernism, Modernity* (Bloomington: Indiana University Press, 2005), Richard Begam and Michael Valdez Moses (eds.), *Modernism and Colonialism: British and Irish Literature* (Durham, NC: Duke University Press, 2007).

3 Douglas Mao and Rebecca L. Walowitz, 'The New Modernist Studies' *PMLA*, 123 (2007): 737–748.

4 L. P. Curtis, *Anglo-Saxons and Celts: A Study of Anti-Irish Prejudice in Victorian England* (Bridgeport, CT: New York University Press, 1968). But see Terence Brown, 'The Literary Revival: Historical Perspectives', *The Literature of Ireland: Culture and Criticism* (Cambridge: Cambridge University Press, 2010), pp. 14–26 for misgivings about the critical orthodoxy around this theme.

5 Seamus Deane, *Strange Country: Modernity and Nationhood in Irish Writing since 1790* (Oxford: Clarendon Press, 1997).

6 Andreas Huyssen, 'Mass Culture as Woman: Modernism's Other', in Tania Modleski, ed., *Studies in Entertainment: Critical Approaches to Mass Culture* (Bloomington: Indiana University Press, 1986), pp. 188–207.

7 Ashis Nandy, *The Intimate Enemy: Loss and Recovery of Self Under Colonialism* (Delhi: Oxford University Press, 1983).

8 L. P. Curtis, *Apes and Angels: The Irishman in Victorian Caricautre* (Newtown Abbott: David & Charles, 1971). R. F. Foster challenges some of Curtis's conclusions in 'Paddy and Mr Punch', *Paddy and Mr Punch: Connections in Irish and English History* (London: Allen Lane, 1993), pp. 171–194.

9 Joseph Valente, *The Myth of Manliness in Irish Culture, 1880–1922*(Champaign, IL: University of Illinois Press, 2010).

10 For a position that argues the inapplicability of the colonial and post-colonial models, see Stephen Howe, *Ireland and Empire: Colonial Legacies in Irish History and Culture* (Oxford: Oxford University Press, 2000).

11 Derek Attridge and Marjore Howes, eds., *Semicolonial Joyce* (Cambridge: Cambridge University Press, 2000).

12 Standish James O'Grady, *History of Ireland: Cuchulain and His Contemporaries*, vol. 2 (London: Sampson, Low, Searle, Marston and Rivington, 1880).

13 *Hurrish: A Study* (1886; New York and London: Garland Publishing Inc., 1979), p. 39.

14 For a reading of the Citizen as an 'indictment of colonial hypermasculinity' see Joseph Valente, "Neither Fish nor Flesh'; or how 'Cyclops' Stages the Double-Bind of Irish Manhood', *Semicolonial Joyce*, pp. 96–127.

15 Douglas Hyde, 'The Necessity for Deanglicising Ireland', *The Revival of Irish Literature* (London: T. F. Unwin, 1894).

16 Declan Kiberd, *Inventing Ireland: The Literature of the Modern Nation* (London, 1995), pp. 25, 31.

17 Samuel Beckett, *Murphy* (1938; London and Montreuil: Calder Publications, 1993), pp. 28–29.

18 Sean Farrell Moran, *Patrick Pearse and the Politics of Redemption: The Mind of the Easter Rising, 1916* (Washington, D.C.: Catholic University of America Press, 1994), p. 160. For an article analysing the anti-modern, aristocratic aspect of Yeats's Cuchulain, see Michael Valdez Moses, 'The Rebirth of Tragedy: Yeats, Nietzsche, the Irish National Theatre and the Anti-Modern Cult of Cuchulain', *Modernism/Modernity* 11.3 (2004): 561–579.

19 The long-standing Weberian association of modernity with 'disenchantment' has been challenged and complicated by recent scholarship. Michael Slater, 'Modernity and Enchantment: An Historiographic Review' in *The American Historical Review* vol. 111, no. 3, (June 2006): 692–716

20 Patrick Pearse, *Plays, Stories, Poems* (Dublin: Phoenix, 1917), p. 44.

21 James Joyce, *Ulysses* (1922; London: Penguin, 1992), p. 15.

22 W. B. Yeats, *The Variorum Edition of the Poems*, ed. Peter Alt and Russell K. Alspach (New York: The Macmillan Co., 1957), p. 328.

23 Yeats, *The Variorum Poems*, pp. 391–394.

24 Kiberd, *Inventing Ireland*, p. 114.

25 Vivian Mercier, 'The Uneventful Event', *Irish Times* (18 February 1956), p. 9.

26 J.M. Synge, *Collected Works*, gen. ed. Robin Skelton, 4 vols. (London: Oxford University Press, 1962–8), pp. iv, 81.

27 Joyce, *Ulysses* (1922; London: Penguin, 1992), p. 6.
28 James Joyce, *Dubliners* (1914; London: Penguin 1992), p. 94.
29 W. B. Yeats, *The Collected Works*, 15 vols. (New York: Scribner, 2001), vol. 2, *The Plays*, p. 158.
30 Gregory Dobbins, *Lazy Idle Schemers*, pp. 10–11.

CHAPTER 5

Marvellous Masculinity: Futurist Strategies of Self-Transfiguration through the Maelstrom of Modernity

Cinzia Sartini Blum

The misogynistic slant of Marinetti's early manifestos established, from the very beginning of the movement, the notorious image of futurism as 'scourge of women', which has been the object of many reductive and dismissive interpretations. The very quality of rhetorical excess characteristic of Marinetti's writing has placed it, to some extent, beyond the reach of critical analysis, as if excess were tantamount to transparency or emptiness. Accounts of the movement's affiliation with fascism, furthermore, have played a major part in framing the discussion of futurism's misogynistic cult of virility as the self-evident corollary of a reactionary ideology.

My essay will question the dominant, reductive image of futurist masculinity, encapsulated in the notorious 'scorn of woman' injunction by the founding manifesto, in order to complicate it on the basis of the argument that Marinetti's exuberant rhetoric magnifies crucial nodes at the heart of the masculine dimensions of literary and cultural modernism. While it is important to acknowledge the presence of multiple, evolving and even contradictory positions in a movement that attracted many different personalities over the course of nearly three decades,[1] my approach can be justified on two major accounts: as the founder, leader, impresario and main literary figure of futurism, Marinetti played a central role in shaping the movement; and the authorial persona he created came to embody the myth of futurist masculinity. A focus on his work and its many apparent contradictions is therefore most suitable for my purpose, which is to find a pattern in multiplicity and contradiction. The pattern will emerge by viewing Marinetti's writings in a complex relationship with the cultural context, which extends beyond the obvious connections with the fascist cult of virility, the overwhelmingly misogynist culture of early twentieth-century Italy and the masculinist undercurrents in modernist culture as a whole. Social theories of decline and interrelated notions of superomism, vitalism and transformationism will provide important points of reference both in my discussion of Marinetti's late-symbolist works, which display the decadent genealogy of the 'hard' futurist man, and in the following analysis of the manifestos which, in constructing the hyperbolic figure of the 'multiplied, metalized' man, symptomatically reveal the same tensions and contradictions that run through the most anxious modernist responses to contemporary changes and challenges. I will then extend my analysis from the manifestos to lesser-studied works so as to address a broad range of modernist themes and concerns: the massification of political and cultural life; the erosion of gender roles; the traumatic impact of industrial warfare; and finally, the connection between the perceived 'emasculation' of Western man and the concomitant exoticisation of 'authentic' masculinity.

Embattled Masculinity

At the origins of futurism there is a programmatic reaction to a widespread sense of crisis and historical dislocation, which in the recently constituted Italian nation, as it belatedly entered a phase of accelerated modernisation after the movement for unification (Risorgimento), was intensified by the impact of destabilising cultural changes related to seismic socioeconomic shifts. An illuminating point of reference, in this context, is provided by turn-of-the-century theories of cultural decline, such as Vilfredo Pareto's 'elite degeneration' thesis – a gloomy critique of declining Western civilisation, fuelled by biological pessimism, political disillusion and growing fears about the impact of the egalitarian tendencies in modern democratic society. Literature commonly characterised as 'decadent' displays close connections with social theories of decline, post-Darwinian ideas of devolution and entropy, and interrelated notions of Nietzschean superomism, Sorelian and Bergsonian vitalism, and Lamarckian Transformationism – the evolutionary theory that posited the transmutation of the species as a result of its adaptive response to the changing environment. Such connections can be highlighted best by focusing on representations of the body in the unsettling fantasies of late-nineteenth century writers, namely, recurrent images of decay, deformity and mutilation, which point to a fragmented, embattled vision of modern reality and subjectivity.[2] This imagery gives expression to fin-de-siècle anxieties generated by a rapidly changing worldview on human identity: anxieties about looming threats, such as the massification of society, racial 'degeneration' and, most notably, the dissolution of sexed identity. Drawing upon the authority of prominent philosophers such as Friedrich Nietzsche and Otto Weininger, writers across national, ideological and intellectual divides represented the ills of modernity – mediocrity, enfeeblement, powerlessness – in terms of effemination or 'de*gender*ation'.³ This pervasive topos suggests that a deep concern with shifting gender roles played a crucial role as a cause of the modern malaise.

Marinetti's pre-futurist work took shape in the cultural mould that I have just described, in particular the French and Italian literary milieus of the fin de siècle. Born of Italian parents in Egypt, the cosmopolitan Marinetti studied law in Italy, received a *baccalauréat ès lettres* in Paris and acquired a reputation as a Franco-Italian poet, writing in the late-symbolist mode epic poems such as *La Conquête des Étoiles* ('The Conquest of the Stars', 1902) and *Destruction* (1904). The poetic persona emerging from these poems is the protagonist of an inner drama that results in the apocalyptic explosion of destructive forces. He is a 'beggar of love', torn between his unappeasable 'hunger' for the Absolute and his disgust for Infamous reality: a frustrated idealist, who draws upon the power of his visionary imagination to launch an offensive against the bastions of the 'impure' Ideal embodied by the stars. In this psychodrama, feminine figures play the role of the desired and abhorred other: the elusive celestial beauty that the stars promised the poet in his youth, and the 'brothel of the flesh' that 'strangles' the 'pure Dream' with sensual ecstasy. The recurrent association of images of decay with female genitals indicates that Woman stands for the material limitations that doom organic life to death and that also contaminate the spiritual realm of the stars, wicked 'courtesans' who taunt the poet with 'their putrid / staring, through the damp slit / of their eyelids, half-closed and like vulvas'.⁴ Woman, in other words, is the embodiment of both the unruliness of nature and the ruling vulgarity of a materialistic, utilitarian society in a world without transcendent values. As such she is, most importantly, the projection of a break, within the poetic subject, between spirit and matter (between the sensual, pragmatic 'I' and his idealist 'Soul'), as well as a figure for the split between self and other – the engulfing chasm between infinite desire and *abject* reality, which is recurrently represented in terms of alienation, wounding, devouring and annihilation.⁵

As a leitmotif of the male literary imagination at the end of the nineteenth century, such imagery has been linked with concerns about shifting gender roles and the commodification of the artist in the consumerist market place.⁶ The fin-de-siècle aesthete attempts to exorcise this double threat through imaginary identification with the feminine, a strategy that involves colonising the feminine body as the locus of artistic creation, sublimating the boundaries it signifies and deploying its subversive power against the dominant cultural discourse. But the fate of decadent heroes such as Joris-Karl Huysmans's dandy, Des Esseintes, shows that feminisation, even as a means of creative transgression, remains a sign of self-division and impotence. Marinetti's symbolist 'I' is comparable to the decadent aesthete in his effort to impose his redeeming creative mark on the engulfing abjection evoked by recurrent images of decay. What distinguishes this pre-futurist persona is the magnitude of the destructive impetus that animates his delirious vision, his tendency to rhetorical surfeit, and overall, his appetite for excess, which will fuel his transformation into the futurist *superuomo* – the 'metalized' embodiment of irrepressible pride, courage and dynamism. Unlike the passive, contemplative dandy, Marinetti's hero seeks to overcome abominable reality through the mobilisation of irrational forces – most notable in sadistic displays of sexual prowess – by means of an empowering symbiotic union with the vital elements of nature (the omnipotent sea, symbolic of the fluid energy of the universe and the chaotic flux of the inner drives) and technology (symbolised by a train launched at frenzied speed towards the unknown). His attempts, however, result in self-destruction: a dissolution of identity that is mirrored by images of the female body and of the amorphous, engulfing crowd in the alienating urban scenario of *Destruction*. It is to avoid this dead end that the poetic 'I' reinvents himself as the leader of a revolutionary avant-garde movement in the 'Founding and Manifesto of Futurism' (1909): by unconditionally identifying with the aggressive forces that drive the technological, capitalist, consumerist society, he joins in the race to the future with the 'artificial optimism' prescribed by his new futurist creed.[7] Still charged with negative connotations in the early imaginary encounter between Marinetti's poetic 'I' and the modern world, mechanical speed and the industrial city thus become, in the manifestos, celebrated emblems of the ambitious cultural project of refashioning the universe in the image of futurism.

Hyperbolic Masculinity: Transfiguring Fragmentation into Multiplication

The movement launched by Marinetti was the most radical, dynamic and organised among the various modernist efforts to redeem modern life through culture.[8] The program outlined by the futurist manifestos, which

Marinetti advertised with a marketing campaign unprecedented for a cultural product, was to assimilate the forces of the technological world as a remedy against the psychological malady caused by the traumatic impact of modern life. While it may seem to imply a contradictory outlook on modernity, this program is *pragmatically* consistent in prescribing strategies for self-expansion that are homologous to evolutionary principles of adaptation and assimilation. Marinetti understood evolution in the Nietzschean sense that life is driven by the 'will to power', a spontaneous, endogenous movement towards limitless expansion and growth of creative energies. There is a patent affinity between Marinetti's brand of vitalism and Nietzsche's theory that life as the will to power is 'nothing but the accumulation and discharge of force' driven by the urge to assimilate.[9] This theory was inspired by the principle of 'insatiability' advocated by zoologist William Rolph – a principle by which Rolph explained all organic functions, from nutrition to evolution.

Marinetti inscribes the principle of insatiability into his work through the leitmotif of ingestion, which in the most striking instances, in keeping with the primitivist tendency shared by much modernist culture, evokes the cannibalistic ritual of eating a powerful enemy – the embodiment of otherness that resists assimilation. The most notable example can be found in 'Un pranzo che evitò un suicidio' ('The Dinner That Prevented a Suicide'), which introduces the 1932 collection of futurist recipes, *La cucina futurista* ('Futurist Cookbook').[10] In this tale of sublimated cannibalism, Marinetti and two other futurist 'sculptors' (described as endowed with 'mouths of charming anthropophagi', 14) create a series of sensual culinary sculptures for the purpose of capturing 'the fleeting eternal feminine' (19). The edible avatars of femininity are intended as treatment for a suicidal friend, who is about to be destroyed by competing insatiable desires: the melancholic call of a dead ideal woman and the dangerous appeal of a living femme fatale. The story reaches a happy ending, predictably, as the lovesick friend is saved by devouring the masterpiece entitled 'The Curves of the World and Their Secrets', a mixture of feminine, natural and mechanical ingredients that fulfils the futurist prescription for absolute (self-) possession. This text can be viewed as a parable about a core principle in the futurist creed. Throughout Marinetti's futurist writings – beginning with the mythopoeia of the founding manifesto, in which the protagonist-narrator is revived by gulping down the 'fortifying sludge' of a factory drain – incorporation reduces the other to a digestible object of consumption and transfigures the subject into a fantastic hybrid organism: the 'multiplied, mechanical man', a Man-Machine fuelled by powerful instinctual forces.

Through incorporation, Marinetti re-subordinates reality to the power of the imagination ('creative genius', as he often calls it) – a power that in the ancient, religious worldview is supernaturally ordained, and in the modern worldview is undone by scientific reason.[11] Marinetti rejects both the religious and the rationalist mode of relating to reality as respectively emptied of and inimical to 'divinity'; at the same time, he replaces faith in an otherworldly God with worship of a worldly 'divine' force: 'energy'. Thus re-ordained and re-inspired, the futurist imagination can re-create the world in the image of the omnipotent 'multiplied man'. The result is a prosopopoeia in which matter is animated by the instinctual drive ('energy') of the will to power and sublimated as 'speed', the new religious/moral principle that can invest the imagination with absolute power.

Tellingly, Marinetti speaks of his imaginative faculty in terms of digestive functions. In the manifesto 'L'uomo moltiplicato e il regno della macchina' ('Multiplied Man and the Reign of the Machine', 1910), envisioning a future in which humans will be immune to all affective and moral poisons, he looks forward to the necessary transformation of the human heart into a digestive organ, 'a sort of stomach for the brain, which will methodically empty and fill so that the spirit can go into action' (*TIF* 300). In another instance, a 'Response to Objections' appended to the 'Technical Manifesto' (1912) in defence of the 'wireless' poetics of imaginative profusion and expressive force, he describes his own creative experience by noting that images flow directly from his body onto the page, through his seemingly detached hand, while his wilful brain, also seemingly detached, impassively observes or lucidly directs the fantastic outpour (*TIF* 56). The role played by his 'commanding brain', he comments, cannot be determined: 'In those moments all I have been aware of, from the physiological point of view, has been a great feeling of emptiness in my stomach' (*TIF* 56). Such images of disconnected and/or disproportionally expanded body parts and functions – including aerodynamic protrusions and the extension of the externalised will 'like a huge invisible arm' (*TIF* 86–87) – are symptomatic of the embattled condition that Marinetti programmatically transfigures into a fiction of power, as shown by the following passage: 'This nonhuman, mechanical species, built for constant speed, will quite naturally be cruel, omniscient, and warlike. It will possess the most unusual organs; organs adapted to the needs of an environment in which there are continuous clashes' (*TIF* 86). Marinetti's prediction follows his specific mention of Lamarck's transformist hypothesis of evolution through adaptation, a reference that offers further support to my argument: by assimilating the clashing pressures of contemporary reality, futurism replaces the bankrupt ideal of ethic and aesthetic harmony with the new 'reign' of the Man-Machine attuned to the 'natural' laws of greedy self-expansion that rule modern capitalist society.

The text that best illustrates this argument is the manifesto in which Marinetti conveys his vision of 'the new religion-morality of speed' ('La nuova religione-morale della velocità', 1916). This vision may be described as animistic in the broad sense that it endows all matter – both organic and inorganic – with the same divine energy. The principle of greed (insatiable self-expansion), which futurism naturalises as the 'instinctual' essence of the entire life of matter and celebrates as the materialistic 'soul' of modernisation, in this text is sublimated and worshipped as speed, 'synthesis of every courage in action', the divine principle of a new religion-morality: '*Speed*, having as its essence the intuitive synthesis of all forces in motion, is naturally *pure*. ... After the destruction of the ancient good and the ancient evil, we create a new good, speed, and a new evil, slowness' (*TIF* 132; emphasis in original). Having imbued the futurist 'analogical intuition' with the divine power of speed, the artist's imagination can then reclaim sovereignty over reality and refashion it into a 'marvellous' creation that cannot be undone by rational, scientific means ('Omnipresence of the wireless imagination = speed. Creative genius = speed', *TIF* 134).

The transformation of division/fragmentation into multiplication/ expansion indeed involves, often in the same text, various modes of fantastic metamorphosis: the 'analogical style' of untrammelled metaphoric transfiguration characteristic of the futurist poetics of shock and awe, 'il *meraviglioso futurista*' (*TIF* 82; emphasis in original), which Marinetti proclaims 'absolute master of all matter and its intense life' (*TIF* 48); the supernatural birth of mythical, exotic heroes, as in the novel *Mafarka le futuriste* (1910), where an embattled African king recreates himself by generating, without any contact with woman, an immortal son; and visions evocative of the kind of scenarios that typically occur in superhuman science-fiction, such as the 'visionary hypothesis' in which futuristic instruments protect 'aerial' men against both nature's poisons (weakness, disease, death) and new technological weapons of mass destruction ('La guerra elettrica', *TIF* 319–325).

These multiple modes of fantastic transfiguration are all driven by an excessive, violent, and potentially self-destructive impetus. But the explosive mix of multiplicity and excess is contained by a consistent unifying strategy: metamorphosis is staged in a gendered scenario defined by clearly drawn battle lines – a proven foundation for the performance of the new futurist hero. In the manifestos the futurist artist is metaphorically transfigured into a warrior whose mission/prize is to 'rape' and 'possess' the mystery of feminised reality. As a mark of decay, impotence and emasculation, femininity is also projected onto everything futurism is supposed to fight against, from old stifling conventions to new debilitating trends. Proustian introspection, for instance, is stigmatised as 'fragmentary, effeminate, ambiguous' (*TIF* 173); pacifist ideals are contemptuously dismissed as a form of 'castration' of the race (*TIF* 290); and academic intellectualism is violently rejected as 'castration' of genius (*TIF* 308). The imagery of sexual dysfunction used to reject non-futurist artistic and political tendencies shores up the affirmation of futurist power: a self-aggrandizing myth in which the revolutionary display of artistic potency is inextricable from the *performance* of hyper-masculinity – the reassuring script of exaggerated stereotypically male behaviour and traditionally masculine traits.[12] Discussions of Futurist hyper-masculinity invariably refer to the notorious example of Mafarka's priapism.[13] An even more telling example is the persona of the futurist Don Giovanni that Marinetti donned by boasting of his power to seduce women, particularly in the autobiographical books he wrote during and immediately after his participation in World War I. This persona deviates from the precepts against love and lust issued by Marinetti in the manifestos that envision the ultimate stage of futurist evolution, the mechanised man immune to all of the weakness of the flesh. As we shall see, in celebrating his military and sexual exploits, Marinetti deploys instead a *presentist* strategy of transformation through performance that betrays the psychological underpinnings and displays the cultural grounding of futurist masculinity.

Heroic Performances

Violence in its various manifestations, thematic as well as rhetorical, is featured prominently in Marinetti's writings. The manifestos were conceived as acts of war: their purpose was to identify and challenge the passéist enemies of futurism, to shock and mobilise audiences into action, and to affirm the physiological, 'hygienic' necessity of war as a natural phenomenon. The interventionist writings collected in *Guerra sola igiene del mondo* ('War, the World's Only Hygiene', 1915) most notably, celebrated war by invoking the evolutionist principle that 'patriotism and love of war' are the sole remedies against decadence and death, the only effective means of individual and collective renewal (*TIF* 289). As illustrated by the mythopoetic narrative in the founding manifesto, both the futurist 'I' (a *superuomo*) and the futurist 'we' (a collective movement) were born in the act of declaring war against passéism; and, in subsequent endeavours, their mettle was professedly tested by a state of constant belligerence. Likewise, according to futurist propaganda in the period leading up to World War I, a new stronger nation was supposed to emerge from the impending conflict. Futurist synthetic theatre was therefore conceived, at this juncture, as a training ground to prepare the Italian 'spirit' for the imminent 'hour of maximum Danger' (*TIF* 113).

The futurists were clearly not alone in propounding this view of war as a means to boost the survival power of individuals and nations. Such a view was in accord with widespread ideologies of social Darwinism, which gave scientific sanction to belligerent imperialism, *laissez-faire* capitalism, eugenics and racism. In the Italian context, theories ranging from Sorel's revolutionary syndicalism to Pareto's view of war as the sole remedy against the advance of socialism supported the myth of violence as a regenerative force, which was embraced by various writers and literary coteries: suffice it to mention Alfredo Oriani, who attributed to war thaumaturgic power, and Gabriele D'Annunzio, who expected from conflict the most effective manifestation of heroic individualism. Arguably, what distinguishes futurism is that it was fundamentally and consistently shaped by Marinetti's 'polemological' Weltanschauung: the notion that war is the basic law of life, as Luciano De Maria famously underscored in his introduction to *Teoria e invenzione futurista* (lxiii).

Marinetti's polemology displays the connections between sexism and belligerent nationalism that run deep through much contemporary Italian literature. But his proclamation of 'scorn for woman' in the founding manifesto, as already noted, has encouraged a reductive approach to the woman's question in futurism – misogyny, from this perspective, is viewed simply as a self-evident manifestation of the movement's proto-fascist ideology. Studies that reject the shibboleth of futurist misogyny, on the contrary, tend to focus on Marinetti's receptivity to women's creative efforts (along with the fact that many female artists were attracted to the movement because of its anti-conventionalism), and are inclined to gloss his dictum as 'denigration of the quietist and sentimental virtues traditionally associated with women'.[14] This interpretation is based on Marinetti's own justification of the infamous phrase as an expression of contempt for the conventional conception of woman and love ('We despise woman conceived as the sole ideal, the divine vessel of love, the poison woman, the tragic plaything, the fragile woman, obsessing and fatal', *TIF* 292).

The futurist discourse on woman and love is much more complex and contradictory than it purports to be. Marinetti's contradictions can be understood in terms of varying but ultimately convergent strategies. On the one hand, he takes on the avant-garde role of formulating a radical blueprint for the future; on the other, he addresses practical concerns, such as the immediate challenges posed by women's emancipation. The ultimate goal – the 'utopia' of immunity to all affective needs – will be attained only when man completes his evolutionary metamorphosis into a superhuman type. But the pragmatist in Marinetti embraces the notion that contemporary man still needs a healthy, ego-boosting 'diet' of seduced women to sustain his masculinity. Despite occasional residues of nostalgia for the lost 'mystery' and 'absolute value' of *amore* (*TIF* 67, 546), the presentist solution reveals a fundamental homology with the utopian goal: in both cases, man is supposed to purge himself of love and redeploy his heart in a purely physiological function.

While the utopian mode is characteristic of the early writings, pragmatism dominates the texts of the war and post-war period. The futurist manual *Come si seducono le donne* ('How to Seduce Women', 1917) and the autobiographical war novel *L'alcova d'acciaio* ('The Steel Alcove', 1921) exemplify the pragmatic reaction to shifting gender roles, and reveal how the underlying anxieties about masculine identity were intensified by the experience of modern warfare. *Come si seducono le donne* – the first and most successful of a number of futurist works in the genre of social-erotic literature, greatly popular immediately after the war – shows that the futurist treatment for embattled masculinity is a purely 'nutritional' experience, whereby man seeks absolute value no longer in an idealised love-object (as the romantic hero would), but rather in the vitality/virility aroused by a sexual object. In short, as a remedy against all fears, both on the war front and the home front, Marinetti prescribes a diet of digestible, bite-size women. In keeping with this strategy, his war memoirs minimise the horror of trench warfare and industrialised killing – a dominant theme in contemporary literature – and maximise the tendency, common in war propaganda, to aestheticise and eroticise destructive violence as a spectacular, exhilarating expenditure of energies.

Patriotic bombast and macho swagger, in fact, set up the dominant mood in Marinetti's novel, which (according to the autobiographical protagonist-narrator) is conceived in a brothel after a night of revelry, and which, tellingly, covers only the final, victorious phase of the war, from the containment of the Austrian offensive in June 1918 to Italy's decisive counteroffensive in October-November of the same year. Marinetti recurrently blends military might with sexual prowess in portraying the 'healthy virility' of Italian soldiers who know how to successfully 'take and hold down their own women and their own mountains'.[15] Encamped in a fortress of boisterous masculinity with his lustful brothers in arms, sustained by frequent sexual sorties and armed with patriotic hatred towards Austria, the fighting artist can confidently deploy the rhetorical arsenal of his 'visionary imagination' (69) to face his challenges: most notably, the 'poison' of passéist moonlight, which Marinetti represents as a more formidable foe than the Austrian army (62–65); and the seductive power of femme fatales like Bianca, his most temperamental lover, whom he compares to a complicated machine gun – the St Etienne, unreliable and prone to overheating (86).

A leitmotif in Marinetti's work, the association woman-machine gun is doubly symptomatic. In identifying fickle femininity with an unreliable deadly weapon, it both reveals and exorcises anxieties about the overwhelming forces that threaten male self-control, on the battlefront of the Great War as well as on the home front, particularly in the battle of the sexes. It is important to keep in mind that the historical context of Marinetti's jubilant representation of war was actually characterised, after the military disaster at Caporetto, by great social unrest. Soldiers' defections and workers' uprisings fuelled fears, among both the authorities and the officers fighting at the front, that a revolution was imminent in Italy.[16] Marinetti's exuberant display of masculine bravado must be measured also against the masculinity crisis that is apparent in cultural and literary responses to the Great War. As women stepped into roles traditionally reserved for men, the collective imaginary registered these changes as a threat to social and moral order.[17] Studies of soldiers' writings, furthermore, reveal psychological reactions characterised by disorientation, passivity and ambivalent attitudes towards aggression. Many veterans were indeed aware that their much-vaunted masculine aggressiveness was little more than a facade; and the phenomenon of decreased libido and impaired potency was widespread.[18] Unlike other narratives about 'the war of iron and gas', Marinetti's writing does not directly address the traumatic impact of industrial warfare.[19] Such an impact, however, is indirectly acknowledged as it is exorcized through an excessive display of sexual prowess. In re-evoking, for instance, the Italians' victorious response to the last all-out attack of the Austro-Hungarian army, Marinetti transfigures the battle into a spectacular gala, and the most 'prodigious' St Etienne into a femme fatale, lethal to the Austrian 'suitors', and yet subdued by the expert hands of her gunner/lover (*L'alcova*, 19). Another example of apotropaic performance is the narrator's seduction of a submissive 'virgin' named Graziella, a triumphant encounter that, significantly, closely follows his debacle with the unmanageable Bianca: with this show of force, the protagonist can reclaim absolute control ('beyond every social, human, divine law') and compare himself to 'a happy cock with the ideal hen of the henhouse' (184–185). The theatrical dimension of this strategy is especially notable in the narrator's conquest of Rosina, a 'well-deserved' 'Prize' from his homeland (38–39). In extolling his mastery of all seduction techniques, the conquering hero describes himself as a gourmet, a military commander, a scientist and a multi-talented artist: one endowed not only with romantic lyricism and 'sculptural' skills, but also with the histrionic ability to change 'souls' as if they were costumes, to suit the moment ('I tossed the soul that I had previously needed on the sofa and I pulled out another one from the depths of my nerves', 39).

It should be underscored that the performance of the futurist hero, in its function, is more akin to ancient forms of ritualistic theatre than to the self-conscious masquerade of modernist anti-heroes such as the protagonists of Luigi Pirandello's plays. Like apotropaic representations in ancient rituals, the futurist performance appears to be invested with magical power.[20] This is best illustrated by the novel's climactic scene: the hero's seduction of personified Italy in his armoured car, the eponymous 'steel alcove'. The fulfilment of the hero's desire for 'perfect fusion' with his homeland is presented as possible though a miraculous event that calls to mind alchemical magic (L'alcova, 54–55). Floating on a 'fetid river' of surrendering enemies, the armoured car functions as a powerful talisman and a crucible (an alchemical vessel) that allows for the materialisation of the beloved Italy, and for the transformation of a morbidly chaotic scenario into a delirious experience of total oneness. Italy's materialisation is realised through the chemistry of myriad fragrances, some carried by winds from all over the homeland, and others collected by the powerful African Simum ('the great perfume wizard', 248) from exotic colonial domains – a fantasy that conjures up a reassuring sense of geopolitical unity/strength. Like the various torrid tales of sexual exploits that pepper Marinetti's re-evocation of the last few months of the war, the ensuing love scene depicts intoxicating exotic pleasures. It should be noted that Marinetti often qualifies the heat of 'wild', 'ferocious' desire as 'African' and 'equatorial' (65). This leitmotif indicates that futurist exoticism – in keeping with the exoticist project of 'recovering 'elsewhere' values 'lost' with the modernization of European society'[21] – counters the perceived 'emasculation' of Western man with the assimilation of the exotic traits of rugged, 'authentic' masculinity.[22] The mixture of eroticism and exoticism also reinforces the reader's impression that Marinetti, in staging masculine prowess, concurrently displays the 'authentic' (primal, magical) transformative force of the futurist imagination and will to power. When considering the function of Marinetti's heroic/erotic performance, let us not forget that futurist theatre was conceived as a 'crucible' for the new 'sensibility' soon to be forged in the great theatre of war (*TIF* 82). As an 'intensified' form of futurism (*TIF* 114), the theatre of war provides the formulas and, most importantly, the agents (patriotic love and hate) to bind chaotic libidinal energies into unifying drives. The battlefield is the stage where the interplay of individual and national identity can best take place, and where libidinal drives can be heroically sublimated. War, in other words, makes it possible for fragmentation, in the individual as well as in the nation, to be transformed into multiplication of force: both regional/class differences among the soldiers and a multiplicity of souls within the hero can be celebrated as 'elasticity', which marks the superiority of the resilient Italian race (individualistic but patriotic, sentimental but audaciously virile, vengeful against the aggressor but compassionate against the defenceless) over the rigid, discipline-worshipping enemy.

Marinetti's contemptuous references to Teutonic rigidity invite a comparison between self-glorifying celebrations of war from the two opposite sides. As Jeffrey Herf argues in his landmark study, the armed male community of the trenches offers a 'utopian alternative to 'lifeless' industrial society' for 'reactionary modernists' like Ernst Jünger, whose work immortalises the dauntless fighting spirit of German troops under the 'storm of steel' of the Great War.[23] How does Jünger's mythicisation of the front experience compare to Marinetti's? The sexual exuberance of Marinetti's boisterous band of brothers points to a significant difference, which can be best understood by viewing war not as 'a testing ground of the true nature of men', but rather as a 'theatre', an exemplary situation that defines the culturally inflected possibility for the performance of heroic masculinity.[24] Jünger's writing (like Marinetti's) displays sadistic violence in metaphoric fashion, through the leitmotif of forcibly violating virginal landscapes. But the sexual overtones of this offensive thrust are muted, in keeping with Jünger's representation of soldiers as armoured against both suffering and sexual gratification.[25] For Marinetti, the soldier's 'mettle' is instead a powerful conduit of 'lust', both sublimated and unabashedly carnal. This contrasts sharply with Jünger's tendency to portray seemingly sexless officers. Given the presence of this tendency in the writings of German *Freikorpsmen*, one may conclude that the contrast between Marinetti's and Jünger's heroes is traceable, at least in part, to culturally specific notions of manhood.[26] The cult of masculinity shared by pro-war discourses has in fact multiple manifestations, which are arguably related to sociocultural differences as well as to the peculiarities of various media and genres. While celebrating sexual exuberance as a *natural* expression of Italian 'genius', Marinetti himself, through the motif of theatricality and through the rhetorical surfeit characteristic of his writing, highlights the *artistry* and *cultural makeup* that play a prominent role in the heroic performance of men at war.

Far from being blatantly transparent, Marinetti's notorious rhetorical excess creates a uniquely extravagant authorial persona, a self-transfiguring embodiment of the futurist *superuomo*, which provides rich insights into the complex, contested cultural circumstances of modernism. If one simply sums up the 'souls' (to use Marinetti's term) of the futurist hero, the result may appear to be a senselessly contradictory formula: metallic hardness is coupled with elasticity; romantic individualism is combined with anti-sentimental technicism; and futuristic attributes are blended with primitive, exotic traits. After careful examination, however, we can conclude that Marinetti produces this paradoxical formula by programmatically casting off the 'old shackles of logic' (*TIF* 52) in order to launch a new, competitive model of masculinity in the maelstrom of modernity.

Notes

1 Silvia Contarini, *La Femme Futuriste: Mythes, Modèles et Représentations de la Femme dans la Théorie et la Littérature Futuristes, 1900–1919* (Presses Universitaires de Paris X, 2006), pp. 22–23.

2 See Kelly Hurley and Gillian Beer, eds., *The Gothic Body: Sexuality, Materialism, and Degeneration at the Fin de Siècle* (Cambridge: Cambridge University Press, 1996); and Susan J. Navarette, *The Shape of Fear: Horror and the Fin de Siècle Culture of Decadence* (Lexington: University Press of Kentucky, 1998).

3 Barbara Spackman, *Decadent Genealogies: The Rhetoric of Sickness from Baudelaire to D'Annunzio* (Ithaca: Cornell University Press, 1989).

4 F. T. Marinetti, *La Conquête des Étoiles* (Paris: «La Plume», 1902); rpt. in *Scritti francesi*, ed. Pasquale Jannini (Milan: Mondadori, 1983), p.115. (Unless otherwise indicated, all translations are mine.) This imagery is recurrent in both the pre-futurist and the futurist writings, and thus points to a persistent concern in Marinetti's oeuvre.

5 I use the expression 'abject reality' in the Kristevan sense that reality, in the modernist imagination, is infested by the 'abject': both repulsive and seductive, the abject is the unconceivable other – an inassimilable outside and an exorbitant inside – which draws the self 'towards the point where meaning collapses' and where subjectivity itself is ultimately destroyed by violent contradictions. Julia Kristeva, 'Approaching Abjection', *Oxford Literary Review* 5.1–2 (1982): 126.

6 Rita Felski, 'The Counterdiscourse of the Feminine in Three Texts by Wilde, Huysmans, and Sacher-Masoch', *PMLA* 16.5 (1991): 1094–1105.

7 In 'La guerra elettrica' (Electrical War, 1915), the 'production of artificial optimism' is embraced as a remedy against 'chronic pessimism'. See Marinetti, *Teoria e invenzione futurista* (hereafter *TIF*), ed. Luciano De Maria, c.1968 (Milan: Mondadori, 1983), p. 324.

8 I refer to Andreas Huyssen's statement that 'a redemption of modern life through culture' was modernism's most ambitious goal. *After the Great Divide: Modernism, Mass Culture, Postmodernism* (Bloomington: Indiana University Press, 1986), p. 210.

9 Keith Ansell-Pearson, *A Companion to Nietzsche* (Malden, MA and Oxford: Blackwell, 2006), p. 525.

10 F.T. Marinetti and Fillia (Luigi Colombo), *La cucina futurista* (Milan: Sonzogno, 1932).

11 For further analysis of the trope of incorporation, see Cinzia Sartini Blum, *The Other Modernism: F. T. Marinetti's Futurist Fiction of Power* (Berkeley: University of California Press, 1996), pp. 93–99.

12 My use of the term 'performance' calls for comparison with Thomas Strychacz's interpretation of *Hemingway's Theaters of Masculinity* (Baton Rouge: Louisiana State University Press, 2003). Strychacz argues that theatricalised masculinity in Hemingway's fictional narratives of manhood-fashioning deconstructs 'the truth, naturalness, and permanence of masculine identity' (11) and 'trouble[s] conventional interpretations of masculine style' (8), thus putting into question the critical tendency to use Hemingway's principles of aesthetic restraint 'to consolidate a philosophy of masculine modernism' (11). Marinetti's fiction and performance of hyper-virility is not to be taken as an attempt to confuse straightforward, essentialist articulations of masculinity. Marinetti rejects nostalgia for any idealised 'lost plenitude' of the past in order to deploy a new, more viable kind of masculine plenitude and not to expose it, in proto-feminist fashion, as a masquerade.

13 In *The Other Modernism* I have argued that Mafarka's violent display of phallic power can be viewed as an exasperated apotropaic reaction to the 'deep, dry black wells' of insatiable lack hollowed out in his own flesh (63), in other words, a defence strategy against the ever-present threat of abjection.

14 Walter L. Adamson, 'Futurism, Mass Culture, and Women: The Reshaping of the Artistic Vocation, 1909–1920', *Modernism/modernity* 4.1 (January 1997): 103. Adamson highlights the importance of women in futurism, which he connects with Marinetti's understanding of and commitment to mass culture. He argues that such a connection underlies Marinetti's call for the emancipation of women' (106). Other scholars view Marinetti's position as equivocal and point to uneasiness about women's emancipation. See Lucia Re, 'Futurism and Feminism', *Women's Voices in Italian Literature, special issue of Annali d'Italianistica* 7 (1989): 254; Spackman, 'The Fascist Rhetoric of Virility', *Stanford Italian Review* 8.1–2 (1990): 95; Blum, *The Other Modernism*, pp. 84–85.

15 Marinetti, *L'alcova d'acciaio: romanzo vissuto* c.1921 (Milan: Vitagliano, 1927), p. 10.

16 Giovanna Procacci, 'State Coercion and Workers' Solidarity in Italy (1915–1918): The Moral and Political Content of Social Unrest', in Leopold H. Haimson and Giulio Sapelli, eds., *Strikes, Social Conflict and the First World War: An International Perspective* (Milan: Feltrinelli, 1992), pp. 146–147.

17 Margaret Randolph Higonnet, Jane Jenson, Sonya Michel and Margaret Collins Weitz, eds., *Behind the Lines: Gender and the Two World Wars* (New Haven, CT: Yale University Press, 1987).

18 Eric J. Leed, *No Man's Land: Combat and Identity in World War I* (Cambridge University Press, 1979), pp. 106, 183.

19 Umberto Rossi, *Il secolo di fuoco: Introduzione alla letteratura di guerra del Novecento* (Roma: Bulzoni, 2008), pp. 97–197.

20 Marinetti's war diaries confirm his superstitious belief in mysterious forces at work in the universe: 'Selections from the Unpublished Diaries of F. T. Marinetti', ed. Lawrence Rainey and Laura Wittman, *Modernism/modernity* 1.3 (September 1994): 18–24. Reliance on forms of talismanic protection such as amulets, rituals and 'magical slang' was common among all front-line soldiers: Paul Fussell, *The Great War and Modern Memory* (New York: Oxford University Press, 1975), p. 36; and Ann P. Linder, 'Magical Slang: Ritual, Language and Trench Slang of the Western Front', www.firstworldwar.com/features/slang.htm.

21 Chris Bongie, *Exotic Memories: Literature, Colonialism, and the Fin de Siècle* (Stanford: Stanford University Press, 1991), p. 5.

22 See Cinzia Sartini Blum, 'Incorporating the Exotic: From Futurist Excess to Postmodern Impasse', in *A Place in the Sun: Africa in Italian Colonial Culture from Post-Unification to the Present*, ed. Patrizia Palumbo (Berkeley: University of California Press, 2003), pp. 138–162.

23 Jeffrey Herf, *Reactionary Modernism: Technology, Culture and Politics in Weimar and the Third Reich* (Cambridge University Press, 2002), p. 80.

24 Strychacz, *Hemingway's Theaters of Masculinity*, p. 11.

25 Leed, *No Man's Land*, pp. 159–161.

26 Klaus Theweleit, *Male Fantasies*, vol. 1, trans. Stephan Conway, Erica Carter and Chris Turner (Minneapolis: University of Minnesota Press, 1987), pp. 52–63.

CHAPTER 6

Surrealist Masculinities: Sexuality and the Economies of Experience

Natalya Lusty

In the *Second Manifesto of Surrealism* Breton proclaimed 'every means must be worth trying, in order to lay waste to the ideas of *family, country, religion*', defiantly signalling surrealism's opposition to the social order as it was being reconstructed in the interwar years. From the late 1920s surrealism became increasingly preoccupied with the transformative potential of repressed and libidinal forces as sites of resistance to hegemonic cultural and social formations. In validating the lived realities of modernity's marginal experiences (childhood, primitive culture, deviant sexuality, criminality, poverty and madness), surrealism sought to disrupt the social and nationalist values informing post-war reconstruction. If surrealism risked cannibalising the experience of those on the periphery of cosmopolitan cultural life, it also gave the disenfranchised a material presence, at the same time reconfiguring the political and aesthetic ground of the movement. The surrealist's turn to marginal experience nevertheless discloses an acute anxiety about the fragmentation and decline of masculine experience itself. While much critical work has connected the violent fragmentation and dismemberment of the female body in surrealist iconography to the mutilations of the male body in the Great War[1], in this chapter I want to reframe the question of surrealist masculine anxiety through the lens of surrealism's recuperation of experience.[2] Surrealism's turn to experience connected the volatile impact of sexuality, eroticism and pornography in the interwar years to its contestation of bourgeois social regulation and a rationalist intellectual tradition that dominated French culture and politics. In contesting both internal domestic policy and the cultural and intellectual imperialism that ideologically reinforced French superiority, the Surrealists re-evaluated marginal 'experience' in an attempt to oppose the regulatory norms around race, class, nationality and sexuality that were becoming sites of intense political and social scrutiny by a revanchist bourgeois state. The policing of social norms was mired in what the historian Carolyn Dean has defined as increasing anxieties about the frail masculine social body in the post-war period.[3]

The emphasis on sexuality within surrealism from the late 1920s on privileged a new kind of subject informed by the emancipation of emotional states, spontaneous or chance experience, and the central role of unconscious desire in mediating the affective and libidinal contours of everyday experience. The concept 'convulsive beauty', although Bretonian in origin, encapsulates the erotic basis of experience more broadly within surrealism in this period.[4] Describing 'convulsive beauty' through the juxtapositions 'veiled-erotic, fixed-explosive, magic-circumstantial', Breton frames aesthetic experience in terms of erotic encounter to describe the shock effect of the surrealist image, but in the process exposes the volatile paradox of experience itself. If non-normative experience became one of the primary agencies of provocation in the post-war years, it necessarily bore the tensions endemic to the competing variants of surrealism in this period. In spite of these differences, surrealist efforts to destabilise fixed categories (of beauty, love, sexuality etc.) are symptomatic of its broader goal to delimit experience. In Bataille's novel, *Story of the Eye* (1928), the concept of inner experience becomes the primary mechanism through which disturbed states of consciousness at the centre of erotic experience are given a material and experiential reality. *Story of the Eye* thus marks Bataille's developing fascination with a heterology that examines transgression, eroticism, sovereignty and expenditure as forms of unintelligible experience but also that which a masculinised 'absolute knowledge' has repressed. For Bataille negative experience reveals a shattered subject that critically destabilises the vertical hierarchies of a masculine economy of philosophical experience that sustain self-mastery and transcendent knowledge. By contrast the 'Recherches sur la sexualité (led by Breton) and begun in the same year that Bataille's novel was published, sets out to investigate a 'collective experience' of sexuality and love, producing in the process an unprecedented series of research documents that disclose the troubling and paradoxical negotiation of sexuality in this period. While the 'Recherches' risked reaffirming the demonstrability of heteronormative male sexuality by marginalising the experience of female and homosexual desire, the discussions reveal a level of affective intimacy that challenge a straightforward recuperation of masculine virile identity. If the threat of emasculation and the decline of masculine authority were at the centre of post-war efforts to heal a war-wounded masculinity and reassimilate men back into civilian life, surrealist responses were not entirely immune to these anxieties. However, by attempting to investigate the limitless varieties of experience in relation to sexuality and desire, surrealism radically contested traditional accounts of masculine experience and the cultural politics that underpinned the repression of men's experience in the name of national reconstruction. As Dean has argued, anxieties about the frail masculine social body in this period often hinged on the desire to protect that body from the 'shame, desecration, and subjugation' that had constituted men's experience of war.[5] The surrealists' investigations of sexual experience reveal a fraught transfiguration of the affective and intimate dimensions of masculine experience that had been irrevocably transformed by the First World War.

Investigating Sex

The 'Recherches sur la sexualité' began as a formal inquiry into the experiences of sexuality among a group of male surrealists. Initiated by Breton, they extended surrealism's ethnographic interest in the devalued or repressed experiences of everyday life, initially established with the experiments at the Bureau of Surrealist Research in 1924.[6] While the Bureau's early activities endeavoured to open up Surrealist research activity to the wider public, the 'Recherches sur la sexualité' were largely confined to formal members of the surrealist group. They initially consisted of six roundtable discussions held over the course of three months at the beginning of 1928. A series of six more group discussions were held infrequently up until 1932, this time including women in some of the discussions, after protests from male members that the discussions were of little value without the perspective of women.[7] In probing so-called deviant sexuality the 'Recherches' encouraged a frank disclosure of the varieties of sexual experience, hoping to contest normative assumptions about sexual proclivities and practices. The first series of discussions were published in *Révolution surréaliste* in March 1928 under the title 'Recherches sur la sexualité, part d'objectivité, determinations individuelles, degré de conscience' ('Research on sexuality: The role of objectivity, individual determinations and degree of consciousness'.) Such claims for the role of objectivity, however, were frequently undermined by the infiltration of literary and psychosexual discourses into participant's responses as well as demonstrative individual prejudices that threatened to close down the investigations altogether. In the discussion of a male partner's awareness – and even evidence – of female orgasm during intercourse, which was the first question posed in the inaugural session, the issue of subjective versus objective experience quickly discloses the obvious strain characterising a good deal of the discussions:

ANDRÉ BRETON A man and a woman make love. To what extent is the man aware of the woman's orgasm? Tanguy?

YVES TANGUY   Hardly at all.

ANDRÉ BRETON   Do you have any objective ways of telling?

YVES TANGUY   Yes.

We are not told what these are.

ANDRÉ BRETON   What does Queneau think?

RAYMOND QUENEAU   There are no ways.

ANDRÉ BRETON   Prévert?

JACQUES PRÉVERT   It depends on the woman.

ANDRÉ BRETON   Do you have any objective ways of telling?

JACQUES PRÉVERT   Yes, yes, yes, yes.

ANDRÉ BRETON Which?

JACQUES PRÉVERT   (*Does not reply.*)

ANDRÉ BRETON   Péret?

BENJAMIN PÉRET   No way. And Breton?

ANDRÉ BRETON   There are only subjective ways, which one can trust to the extent that one can trust the woman in question.

BENJAMIN PÉRET   I agree with Breton.[8]

Here the difficulty in establishing 'objective' knowledge of female orgasm directly highlights the tension between the reflexive forms of male sexual experience investigated in the discussions and the erotic experience of the female 'other' which surrealist aesthetic ideology frequently idealised. The consternation expressed over the objective verification of a woman's orgasm and the assumption that evidence of male orgasm is always indisputable (the subject of the following question) disclose a pervasive confusion around female orgasm consistent with contemporary psycho-sexual discourses. Such discourses tended to reinforce an androcentric model of sexual pleasure with male emission as the incontrovertible proof that orgasm had taken place. Female sexual experience, on the other hand, was invariably defined in terms of receptivity, with female orgasm reduced to anatomical enigma.[9] The discussion of female orgasm in the 'Rechearches' reinforces a normative discourse on the obscurity of female orgasm as well as well as a pervasive anxiety around women's potential duplicity in the sexual act.

Returning to the topic of orgasm in the second session, the discussion of the evidence of male orgasm takes an unexpected turn when Raymond Queneau confesses to experiencing orgasm without ejaculation, to which Breton responds: 'These can only be pathological cases' (24). Louis Aragon, quick to combat Breton's reductive assumption, replies: 'I must point out that for the first time during this discussion the word 'pathological' has been brought up. That seems to suggest that some of us believe in the idea of the normal man. I object to this idea' (24). According to Elisabeth Roudinesco 'the Surrealist inquiries into sexuality ... read as parodies of the case histories being published at the same time in the *Revue française de psychoanalyse*', making use of a psychoanalytic vocabulary 'which gave their exchanges a technical cast'.[10] While the technical language and the confessional nature of the discussions often suggest 'a kind of ongoing therapy' (17) for the group, the discussions also reveal a degree of resistance to the therapeutical value of psychoanalysis, signifying a tension between the clinical foundations of the psychoanalytic movement and the Surrealist's unorthodox use of psychoanalytic concepts. In the discussion on masturbation in the sixth session, Breton makes this position clear:

> Strictly speaking [masturbation] has never been loathsome for me. ... It did not become completely acceptable to me until the day I learned from a work of Wittels on Freud that certain psychoanalysts of the Zurich school recommend it as therapeutic in some cases. Since then I have only seen it as a cure, and am thus prejudiced against it as I am against cures in general. (89–90).

While the surrealists certainly absorbed the technical language of psychoanalysis, drawing on the central Freudian concepts of repression, fantasy and the unconscious to establish its politics of revolt, the 'Recherches' broke with the spirit of the 'talking cure' in shifting the emphasis from the individual to the group. In this sense the experimental impetus of the discussions reveal the influence of ethnography as much as psychoanalysis, first-hand experience as much as unconscious motivations. Such an interdisciplinary approach facilitated an understanding of cultural research in terms of 'a contested reality'[11] in which the 'Recherches' become exemplary of a collective experience defined in opposition to the social taboos and cultural hypocrisies around sexuality that dominated French life.

The tensions between individual experiences nevertheless frequently unsettle the collective effort to establish detached, objective inquiry. Aragon's objections to Breton's use of the term 'pathological' and its assumption of a stable benchmark for experience – that of 'a normal man' – reveals masculinity itself to be a site of contestation within the group. This becomes an even greater source of conflict when the discussion moves to the subject of male homosexuality. Although the group agree to endorse 'everything to do with perversity and experiment' (39),

Breton nevertheless launches a condemnation of male homosexuality, indeed a refusal to pursue it as a topic of discussion. Breton's views on this subject, however, are by no means straightforward or even consistent – he excuses the Marquis de Sade's homosexual proclivities on the grounds that for him 'freedom of morals was a matter of life and death' (5–6). Michael Richardson has usefully pointed to the distinction between *homosexualité* (sexual practices) and *pédérastie* (the cultural affectations of homosexuality) in this period, suggesting Breton's attitude is indicative of the latter.[12] I would argue, however, that the vocal opposition to Breton's views by several prominent members of the group suggests a level of prejudice across both domains. While Man Ray contends that there is no 'great physical distinction between the love of a man for a woman and homosexuality', Aragon defines homosexuality 'as a sexual inclination like any other'. Aragon, moreover, directly challenges Breton's moral containment of homosexuality: 'The discussion is becoming reactive. . . . I want to talk about all sexual inclinations' (27). Faced with this opposition, Breton threatens to walk out, conceding his 'obscurantism on this subject' (28). The group are brought to order by the possibility of Breton's abandonment and readily move on to another topic. In this exchange Breton's emotionally volatile and paranoid response suggests a classic case of homosexual panic that reinforces the homosocial bonds of the group in spite of members' forceful opposition to his views. But it also indicates how a surrealist idealisation of heterosexual, romantic love was continually threatened by 'individual determinations' that rendered an investigation of sexual experience antithetical to Breton's elevation of romanticised forms of love. As Dawn Ades suggests, 'rather than affirming any constant elevation of a surrealist concept of love, there is . . . a constant interplay between pessimism and optimism, hope and despair in the face of sexual experience.'[13]

The surrealist investigations of sexuality are groundbreaking in terms of the candour and genuine sense of inquiry about an area of life that still remained largely taboo. The absence of women during the early sessions and Breton's violent reaction to the discussion of male homosexuality preclude the group's more generalised ambition of uncovering 'collective experience', revealing the blind spots of the ethnographic and political ethos of the movement. Breton's dogmatic arbitration similarly discloses a repressed anxiety about the role and representation of sexuality in the movement rather than an openness to the spirit of objective research. And yet the discussions tell us something crucial about the way the movement attempted to extend the very notion of 'experience' beyond individual affective responses. In turning to the experience of the group or closed community, newly valued in the emerging disciplines of ethnology and anthropology, surrealism struggled to situate 'individual determinations' in relation to the prescribed bonds of masculine intimacy driving the avant-garde coterie dynamic. At the beginning of the sixth session, Artaud, a late participant in the first series of discussions, astutely surmises the complexity – and the limitations – of the entire project:

> I tend to see the realm of sexuality as personal, as something quite individual and private. ... In investigations like this one, for most people a degree of ostentation inevitably intrudes. There is thus also the problem of whether such an investigation can distinguish between people who are being sincere and those who are not. (85)

If the 'Recherches' began with an implicit male anxiety about simulated orgasm and women's duplicity in the sexual act, Artaud reminds the group that duplicity may be elsewhere. As such Artaud draws attention to one of the central tensions of the 'Recherches' – the desire for an account of 'authentic' experiences of sexuality versus the performance of bravado that drives and indeed sustains the homosocial bonds that underpin the closed community of research participants. According to Michael Stone-Richards the sense of communal activity established by the surrealists owes its very inception to an 'ethics of experience' that defines the 'elective affinities' and 'affective bonds' of the coterie structure as 'a form of exemplary validity' outside the contractual social bonds associated with representational politics.[14] He writes:

> The ethical space constituted by such a mode of exemplarity is a possible movement toward a possible political realm. It can only be a possible movement toward a possible political realm as the group is a form of community with a difference, not least because, within the affective bonds of the group, the group permanently runs the danger of projecting its own narcissistic ideal as *the* ideal. (306–7)

Drawing attention to the potential for 'ostentation' created by the group dynamic, Artaud reveals how the group's 'narcissistic ideal' continually threatens the sense of detached inquiry driving the investigations and its usefulness for political transformation. That Breton regarded the 'Recherches' as a failure might further indicate that the tensions between liberation and censorship that cloaked the group's responses could never be adequately resolved.

These tensions are also symptomatic of how the movement's political and ethical goals were forged around the flux and instability that pertains to the phenomenology of experience. The sense of conflict and terminal crisis that plagued the constitutive parameters of the surrealist group throughout the years was a crisis *between* men, always involving male members of the group.[15] The 'Recherches' thus become an instructive microcosm for the possibilities and failures of a communal fidelity to 'the truth' of experience. This crisis might be recast then in terms of the tension between the cultivation of a *sensus communis*[16] that ensured the ethical and political ideals of the group against the plurality of responses to experience that continually extended the life of the movement but also paradoxically threatened to destabilise the communal bonds with which the group's power was forged. The absence of women from all but three of the twelve sessions signals masculine sexual experience as the primary object of inquiry, albeit one that revealed an ongoing struggle for alternative forms of masculine intimacy and communication in the face of idealised notions of what it meant to be a man in post-war France. The cataloguing of desires, experiences and attitudes towards sexuality provide an insight into the surrealists' struggle to broaden the very parameters of masculine experience against the tide of an increasingly alienated consciousness that had all but diminished both empirical and transcendent forms of communicable experience.[17] While liberation and censorship operated simultaneously in the 'Recherches', Bataille's turn to erotic experience is no less mired in the antinomies of transgression and interdiction, but in ways that more overtly celebrate the violent emasculation of heroic masculinity.

Stories of the 'I' / Stories of Experience

Roland Barthes's structuralist reading of *Story of the Eye* famously produces a conflation of the erotic and the linguistic: '*Story of the Eye* is not a deep work. Everything in it is on the surface; there is no hierarchy. The metaphor is laid out in its entirety; it is circular and explicit, with no secret reference behind it.'[18] In privileging form over content Barthes institutes his own interpretive hierarchy by diminishing the novel's representation of erotic experience, suggesting that Bataille's achievement is the transformation of 'all experience into language that is *askew*' (127). It is not surprising that Barthes's reading rests almost entirely on his close attention to Part One of the narrative, 'The Tale'. When read through the autobiographical and analytical scaffolding of Part Two, 'Coincidences', a purely textualist reading becomes more difficult. Framed by an autobiographical account of traumatic childhood memory, Bataille's novel signifies the erotic imagination in terms of childhood trauma, paternal impotence and loss. The importance of this frame for the structure of the entire work is reinforced by Bataille, who strategically leads us there in terms of indirectly accounting for the obsessions played out in Part One of the narrative:

> While composing this partly imaginary tale, I was struck by several coincidences, and since they appeared indirectly to bring out the meaning of what I have written, I would like to describe them.[19]

What follows in this section is an analytic confession of sorts, in which a narrator (who may or may not be Bataille but who is decidedly not the narrative voice in Part One) explains the preceding narrative as a composite of sexual obsessions and deviations, within the context of memories of a traumatic adolescence. The recollection of childhood trauma in Part Two – a blind and paralysed syphilitic father, whose tabetic symptomology produced shrieks of unbearable pain and uncontrollable urination and defecation in front of his son, *and* a depressed, suicidal mother, whom the young narrator rescues from a series of attempted suicides – might well be the scandal of this text.[20] In other words traumatic childhood experience discloses the force of experience to the shaping of the imaginative writing in Part One and to read one part without the other misses the critical import of Bataille's interest in experience. Like the dream fragment that was produced as part of Bataille's cure with his psychoanalyst Adrien Borel in 1927, the year that Bataille began writing *Story of the Eye* with Borel's encouragement, and which echoes the substantive content of the analytic frame, we have no way of verifying the accuracy of the autobiographical details established in 'Coincidences'. Furthermore Bataille warns us not to read the events of 'The Tale' in mimetic relation to the autobiographical details of 'Coincidences' ('these memories and coincidences only indirectly account for the meaning of the story'). As a writer who treats meaningfulness with suspicion, Bataille should make us wary of taking the second section of the novel at face value – but this section also warrants closer scrutiny since it obviously forms an important framing device for Bataille's own intellectual and imaginative concerns. It is also integral to his turn to fictional writing as part of his analysis with Borel.[21] How might the novel attempt to come to terms with 'experience' in ways that connect the analytic and creative dimensions of the entire narrative?

If Part Two is structured as a form of analytic reflection involving previously repressed childhood memories, Part One pertains to the genre of the erotic quest, expounded through a series of obscene erotic encounters and spectacles that propel the narrative fantasy towards its climactic scene of sexual debauchery and transgression. In all of these scenes the narrative imparts a repetitive logic of eroticism in which death illuminates the meaning of the erotic experience for the central protagonists, the narrator and Simone. As the erotic quest intensifies, the narrator declares: 'We had abandoned the real world, the one made up solely of dressed people. ... Our personal hallucination now developed as boundlessly as perhaps the total nightmare of human society' (29). As 'hallucination' and 'nightmare', distanced from the real world (what Barthes refers to as the narrative's movement within 'a kind of essence of make-believe'), the first part of the narrative privileges the role of the imagination in converting obscene obsessions into 'intellectual violence'. The acts of sexual debauchery are thus framed through the altered states of consciousness ('hallucination', 'nightmare') and point to Bataille's interest in eroticism as central to his development of a concept of heterogeneous experience.

Part One also explores a series of linguistic transgressions through the metaphor of the eye which drive the sexual obsessions of the novel's protagonists. In the chapter titled 'Simone', this metaphorical chain becomes a verbal game that recalls the use of word association in the analytic session:

> Upon my asking [Simone] what the word *urinate* reminded her of, she replied: *terminate*, the eyes, with a razor, something red, the sun. *And egg?* A calf's eye, because of the colour of the head (the calf's head) and also because the white of the egg was the white of the eye, and the yolk the eyeball... She played gaily with words, speaking about *broken eggs*, and then *broken eyes*, and her arguments became more and more unreasonable. (34)

Within the formal construction of the metaphorical associations of globular objects (eye, egg, sun), we have the deranged experience of erotic obsession in which the objects signify the alluring and destructive experience of evacuation and death ('*urinate*, '*terminate*'). And as Barthes reminds us, the erotic theme in the novel is 'never directly phallic' but rather the eye, which 'we know to have been the Father himself, blind, his whitish globes turned up in their sockets as he pissed in front of his child' (122). But just as Barthes readily admits the autobiographical contamination of 'The Story' through the account in 'Coincidences' he closes down the possibility of deciphering its meaning. And yet the narrator insists on connecting his sexual obsession with traumatic childhood memory:

> [U]pon locating the breaking point of the conscious or, if you will, the favourite place of sexual deviation, certain quite different personal memories were quickly associated with some harrowing images that had emerged during an obscene composition. (72)

Erotic transgression ('sexual deviation'), thus emerges in the text through autobiographical experience and the implicit analytic session as a moment in which the subject – or 'I' – is torn from itself, just as in the final moments of 'The Story' the eye is torn from the priest's socket. The enucleated eye, a symbol throughout Bataille's oeuvre for a declining masculinist tradition, is returned to the female body's lowest orifices, the vagina and anus. As a symbol of Enlightenment rationality, the eye becomes debased and feminised through its association with the 'low'. Simone's insertion of an array of ovoid objects into her vagina (eggs, an eye and a bull's testicle) symbolically represent the female genitals as a vagina dentata, challenging an understanding of female genitals as simply lack, signifying instead their power to castrate and consume. In this way, as Barthes suggests, the phallic is destabilised as the dominant signifier in the text. The blinding of the priest (Father), later linked to the narrator's 'personal memories' of his blind, syphilitic father, enacts the emasculation of paternal authority, in the same way that the pseudonym Bataille used for the novel, Lord Auch (literally, Lord 'to the shit house'[22]), severs authorial presence from the name of the father, tying it instead to base matter. In severing the patrilineal origins of the authorial subject, Bataille enacts a critical blinding of hegemonic forms of masculine power, although as we shall see, this does not entirely foreclose the possibility of the son's renewed virility.

The excessive and debauched nature of the erotic quest, one in which experience is defined in terms of hallucination and nightmare, equally subverts the traditional function of the quest narrative as a source of self-discovery, one invariably conceived in terms of a masculinised heroic journey. It thus pointedly disrupts the romanticised adventures of the wandering surrealist's enchanted quest for self-knowledge, one that proceeds through the marvellous encounters of everyday urban experience (the real world). The theme of the enchanted quest structures the key surrealist prose narratives, Aragon's *Paris Peasant* (1926) and Breton's *Nadja* (1928). Instead Bataille's exploration of violence, bodily excess, delirium and eroticism point to the irrational, dark side of humanity ('the total nightmare of human society') and modes of experience that have been relegated as outside a democratic, bourgeois world order ('the real world ... of dressed people'). The novel's exploration of transgression, eroticism and death are forms of unintelligible experience that 'absolute knowledge' has repressed. If for Bataille erotic experience tears the subject from itself and transgresses the limits of intelligible subjectivity, it forms the basis of what he would later outline as 'inner experience', but which he also notes had first been developed as early as 1924.[23] In *Inner Experience* Bataille writes: 'Experience, its authority, its method do not distinguish themselves from ... contestation' (12). Experience, for Bataille, is a contestation of the self and the world, a form of negativity that does not negate the human subject and its community but rather questions the very ground of an epistemological certainty that reduces experience to philosophical transcendence. Experience is everything for Bataille, or rather a refusal to limit experience in ways that contain the subject's totality of possibility – 'in experience there is no longer a limited existence' (27). Or as Kristeva reminds us, negative experience is what absolute knowledge (philosophical knowledge) has repressed: 'Bataille rediscovers negativity in that repressed moment of absolute knowledge that is experience.'[24]

For Bataille, the very foundation of absolute knowledge (a Hegelian absolute knowledge no less) represses negative experience precisely because it represents the discontinuity that intelligible subjectivity and intellectual mastery must overcome. The operation of discontinuity as it informs our experience of the world is located, for Bataille, in eroticism and death – the central narrative experiences driving the first section of *Story of the Eye* – since these experiences constitute the philosophical acknowledgement of the death of God and the shattering of a unified and knowable subject. Bataille's shattered subject is an assault on the vertical hierarchies that sustain a masculine economy of experience as erect and phallic. In the first part of the text this is made parodically clear through the figure of the bullfighter, Granero. Described as 'a very manly Prince Charming' and one of the 'best matadors in Spain', Granero is the story's supremely hyper-masculinised figure, until his caricatured virility is violently assaulted 'under the blinding sun' by the bull's horn, which rips his right eye from its socket, leaving it 'dangling from his head' as a throng of men rush to haul his body away (53). In a scene that recalls the wounded and dismembered male body of the Great War, who is rescued from the battlefield by his fellow soldiers, Granero becomes the supremely emasculated heroic man at the same moment that Simone bites into the raw testicle of a slaughtered bull as she climaxes to orgasm. The narrator's confession of his 'ancient obsession' with eyes, eggs and testicles, all of which are either inserted into a female body or violently displaced from a male body, or both, thus connects the formlessness of base matter with the fragmentation and destruction of the masculine virile body.

While part one enacts an obscene erotic quest that has no meaning, no self-knowledge beyond the imaginative realm (a world of make-believe), part two moves in the opposite direction, providing an analytical and autobiographical frame that thwarts the enterprise of meaninglessness but without fully restoring the absence, the lack of self-mastery, meaninglessness invokes. In other words the two parts of the narrative provide a refusal of dialectical synthesis (of imagination and experience) but nevertheless restore the importance of inner experience as that which constitutes a reality beyond the horizon of intelligibility. In this sense *Story of the Eye* is an experience-book (in Foucault's sense of the term[25]), a work of fiction that rests on the reality of experience as that moment in which the subject is torn from the 'truth' of itself. The self, or 'I', in Bataille's fiction is thus defined through an experience of presence and absence, one that corresponds to the pseudonymous status of the author: through the action of *glissement* (sliding) the autobiographical narration is severed from the name of the author, even while presenting the experience of the author as foundational to the truth of its fiction.

Presence and absence tied to eroticism and death also correspond to the operation of transgression and interdiction that set in play a series of binary relations ('high' and 'low', ideal and real, virility and emasculation) that inform many of the essays composed for *Document* that immediately followed *Story of the Eye*. In these essays Bataille makes clear how any set of binary relations are always fundamentally unstable insofar as one set of terms reveals a dependency on the other, a process that signals destabilising contamination rather than a unifying dialectic. As such they invoke Bataille's own privileged use of the term *glissement*, a concept that designates a simultaneous movement in opposite directions, so that each term contaminates the other but forecloses the possibility of synthesis. Bataille's obsession with the operations of emasculation and virility suggest a particularly illuminating example of how these operations come to function in the wider trans-allegorical structure of his early writing in ways that sustain the double movement of masculinity as impotent and all powerful. In his essay 'The Lugubrious Game' (1929) Bataille provides a reading of Dali's painting of the same name as centrally concerned with the theme of castration as a pivotal experience of both emasculation and virility. Providing a schematic diagram complete with interpretive notes that lay out the psychoanalytic schema of the painting, Bataille reads 'the laceration of the upper part of the body' of the central figure as principally concerned with the experience of emasculation provoked by 'dreams of virility of a puerile and burlesque temerity'.[26] It is, however, the representation of a faecal stain in the underwear of a man in the lower right hand corner of the painting, that signifies, for Bataille, a new kind of experience of virility: 'a new and real virility is rediscovered by this person in ignominy and horror ...' (29). Since horror, for Bataille, always invokes a loss of ego and self-identity that also touches upon a vertiginous experience of joy, Bataille identifies the ignoble *skid mark* in Dali's painting as a sign that the soiled subject has passed through the experience of emasculation and out the other end, so to speak, redefining virility as a facing up to the experience of shame and horror. Here the anal-sadistic disruption of the social order, which also preoccupies the climactic scene of the first part of *Story of the Eye*, redefines virility as a facing up to the shame and horror of human impotence. It is not surprising then that Bataille triumphantly succumbs to Breton's infamous accusation; as 'the excremental philosopher', he finds in shit (and all base matter) a reformed tumescence that contaminates an Icarian flight of virile transcendence. For Bataille there is no existence without excretion, no possibility of a virile masculine subject without the possibility of its putative emasculation.

How might Bataille's autobiographical disclosures in 'Coincidences' function as a way to confront the ignominy and horror of an Oedipal experience that left Bataille obsessed with violent eroticism, resulting in his analysis with Borel? As Allen Stoekl suggests, Bataille's transformation of morbid and dangerous sexual experience into an 'intellectual violence' through writing reformulates his entire thinking around a heterodox theory that he begins to elaborate in earnest after writing *Story of the Eye*.[27] While sections of the text overtly invoke the scene of analysis, Bataille would later disclose the entire work's birth as the result of this analysis with Borel: 'the first book I wrote [*Story of the Eye*] ... I was able to write it only when psychoanalysed, yes, as I came out of it. And I believe I am able to say that it is only by being liberated in this way that I was able to write' (99). But Bataille's text is neither simply analytic confession nor autobiographical revelation – far from it. The operation of imagination and experience in the two parts of the text disclose the porous boundaries of the self against the desire for absolute knowledge in the face of its impossibility. In other words *Story of the Eye* refuses assimilation into a singular meta-narrative but rather defines traumatic experience as the site of a ruptured subjectivity in which meaning can never be fully realised. Similarly, erotic transgression in the novel does not function without the interdiction or limit that demarcates its threshold crossing, producing both an experience of anguish in the crossing of that limit that is no less marked than the desire (pleasure) to break the taboo. For Bataille the anal-sadistic destruction of idealised form operates as a contestation of the symbolic order to give experience over to an inaccessible 'real', an 'inner experience' that thwarts the enterprise of fully integrating traumatic experience into a teleological narrative. Experience is thus simultaneously inner and exterior to the self. The son's virility might thus be constituted as a refusal to ameliorate the shame and horror induced by the Great War, which decimated masculine experience and exposed the fragilities of an all-powerful male body.

Conclusion

Towards the end of 'The Lugubrious Game' essay Bataille turns to the figure of the soldier as the quintessential docile body of the state, as a metaphor for the habitual and orthodox forms of intellectual and aesthetic culture that were resurrected in the post-war years:

> Taking into account trickery, human life always more or less conforms to the image of the soldier obeying commands in his drill. But sudden cataclysms, great popular manifestations of madness, riots, enormous revolutionary slaughters – all these show the extent of the backlash (26–27).

Tellingly Bataille invokes the slaughtered bodies of the Great War even as he names that carnage as the very sign of a crisis of consciousness and revolt that followed in its wake. Undoubtedly a great deal of surrealist work responded to the fragmentation and destruction of the male body and psyche in the wake of the Great War, but above all it opposed efforts to make of that body and of that experience the docile agent for state rehabilitation and conformity that underwrote French national efforts to re-masculinise soldiers according to the demands of civilian life – through the institutions of 'family, religion, country' – the very site of Breton's opposition in the second manifesto. Surrealism's turn to experience formed part of its commitment to experimentation, uniting the imagination with the protean forms of individual and collective desire. The quotidian was therefore opened up to the realm of expectancy and possibility as a political response to a diminished post-war reality governed by the illusion of orderly reconstruction. As Blanchot reminds us, 'Surrealist *experience* is experience of experience, whether this be found under a theoretical or practical form: an experience which dismantles and dismantles itself, to the extent that it develops and, developing, interrupts itself.'[28] Despite the very different economies of 'experience' mapped by Breton and Bataille in their respective projects, they remained alert to the self-perpetuating illusions of politics and art in the interwar period. As Martin Jay notes, 'we have to be attentive to the various ways in which different concepts of experience – negative as well as positive, limit as well as ordinary, non-subjective as well as subjective – prevent us from ever having a simple foundational version on which to base an epistemology or from which to launch a politics'.[29] It was surrealism's scepticism towards what remained of human experience, including the restrictive forms of politics offered by the Right and the Left,[30] that precipitated its efforts to explore the limitless varieties of experience as the founding impetus for its transformation of art and politics .

Notes

1 For various discussions on this theme see Katharine Conley, *Automatic Woman: The Representation of Women in Surrealism* (Lincoln: University of Nebraska Press, 1996); Natalya Lusty, *Surrealism, Feminism, Psychoanalysis*, (Aldershot: Ashgate, 2007); Amy Lyford, *Surrealist Masculinities: Gender Anxiety and the Aesthetics of Post World War I Reconstruction in France* (Berkeley: University of California Press, 2007); Susan Rubin Suleiman, *Subversive Intent: Gender, Politics and the Avant-Garde* (Cambridge, MA: Harvard University Press, 1990).

2 Amy Lyford's impressive study of surrealism and masculinity in post-World War One reconstruction investigates the paradox of surrealist representations of masculinity, which she argues 'simultaneously visualized and disavowed male trauma in the interwar years', *Surrealist Masculinities*, p. 13. While I find much of Lyford's analysis and argument compelling, I do not agree with her rather pessimistic conclusion that 'surrealists' feminized, marginal, or deviant images prepared the way for postwar social regulation' nor that they 'delivered the unconscious to the technocrats by reconstructing the gendered human subject', pp. 187–188. For an alternative reading of the impact and legacy of surrealism on the various Left movements and intellectual formations of the twentieth century, see Michael Sherringham, *Everyday Life: Theories and Practices from Surrealism to the Present* (Oxford: Oxford University Press, 2006).

3 Carolyn J. Dean, *The Frail Social Body: Pornography, Homosexuality, and Other Fantasies in Interwar France* (Berkeley: University of California Press, 2000). Dean argues that post-war anxieties about the masculine social body were intrinsically tied to fears of French cultural decline after the Great War, precipitating 'a new relationship between the metaphorically masculine social body and sexual politics that derived from a new and complex displacement of that violence into ... increasingly fantastic constructions of the dangers of so-called perverse sexuality', p. 14.

4 The term 'convulsive beauty' first appears at the end of *Nadja* (1928) ('beauty will be convulsive or it will not be'), p.160, André Breton, *Nadja*, c.1928, trans., Richard Howard (New York: Grove Press, 1960), but received its fullest definition at the beginning of *Mad Love* (1937), where Breton writes, 'convulsive beauty will be veiled-erotic, fixed-explosive, magic-circumstantial, or it will not be'. Breton, *Mad Love*, c.1937, trans. Mary Ann Caws (Lincoln: University of Nebraska Press, 1987), p. 19.

5　Carolyn Dean, 'History, Pornography and the Social Body' in Jennifer Mundy, ed., *Surrealism: Desire Unbound* (Princeton: Princeton University Press, and Tate Publishing, 2001), p. 228. Judith Surkis has also shown that fears over the rapid spread of venereal disease in the interwar years 'embodied an internal threat to the nation's sexual health, which served to justify concrete measures to maintain and police its corporeal integrity.' She argues that '[v]enereal disease was not merely a convenient metaphor for the fragility, permeability, and instability of French masculinity' but 'anchored diffuse concerns about who could and should qualify as a French man in specific bodies'. See 'Enemies Within: Venereal Disease and the Defense of French Masculinity Between the Wars', in Christopher E. Forth and Bertrand Taithe, eds., *French Masculinities: History, Culture and Politics* (Basingstoke: Palgrave, 2007), p. 116.

6　The Bureau of Surrealist Research was a short-lived experiment, lasting from October 1924 to April 1925. A press release for the Bureau published in *La Révolution surréaliste* in early 1925 promoted the intention of creating 'true surrealist archives' of dream accounts, automatic writing and strange and disturbing occurrences, inviting members of the public to participate in these activities.

7　See José Pierre, ed., *Investigating Sex: Surrealist Discussions, 1928–1932*, trans. Malcom Imrie (London: Verso, 1992). Breton initially defended the exclusion of women on the grounds that male participants would be less inhibited and more inclined to be candid in their responses.

8　Pierre, ed., *Investigating Sex*, p. 3.

9　The subject of female orgasm is returned to in the Seventh Session, where the discussion turns to the distinction between clitoral, vaginal and uterine orgasm. Breton argues that 'very, very few' women experience orgasm through clitoral stimulation alone – he suggests 5%, while Jean Caupenne (a brief associate of the group) refutes Breton's assertion, claiming, 'The very high percentage of women who do not have orgasms must derive from the fact that they only have normal sexual relations, in which the clitoris is neglected.' Pierre, ed., *Investigating Sex*, pp. 104–105.

10　Elisabeth Roudinesco, *Jacques Lacan and Co. A History of Psychoanalysis in France, 1925–1985*, trans. Jeffrey Mehlman (Chicago: University of Chicago Press, 1990), p.17.

11　James Clifford, 'On Ethnographic Surrealism', in *The Predicament of Culture: Twentieth-Century Ethnography, Literature and Art* (Cambridge, MA: Harvard University Press, 1988).

12　Michael Richardson, 'Seductions of the Impossible: Love, the Erotic and Sacrifice in Surrealist Discourse', in *Theory, Culture, Society*, Special Issue on Love and Eroticism, 15.3–4 (1998): 390.

13　Dawn Ades, 'Afterword', in Pierre, ed., *Investigating Sex*, p. 201.

14　Stone-Richards draws on Monnerot's characterisation of surrealism as a *Bund*, a kind of outsider community opposed to *Gesellschaft* and *Gemeinschaft*, contract-based and community-based social formations respectively. 'Failure and Community: Preliminary Questions on the Political in the Culture of

Surrealism', in Spiteri and LaCross, eds., *Surrealism, Politics and Culture* (Aldershot: Ashgate, 2003), pp. 306–308.

15 It is only after the purge of male members from the group in the late 1920s, that women begin to take on a more significant role in the movement, often as a result of Breton's conscious efforts to recruit them.

16 Stone-Richards uses Kant's formulation, *sensus communis*, to describe the expansion of thinking from the viewpoint of the other, p. 306.

17 This is, of course, also the subject of Walter Benjamin's lament in his essay, 'The Storyteller': 'Was it not noticeable at the end of the war that men returned from the battlefield grown silent – not richer, but poorer in communicable experience? A generation that had gone to school on a horse-drawn streetcar now stood under the open sky in a countryside in which nothing remained unchanged but the clouds, and beneath these clouds, in a field of force of destructive torrents and explosions, was the tiny fragile human body.' 'The Storyteller: Reflections of the Work of Nikolai Leskov', in *Illumations*, trans. Harry Zohn (London: Fontana Press, 1992), p. 84.

18 Roland Barthes, 'The Metaphor of the Eye', trans. J. A. Underwood, in Georges Bataille, *Story of the Eye* (London: Penguin, 1979), p. 123.

19 George Bataille, *Story of the Eye*, trans. Joachim Neugroschal (London: Penguin, 1979), p. 69. First published in 1928. My reading is taken from the English translation of the original French text published under the pseudonym, Lord Auch in 1928.

20 Andrea Dworkin famously accused Bataille's novel of being merely 'high class pornography.' Her reading was almost exclusively drawn from Part One of the novel. For an excellent feminist critique of Dworkin's critique, see Suleiman, *Subversive Intent*.

21 According to Michel Surya, Bataille's biographer, this was an unconventional analysis and Borel was experienced in working with writers and artists. Michel Surya, *Georges Batailles: An Intellectual Biography*, trans. Krzystof Fijalkowski and Michael Richardson (London and New York: Verso, 1992), p. 97.

22 *Auch* is short for *aux chiottes*; in French slang it means to send someone to the toilet by telling them off.

23 Georges Bataille, *Inner Experience*, trans. Leslie Ann Boldt (Albany: State University of New York Press, 1988), p. xxxvi. First published in 1958.

24 Julia Kristeva, 'Bataille, Experience and Practice', in Leslie Anne Boldt-Irons, ed., *On Bataille: Critical Essays* (Albany: SUNY Press, 1995), p. 239.

25 In accounting for the importance of experience in his own work, Foucault suggests 'experience is always a fiction, something constructed, which exists only after it has been made, not before; it isn't something that is "true", but it has been a reality'. See 'How an 'Experience-Book' is Born', in *Remarks on Marx: Conversations with Duccio Trombadori*, trans. R. James Goldstein and James Cascaito (New York: Semiotext(e), 1991), p. 27.

26 Georges Bataille, 'The Lugubrious Game', in Allan Stoekl, ed., *Visions of Excess: Selected Writings, 1927–1929* (Minneapolis: University of Minnesota Press, 1985). First published as 'Le 'Jeu lugubre" in *Documents*, Paris, no. 7 (December 1929): 29.

27 'Introduction' in *Visions of Excess*, p. x.
28 Maurice Blanchot, 'Le demain jouer', from *L'Entretien infini*, cited in 'Failure and Community', in Spiteri and LaCross (eds.), *Surrealism, Politics and Culture*, p.115.
29 Martin Jay, 'The Limits of Limit-Experience', in *Cultural Semantics: Keywords of Our Time* (Amherst: University of Massachusetts Press, 1998), p. 77.
30 Although in 1933 Breton formally split with the French Communist Party, the most prominent Left movement in France, and aligned with Stalinist communism, this came at the end of a long and difficult history between the surrealists and the PCF. After this, Breton's politics moved to the far-Left. In 1935 Breton and Bataille co-founded the anti-fascist group, Contre-Attaque, united in their efforts to oppose official forms of politics.

PART III

New Men

CHAPTER 7

The New Womanly Mensch? Modernism, Jewish Masculinity and Henry Roth's Call It Sleep

Maren Linett

In James Joyce's *Ulysses* (1922), the men in Barney Kiernan's pub mock Leopold Bloom for the impaired masculinity they believe accompanies his Jewishness. One of the men in the pub asserts that, when they are becoming parents, 'every jew is in a tall state of excitement, I believe, till he knows if he's a father or a mother'. Discussing Bloom's solicitous behaviour when his wife, Molly, was pregnant with their second child, the character called 'the citizen' asks, 'Do you call that a man?'

> – Well, there were two children born anyhow, says Jack Power.
>
> – And who does he suspect, says the citizen.
>
> Gob, there's many a true word spoken in jest. One of those mixed middlings he is. Lying up in the hotel Pisser was telling me once a month with headache like a totty with her courses.[1]

In this passage from the 'Cyclops' chapter, Bloom is impugned for being like a woman not only emotionally, but also biologically. He is overly solicitous of his wife, and what is more, he is so identified with her that he stands a chance of becoming a mother when she gives birth; he cannot have fathered his children; and he gets a monthly period. He is a 'mixed middling' – neither woman nor man.

In this scene Joyce is playing with antisemitic discourses hundreds of years old (the idea that Jewish men menstruate was popular during the Middle Ages) but given renewed life during the late-nineteenth and early-twentieth centuries, when sexology was all the rage. Scholars such as George Mosse and Sander Gilman have documented 'sociological and race-based medical theories [about] the Jewish male body [that] figured it as weak, diseased, and degenerate when compared to an idealized masculinity of European culture. During the *fin de siècle*, the inferiority of Jewish male physicality was often [ascribed to] a feminized racial essence.'[2] This prejudice is exhibited by Wyndham Lewis when he comments succinctly in *Hitler* (1931) that Jews are '[f]eminine, and in many ways unpleasant'.[3]

The image of the feminised Jew gained support from major thinkers in the United States and Europe. Henry Adams used an image of a synagogue to describe himself as branded, like a man 'circumcised in the Synagogue by his uncle the high priest, under the name of Israel Cohen'.[4] As Rachel Blau DuPlessis points out (following Freud), circumcision is imagined as a sort of castration; so Adams's assertion connotes emasculation. In *The Joyful Wisdom*, Friedrich Nietzsche compared 'the adaptability of women and Jews'.[5] The most extreme and detailed expression of the belief that Jewish men are feminine can be found in Otto Weininger's *Sex and Character*, published in German in 1903 and in English in 1906. Weininger asserts that '[i]t would not be difficult to make the case for the view that the Jew is more saturated with femininity than the Aryan to such an extent that the most manly Jew is more feminine than the least manly Aryan.'[6]

In *Ulysses*, Bloom's alleged womanliness briefly becomes a positive attribute in the magical world of 'Circe'. There, medical sexologists examine Bloom, one declaring that he has done a 'pervaginal examination' and found Bloom to be '*virgo intacta*'.[7] Another doctor chimes in, announcing that 'Professor Bloom is a finished example of the new womanly man.' This doctor concludes by saying '[h]e is about to have a baby', after which Bloom 'bears eight male yellow and white children'.[8] Joyce's playful attitude towards the femininity of Bloom invites readers to approve of femininity in men – up to a point. Joyce reportedly said that Jewish men are 'better husbands than we are, better fathers and better sons'.[9] However, after the long day during which Molly, as Bloom knows, has a sexual liaison with Blazes Boylan, Bloom demands that she bring him breakfast in bed the next day instead of their usual practice in which he serves her. His demand may represent a redemptive assertion of masculine dominance; perhaps Bloom is learning to overcome his femininity.

Through its playfulness, power and ambiguity, Joyce's representation of Bloom's femininity brought the gender of Jewishness into the center of literary modernism. By the time Henry Roth began writing his modernist immigrant novel *Call It Sleep* (1934) in 1930, the literary scene he sought to enter was peppered with feminised male Jewish characters. Influential examples in addition to Bloom include Louie Marsellus from Willa Cather's *The Professor's House* (1925), Jay Gatsby from F. Scott Fitzgerald's *The Great Gatsby* (1925) and Robert Cohn from Ernest Hemingway's *The Sun Also Rises* (1926).

Confronting such characters and writing an experimental autobiographical novel about growing up Jewish on the Lower East Side of New York

City – a novel Irving Howe called 'one of the few genuinely distinguished novels written by a 20th-century American'[10] – Roth could hardly sidestep the issue of the gendering of the Jewish man. Instead, clearly provoked by the array of feminised fictional Jews (as well as by the contours of his own childhood), Roth wrestled with this issue, crafting his novel around a hyper-masculine, brutal father and a timid, often terrified son who clings to the only source of comfort in his world – his mother. Through the conflicts between Albert Schearl and his son David, Roth depicts a conflict about the shape of Jewish masculinity.

In his brilliant study *Unheroic Conduct*, Daniel Boyarin has connected the stereotype of the womanly Jewish man to the ideal of *edelkayt* (nobility) enshrined in Talmudic culture, suggesting that 'there is something correct – although seriously misvalued – in the persistent European representation of the Jewish man as a sort of woman.'[11] With Boyarin's claims in mind it is tempting to seek in *Call It Sleep* an affirmation of the masculine delicacy valued in Talmudic culture. Albert Schearl's rage, primitive jealousy and physical roughness suggest a view of normative Western masculinity as brutality, whereas David's enforced gentleness offers new possibilities for Jewish masculinity. Perhaps David, through his close relationship to his mother, will replace his father's pitiless violence with a compassionate *edelkayt*. Perhaps he will become a counterpart to Joyce's 'new womanly man': a new womanly *mensch*. Since the novel ends while David is still a child, this reading remains possible. But the particular representations of violence in the novel suggest that it is at least as likely that the son of such a father will repeat the cycle: that his victimisation will lead him not to eschew violence but to enact it. The plot of *Call It Sleep* thereby thrusts femininity into the background. At the same time its experimental form – especially in the final section – resists the authoritarian masculinity embodied in Albert Schearl, making way instead for a formal inclusivity and a non-phallic subjectivity.

Modernist Jews

Roth read *Ulysses* in 1925, having borrowed a copy that his mentor (and later lover) Eda Lou Walton had smuggled from France. Although Roth much later objected to Joyce's pyrotechnics and what he saw as the insufficiently authentic Jewishness of Bloom, in 1925 he was amazed and inspired by the novel. Roth's biographer Steven Kellman writes that

> *Ulysses* taught Roth that the plots and characters of fairy tales need not be the only formula for literature, and that ... ordinary urban existence could bear the gravity of myth. 'What I gained', Roth would recall, 'was this awed

realization that you didn't have to go anywhere at all except around the corner to flesh out a literary work – given some kind of vision of course. ... It
was a tremendous impetus toward writing.'[12]

Roth found in Joyce's technical mastery the key to unlock his own
experience as the son of a violent immigrant father and transform it
into literature. He wrote of Joyce, 'it was language, language, that could
magically transmogrify the baseness of his days and ways into precious
literature.'[13]

As Brian McHale has pointed out, critics regularly describe *Call It Sleep*
as Joycean. McHale compares the parallel aesthetics of *Call It Sleep* and
Ulysses and explores the similarities between David Schearl and Leopold
Bloom. 'An observer and outsider, an urban wanderer, David is moreover,
also like Bloom, a specifically *Jewish* wanderer – the modern city-dwelling
Jew.'[14] I suggest that for Roth, Bloom's salient features were not only his
status as a Jewish wanderer but also his 'Jewish' femininity, a gendering
that helped motivate Roth's portrayal of both the feminised David Schearl
and the hyper-masculine Albert Schearl.

Like Bloom, the Jewish men in *The Professor's House*, *The Great Gatsby*
and *The Sun Also Rises* are feminised by their obsessive desire for and
attention to women and their purportedly unmasculine attention
to material details. Roth is very likely to have read these novels[15]; but
beyond the question of direct influence, I want to sketch an atmosphere
in which Jewish masculinity was seen as impaired and in which this
impairment was viewed as a complex and valuable theme for literary
exploration.

In Willa Cather's *The Professor's House*, the Jewish Louie Marsellus mar-
ries Rosamond, one of the daughters of the protagonist, Godfrey St. Peter.
While the dominant strands of antisemitism in Marsellus's representation
inhere in his inauthenticity, his usurpation of Tom Outland's creativity
and his relationship to money, he is also feminised by his relations to his
wife.[16] Two aspects of Louie's characterisation mark him as unmasculine.
The first is his selection of all of Rosamond's clothing. Although St. Peter
approves of Louie's choice of lavender clothes for Rosamond and she is
proud that her husband 'selects all [her] things', the novel directs us to
read Louie's interest in her clothing as unmasculine.[17] In the section 'Tom
Outland's Story', Tom tells a story about a Mr. Bixby who accompanied
his wife to buy a dress. 'That seemed to me very strange. In New Mexico
the Indian boys sometimes went to a trader with their wives and bought
shawls and calico, and we thought it rather contemptible'.[18] Tom continues the story with clear disdain. Because Tom is the text's and St. Peter's

hero, his mockery of Bixby instructs us how to view Louie's selection of Rosamond's clothing.[19]

The second way Louie is feminised is by his embrace of Tom Outland's memory. Tom was his wife's former fiancé, but he was killed in World War I. In a scene that combines Louie's unmanly interest in clothes with a lack of masculine competitiveness, Louie enters St. Peter's study and finds a blanket Tom's friend had brought up from Mexico. He 'pounces upon' the blanket and pronounces it a 'proper dressing gown'. When St. Peter tells him the blanket was Outland's, Louie is intrigued:

> 'Was it Outland's indeed?' Louie stroked it and regarded it in the glass with increased admiration. 'I can never forgive destiny that I hadn't the chance to know that splendid fellow.'
>
> The Professor's eyebrows rose in puzzled interrogation. 'It might have been awkward – about Rosie, you know.'
>
> 'I never think of him as a rival,' said Louie, throwing back the blanket with a wide gesture. 'I think of him as a brother, an adored and gifted brother.'[20]

Louie's donning and stroking of the blanket are coded as feminine. His professed adoration of Rosamond's former fiancé strikes St. Peter as puzzling because it lacks any hint of masculine possessiveness. Indeed, Louie and Rosamond are having a new house built and calling it 'Outland'. The extent to which Louie identifies with Rosamond's love for Outland rather than seeing Outland as a rival (albeit a dead one) suggests a fundamental femininity.

In F. Scott Fitzgerald's *The Great Gatsby*, Jay Gatsby's adoration of a woman results in a similar unmasculine attention to material details. In this case, Jay Gatsby organises his life around the hope that he can win back his former love, Daisy Buchanan. He buys and decorates a mansion and throws elaborate parties designed to attract her. As Walter Benn Michaels points out, Gatsby, whose name was formerly James Gatz, is almost certainly a Jewish man, originally poor, who changed his name to assimilate into a wealthier tier of American society. Now that he is wealthy, he shows an excessive attention to clothes: 'he opened for us two hulking patent cabinets which held his massed suits and dressing-gowns and ties, and his shirts, piled like bricks in stacks a dozen high.' Gatsby tells Nick and Daisy, 'I've got a man in England who buys me clothes. He sends over a selection of things at the beginning of each season, spring and fall.'[21]

His attention to clothing seems warranted when Daisy buries her head in the pile of shirts and cries 'stormily': 'It makes me sad because I've never

seen such – such beautiful shirts before.'²² Much as Rosamond is proud of
her husband's taste in picking out her clothes, Daisy responds to Gatsby's
sartorial extravagance. But in both cases readers are meant not to share
the women's approval. The pink suit in which Gatsby goes to visit Daisy
proves to Tom Buchanan that he could not have been an 'Oxford man'.²³
Meredith Goldsmith writes that the colours of Gatsby's shirts 'violate
normative masculine dress codes of the period'.²⁴ She further claims that
'Gatsby's efforts at sartorial and commodity self-fashioning situate him
within a distinctly feminized and middle- to working-class mode of identity construction.'²⁵ Much as Marsellus represents the decline in values of
contemporary society, Gatsby represents a threat to a culture of class stability and propriety.

The feminization of Robert Cohn in *The Sun Also Rises* is more blatant
than the feminisation of Marsellus and Gatsby, in spite of the fact that
he is a skilled boxer and that Jake Barnes assures us, 'I do not believe he
thought about his clothes much.'²⁶ Cohn's feminisation emerges from his
emotional investment in sex and his inability to keep his love for Brett
Ashley in check. In contrast to Jake, who loves Brett deeply but suffers stoically, Cohn's emotions spill out willy-nilly. After Cohn meets Brett, Jake
demonstrates his masculine restraint by repeating, 'she's very nice', while
Cohn gushes that she has 'a certain fineness. She seems to be absolutely
fine and straight' and tries to find a name for the quality.²⁷ After having a
weekend affair with her, he becomes very nervous about seeing her again.
'At dinner that night we found that Robert Cohn had taken a bath, had
had a shave and a haircut and a shampoo, and something put on his hair
afterward to make it stay down. He was nervous. … I have never seen a
man in civil life as nervous as Robert Cohn – nor as eager.'²⁸

Cohn later hangs around Brett, prompting her fiancé to complain that
he 'follow[ed] Brett around like a steer all the time'; '[h]e hung around
Brett and just *looked* at her. It made me damned well sick.'²⁹ The image of
the castrated bull explicitly links Cohn's romantic attachment to emasculation. Discussing Cohn with Brett, Jake remarks that '[h]e can't believe
it didn't mean anything.'³⁰ Cohn eventually beats up Brett's new lover, a
young bullfighter, in a show of physical strength that paradoxically only
confirms his status as a 'steer' who treats sex and love as the pinnacle of his
existence.³¹

In a thorough exploration of the novel's taxonomy of the 'real man'
and the counterfeit, Todd Onderdonk remarks that Cohn's 'accentuated
Jewishness … functions here less as a denigrated racial category than as
evidence of gender inauthenticity.'³² Onderdonk offers an astute analysis

of Cohn's feminisation; I question, though, his distinction between racial category and gender inauthenticity. As modernist fiction demonstrates, impaired masculinity is a crucial *component* of racialised Jewishness.

Call It Sleep

Given a literary and cultural climate that stressed the feminisation of Jewish men, it is not surprising to find that from the first pages of *Call It Sleep*, David Schearl is linked to women. Roth's stated themes centred more on the urban, immigrant, working-class experience than on gender, and critics have in turn focused their readings mainly on issues of heritage, religion, class and language. But viewing the novel in terms of its representations of gender allows us to understand Roth's implicit response to the feminised Jews of modernism and his understanding of cyclic violence.

A minor scene in the novel indicates that Roth did remark the feminisation of certain racial categories of men. David gazes at a sign for the local laundry, which reads 'Charley Ling'. The proprietor is Chinese, and David wonders about his first name: 'Charley, American name. Just like Charley in school. But something else maybe, like Yussie is Joey.'[33] Then he shifts his gaze to the last name: 'L-i-ng. Ling. Ling-a-ling. Is Jewish. Can't be. Ling' (174). Although he concludes that Mr. Ling cannot be both Jewish and Chinese, he does consider an identity between himself and the proprietor. His friend Izzy soon remarks, 'Like a lady, he looks. . . . Wod a big tail he's god on his head' (175). In the early-twentieth century Jews were commonly classed as an 'Oriental' people. Izzy's assertion that the Chinese man looks like a lady, along with David's speculations about Mr. Ling, confirms Roth's awareness of gendered racial categories.

Roth contributes to the creation of a gendered, modernist Jewishness by delineating a conflict between David/femininity and Albert/masculinity. In the prologue he shows David as a toddler in his mother Genya's arms and then, when his father directs her to put him down, clinging to her skirt (14). In the novel's first chapter, David is asked by a neighborhood boy, 'Who you like bedder, ladies or gents?' David answers 'ladies', while the other boy says he 'likes [his] fodder bedder' (21). This snippet of dialogue serves a crucial function: to generalise David's connection with his mother, suggesting that he seeks solace not only from her, but from women in general. Like Leopold Bloom, who returns after his hard day of expulsion and wandering to the 'promised land' of Molly's 'rump', David views femininity as a place of refuge.[34]

Because he is a child, David's obsession with a woman – his mother – is distinct from the obsessions of Jay Gatsby with Daisy Buchanan and Robert Cohn with Brett Ashley. But given the way Roth portrays David's fixation, we may legitimately view it on a continuum with the other characters. In his much later and also autobiographical novel, *A Diving Rock on the Hudson* (1995), Roth's alter ego, the elderly writer Ira Stigman, comments on his representation of his young self: he realises how 'little in so many ways the adolescent juvenile he portrayed, or strove to re-create, resembled the 'normal' youngster of that age and period. [T]he greatest difference ... was in ... his way of mooning about the opposite sex, about females.'[35]

Like Ira and the modernist Jews I've described, David Schearl cannot keep his feelings about 'his' woman in check. He is at intervals overwhelmed by his need for and possessiveness of his mother. Sitting in the kitchen with her, he thinks, 'But if only the air were always this way and he always here alone with his mother. He was near her now. He was part of her. The rain outside the window set continual seals upon their isolation, upon their intimacy, their identity. ... He watched her every movement hungrily' (68). When his mother asks if he'd like a younger sibling, saying 'it would give you something else to look at besides your mother', David answers 'I don't want to look at anything else' (38). When he sees his father's workmate Luter 'staring at his mother, at her hips', he becomes aware of her body in a new way, feeling 'bewildered, struggling with something in his mind that would not become a thought' (40); later, thinking again of Luter, he has to tell himself to look away from her breasts as she bends to mop the floor (64). Luter tells Genya, 'Do you know I have never seen a child cling so to his mother?' (41).

In one important scene, when boys in the neighborhood brag that they have seen a naked woman, he realises it was his mother bathing. 'The rush of shame set his cheeks and ears blazing like flame before a bellows. ... He stood with feet mortised to the spot, knees sagging, quivering' (294). David feels injured: 'Like flying hail against his nakedness their sharp cries stunned and flayed him' (295). There is an obvious Oedipal component to David's obsession with his mother, which has been well analysed;[36] for my purpose here, what is most important is the close association between David and femininity. His mother's nakedness becomes his own, flayed by the boys' 'sharp cries'. His knees sag in an allusion to T. S. Eliot's Jewish Bleistein.[37] He takes on himself the shame of being exposed.

While the adult Jewish characters' need of women makes them seem, in the misogynist terms of their novels, contemptible, David's need of his mother seems at first justified. His father brutalises him, his playmates bully him. His mother is the only kind force in his world. But the Oedipal attraction and the intensity of his need for her fuse to invite readers to feel at least as much discomfort with as sympathy for David's relationship to Genya. The novel implies, in part through his father's articulations of disdain for his 'mama's boy', that by the age of eight, David should be out-growing his dependence on his mother rather than revelling in it.[38] In this way, the novel invites readers to scorn David's dependence on his mother, and by implication, his connection to women.[39]

Indeed, the arc of the narrative reinforces this disdain by positioning Genya as that which must be left behind in order for David to find tran-scendence. Elaine Orr insightfully describes the scene after David has heard that the boys saw his mother naked. He runs to his apartment, but instead of entering, passes his door and goes up for the first time to the roof, where he finds a kind of peace usually reserved for his times with his mother. 'As the boy by-passes Genya and bounds up the final flight of stairs, he rends the narrative pattern of return. ... [The mother] must be there to leave, and then her meaning in the process is at an end.'[40] After this David's trajectory moves outward, centring on two incidents where he inserts metal, phallic objects into the streetcar tracks.

In the first instance, David is goaded by some Gentile boys to throw a zinc sword down onto the streetcar tracks. As Wendy Zierler points out, 'phallic images of swords and rods and images of male sexual release fig-ured as light, power, even transcendence, abound in the novel.'[41]

> The point of the sheet-zinc sword wavered before him, clicked on the stone as he fumbled, then finding the slot at last, rasped part way down the wide grinning lips like a tongue in an iron mouth. He stepped back. From open fingers, the blade plunged into darkness.
> Power!
> Like a paw ripping through all the stable fibers of the earth, power, gigantic, fetterless, thudded into day! And light, unleashed, terrific light bellowed out of iron lips. The street quaked and roared, and like a tor-tured thing, the sheet zinc sword, leapt writhing, fell back, consumed with radiance. (253)

Zierler describes this scene as allying 'power, light, and transcendence' with 'a rather violent version of male sexuality and orgasm – with David's sword wavering before him, plunging into the dark lips of the rail tracks, 'ripping through the stable fibers' of the (female/mother) earth, ending with the consummation of radiance.'[42]

The second scene of 'power!' is more dramatic: David runs away from his father's accusation that he is the son of a Gentile Genya was involved

with before coming to America, and dips a milk ladle into the rail. This
time, since he does not let go of the ladle, he is knocked unconscious, and
his dream-state and the multiple languages and dialects spoken around
him give Roth the opportunity to magnify his stream-of-consciousness
experiment. The milk ladle connects David to his father, who works as
a milkman, and its function as the implement of transcendence brings
David closer to his violent father. Leslie Fiedler notes that David has
'usurped the paternal role ... thrusting a milk ladle into a dark gap in
the earth'.[43] Lynn Altenbernd also comments on the sexual imagery: 'The
phrase "in the crack be born"... when considered in conjunction with
David's posture as he straddles the slotted rail to insert the dipper's handle between "the long, dark, grinning lips ... like a sword in a scabbard"
clearly suggests an insemination that will assure the rebirth of the self-
created creator.' Altenbernd adds in a footnote that Roth 'was no doubt
aware that the Latin for *scabbard* is *vagina*'.[44]

Transcendence at the end of *Call It Sleep*, then, means that David flees
the safety of the mother for the exaltation and danger of phallic power,
transforming the maternal substance of milk into the father's milk ladle/
sword. '*Power! Incredible, barbaric power! A blast, a siren of light within
him, rending, quaking, fusing his brain and blood to a fountain of flame,
vast rockets in a searing spray! Power!*' (419). Here David, even as he writhes
helplessly in its grip, claims power for himself.[45]

Linking David to women, then, does not make *Call It Sleep* a feminist
response to the more misogynistic portraits of feminised Jews. Femininity
in the novel becomes mostly a place from which to hide from masculinity,
which is portrayed as full of violence and coercion. Portraying femininity
as a refuge, even though it gives femininity a positive valance, means that
it cannot be an integral part of masculine development, but a space that
must remain outside it. David has only a slim chance of redirecting his
momentum, of integrating femininity into his identity to become a 'new
womanly *mensch*'.

Indeed, the novel invites us to explore the links between the fear that
keeps David at his mother's skirts and the fear that lurks in his father's
psyche and seems to prompt him to violence. We wonder, for example,
about the source of Albert's rage when, after David has hurt his friend
Yussie and Albert has beaten David, he rants to Genya that David will
hurt him someday: "I'm harboring a fiend!' the implacable voice raged. 'A
butcher! And you're protecting him! Those hands of his will beat me yet! I
know! My blood warns me of this son! Look at this child! Look what he's
done! He'll shed human blood like water!" (85). This expression of fear

in the domineering father asks us to question the origin of his violence, and then necessarily to doubt whether his equally scared son will find the strength to inhabit a gentle *edelkayt*.

In *A Diving Rock on the Hudson*, Ira Stigman describes his father's feelings of inadequacy as the source of his rage: 'Provocations I must have afforded in plenty, without any doubt. But the little man, pathetic, deeply troubled little man, frustrated by his inadequacy, haunted by fear of ridicule, undoubtedly a rejected child himself, lost all self-control in administering chastisement'.[46] Roth's father was, as he says here, a small man; in *Call It Sleep*, Albert is large, imposing and muscular. But Albert is motivated by the same insecurity Roth detected in his father. David notices that Albert's sharp calls for his wife ('Genya!') are really cries for reassurance: 'Always he seemed to need reassurance, always he seemed reassured' by her reply (241).

This genealogy of Albert's violence draws our attention to the violence that the usually timid David commits. These eruptions of rage suggest that David may continue to replicate his father's transformation of fear into violence. In fact, when we learn that Albert let his own father be gored to death by a bull without 'lift[ing] a finger' to help him because the father had struck Albert that morning, we assume that Albert too is the son of an abusive father, that we are witnessing an unholy legacy passed down from generation to generation. One of David's eruptions of rage occurs when he is telling his neighbour Yussie to leave his house.

> 'Get otta here!' hissed David frantically. 'Go in yuh own house!'
> 'I don' wanna', said Yussie truculently. 'I c'n fight-choo. Wanna see me?' He drew back his arm, 'Bing!' The point of the clothes hanger struck David in the knee, sending a flash of pain through his whole leg. He cried out. The next moment, he had kicked at Yussie's face with all the force in his leg.
> Yussie fell forward on his hands. He opened his mouth but uttered no sound. Instead his eyes bulged as if he were strangling, and to David's horror the blood began to trickle from under his pinched white nostrils. (82)

Using words like 'hissed' and 'frantically', Roth stresses the position of powerlessness from which David tries to persuade Yussie to leave. When it doesn't work, David's feeling of powerlessness intensifies, setting the stage for his overreaction to Yussie's 'bing' on his leg. The wording of the sentence, 'the next moment, he had kicked at Yussie's face with all the force in his leg', stresses a pre-conscious eruption of violence rather than a calculated reprisal. And David's 'horror' at Yussie's blood caps the picture of a child acting out of a helpless, instinctive rage.

A second scene repeats the salient aspects of the incident with Yussie. David is outside his apartment building and neighborhood kids taunt him, implying, as does his father, an infantilising relationship to his mother: 'cry baby, cry baby, suck your mudder's tiddy'. Then the boys begin to close in on him.

> And suddenly a blind, shattering fury convulsed him. Why were they chasing him? Why? When he couldn't turn anywhere – not even upstairs to his mother. He wouldn't let them! He hated them! He bared his teeth and screamed, tore loose from the boy who was dragging at his belt and lunged at him. Every quivering cell was martialed in that thrust. Before his savage impact, the other reeled back. ... His head struck first, a muffled distant jar like a blast deep underground. His arms flopped down beside him, his eyes snapped shut, he lay motionless. With a grunt of terror, the rest stared down at him, their faces blank, their eyes bulging. David gasped with horror and fled toward his house. (91)

Here David does realize his anger before he acts ('He wouldn't let them!') but the imagery accompanying the description of his lunge suggests a primitive rage: he 'bared his teeth and screamed', and 'every quivering cell was martialed in that thrust'. The impact is described as 'savage' and again David is struck with 'horror' at what he has done.[47]

Roth has given us a genealogy of violent sons of violent fathers, each coming from a place of fear. Victimisation, the novel demonstrates, does not lead to gentleness but to outbursts of rage. The *edelkayt* readers may hope David will grow into seems far off as he leaves behind the softness of femininity as embodied in his mother and employs the two phallic objects to acquire transformative power. The conflict between the timid, feminine boy and the brutal, masculine father is settled in favour not of either party but of brutality. The novel does not offer a way to view femininity as a part of masculine fulfilment: femininity may be a place from which to develop into masculinity, but it must be transcended.

In one important sense, *Call It Sleep* offers an antidote to other modernist representations of impaired Jewish masculinity: although David is linked to women, Albert is the apotheosis of normative Western masculinity. Albert is, unlike Louie Marsellus, possessive and jealous; also unlike Louie, who adores his wife, and unlike Jay Gatsby and Robert Cohn, who ardently wish to marry their beloveds, he views a wife as a 'stone around [one's] neck' (76). With his physical strength and simple working-class clothes, he is the opposite of effete characters like Gatsby and Marsellus. Likely in response to the feminine Jewish man in cultural circulation as well as to his own childhood, Roth depicts Albert's masculinity as exaggerated. In David the novel confronts the alleged femininity of Jewish men, showing the enforced timidity that must characterise the son of a man like Albert, but also strongly hinting at a path that will lead David from this place of fear and victimisation to the status of rageful oppressor.

But *Call It Sleep* misses its chance to revalue femininity, to posit it as an integral part of masculine identity, to present David Schearl as the 'new womanly *mensch*' who would speak back to the misogynist portraits of feminised Jewish men along lines later offered by Daniel Boyarin. It misses its chance, too, to redefine masculinity: in spite of the sense throughout the novel that the hypermasculinity of Albert Schearl is barbaric, it tenders little hope, and offers no model, of any other kind of masculinity that might replace it. There is a strong sense of self-loathing in the representation of Roth's fictional alter ego, David: from feminised victim he stands to become masculine victimiser. On the level of plot, the novel fails to find a way out of that dichotomy.

Formally, however, the novel suggests quite a different trajectory. Its last, most experimental section, 'The Rail', rejects the phallic power that David, in that very section, both enlists and succumbs to. In direct contrast to the dictatorial approach of Albert Schearl, 'The Rail' refuses linear, authoritarian narration; insists upon a multilingual, accented, disparate throng of people and their voices; credits David's dreamlike, poetic, half-conscious musings; and accepts multiple accounts of what is 'really' happening. This avant-garde and inclusive narrative style conjures the journey into *edelkayt* David is unlikely to take. The final section thereby offers readers, on the level of form, a glimpse of an alternative way to imagine a more balanced and inclusive gendering: rather than serving masculinity merely as a starting point or temporary refuge, femininity could be incorporated into the body of the man in the way that the multiple languages, dialects and perspectives of 'The Rail' are incorporated into the body of the text. While David moves in and out of consciousness, the narrative style hints at a possibility that for him is as elusive as the '*ember in a mirror swimming without motion in the motion of its light*' (430).

Notes

I would like to thank Jennifer William, Aparajita Sagar, and the editors of this volume for their helpful suggestions about this essay.
1 James Joyce, *Ulysses*, ed. Hans Walter Gabler (New York: Vintage Books, 1986), p. 277.
2 Neil Davison, *Jewishness and Masculinity from the Modern to the Postmodern* (New York: Routledge, 2010), p. 3.

3 Wyndham Lewis, *Hitler* (London: Chatto and Windus, 1931), p. 41.

4 Quoted in Rachel Blau DuPlessis, *Genders, Races, and Religious Cultures in Modern American Poetry, 1908–1934* (New York: Cambridge University Press, 2001), p. 142.

5 Ritchie Robertson, 'Historicizing Weininger: The Nineteenth-Century German Image of the Feminized Jew', in Bryan Cheyette and Laura Marcus, ed., *Modernity, Culture and 'the Jew'* (Stanford: Stanford University Press, 1998), p. 28.

6 Otto Weininger, *Sex and Character* (New York: G. P. Putnam's Sons, 1906), p. 306.

7 Joyce, *Ulysses*, p. 402.

8 Ibid., p. 403.

9 Quoted in Richard Ellmann, *James Joyce* (New York: Oxford University Press, 1982), p. 373.

10 Irving Howe, 'Life Never Let Up', *The New York Times Book Review* 69.43 (26 October 1964), p. 1.

11 Daniel Boyarin, *Unheroic Conduct: The Rise of Heterosexuality and the Invention of the Jewish Man* (Berkeley: University of California Press, 1997), p. 3.

12 Steven G. Kellman, *Redemption: The Life of Henry Roth* (New York: W. W. Norton & Co., 2005), p. 89.

13 Quoted in ibid., p. 89.

14 Brian McHale, 'Henry Roth in Nighttown, or, Containing *Ulysses*', in Hana Wirth-Nesher, ed., *New Essays on Henry Roth* (New York: Cambridge University Press, 1996), p. 79.

15 It is likely that Roth read Cather, although I cannot guarantee that he read this particular novel. His biographer Steven Kellman says that Roth almost certainly read *The Great Gatsby* and *The Sun Also Rises* (personal correspondence, 21 April 2011). In his biography, he mentions a comment Roth made about bullfighting: 'They attended a bullfight, and Roth was revolted: "It's pitiful, disgusting, and it stinks, and so does Mr. Hemingway for pearling it over with glamor" (*Death in the Afternoon*, Hemingway's tribute to bullfighting as tragic ritual, had been published in 1932).' Kellman, *Redemption*, 123. Roth's comment could also refer to *The Sun Also Rises*.

16 Although he doesn't address the characters' femininity, Walter Benn Michaels offers a striking reading of *The Professor's House*, *The Great Gatsby* and *The Sun Also Rises*, pointing out a plot dynamic that leads readers to want the Gentile women to be 'saved' from the Jewish men. See *Our America: Nativism, Modernism, and Pluralism* (Durham: Duke University Press, 1995), p. 7.

17 Willa Cather, *The Professor's House* (Lincoln: University of Nebraska Press, 2002), pp. 81–82.

18 Ibid., p. 231.

19 In a larger sense, Louie Marsellus represents the antithesis of Tom Outland. See Donald Pizer, *American Naturalism and the Jews: Garland, Norris, Dreiser, Wharton, and Cather* (Urbana: University of Illinois Press, 2008), pp. 63–64.

20 Cather, *The Professor's House*, pp. 162–163.

21 F. Scott Fitzgerald, *The Great Gatsby* (New York: Scribner, 1925), p. 93.

22 Ibid., pp. 93, 94.

23 Ibid., p. 122.

24 Meredith Goldsmith, 'White Skin, White Mask: Passing, Posing, and Performing in *The Great Gatsby*', *Modern Fiction Studies* 49.3 (Fall 2003): 458.

25 Goldsmith, 'White Skin, White Mask', p. 460.

26 Ernest Hemingway, *The Sun Also Rises* (New York: Scribner, 1954), p. 52.

27 Ibid., p. 46.

28 Ibid., p. 103.

29 Ibid., pp. 146–147.

30 Ibid., p. 185.

31 Neil Davison notes that 'Hemingway confronted his own gender trouble by positioning Cohn as a barometer of racial feminine essence, even when it is ironically disguised as Jewish athletic bravado.' See Davison, *Jewishness and Masculinity*, p. 21.

32 Todd Onderdonk, '"Bitched": Feminization, Identity, and the Hemingwayesque in *The Sun Also Rises*', *Twentieth-Century Literature* 52.1 (Spring 2006): 73. For another interesting analysis of Hemingway's gender trouble, see Richard Fantina, *Ernest Hemingway: Machismo and Masochism* (New York: Palgrave Macmillan, 2005).

33 Henry Roth, *Call It Sleep* (New York: Farrar, Straus and Giroux, 1991/1996), p. 174. Further references to this edition will be cited parenthetically in the text.

34 Joshua Miller too reads David's home as coded feminine: 'The Schearl home is coded as feminine and Yiddish-speaking, as David's mother is the abiding domestic presence'. See Joshua Miller, *Accented America: The Cultural Politics of Multilingual Modernism* (New York: Oxford University Press, 2011), p. 244.

35 Henry Roth, *A Diving Rock on the Hudson* (New York: St. Martin's Press, 1995), p. 5.

36 The following are among the critical articles that analyse the Oedipal strands of the novel: Richard Fein, 'Fear, Fatherhood, and Desire in *Call It Sleep*', *Yiddish* 5.4 (1984): 49–54; Lynn Altenbernd, 'An American Messiah: Myth in Henry Roth's *Call It Sleep*', *Modern Fiction Studies* 35.4 (Winter 1989): 673–687; Anna Petrov, 'Fear of a Dominant Male in Henry Roth's *Call It Sleep* and Bernard Malamud's *The Tenants*, *Studies in American Jewish Literature* 17 (1998): 142–151; three essays in *New Essays on* Call It Sleep, ed. Hana Wirth-Nesher (New York: Cambridge University Press, 1996): Leslie Fiedler, 'The Many Myths of Henry Roth', pp. 17–28; Werner Sollors, '"A world somewhere, somewhere else": Language, Nostalgic Mournfulness, and Urban Immigrant Family Romance in *Call It Sleep*', pp. 127–182; and Karen Lawrence, 'Roth's *Call It Sleep:* Modernism on the Lower East Side', pp. 107–126.

37 'Burbank with a Baedeker, Bleistein with a Cigar' was published in *Poems* (1920). One stanza reads: 'But this or such was Bleistein's way: / A saggy bending of the knees / And elbows, with the palms turned out / Chicago Semite Viennese'.

38 Even though readers are not prone to agree with Albert's statements, their presence in the text has its effect, and readers find themselves agreeing with him at times. His paranoia about Genya, for example, seems to have some basis in reality. David *may* be his son, but the evidence that he may not be, which Albert lays out in the final section, does seem worth considering.

39 Kellman writes of Roth's struggles with his own connections to women: he lamented his status as a 'kept man' with Eda Lou Walton, and deplored the incest he committed with his younger sister and a younger cousin. He viewed the incest with intense disgust, seeing it as a sign of deficient masculinity.

40 Elaine Orr, 'On the Side of the Mother: *Yonnondio* and *Call It Sleep*', *Studies in American Fiction* 21.2 (Autumn 1993): 220.

41 Wendy Zierler, 'The Making and Re-making of Jewish American Literary History', *Shofar* 27.2 (Winter 2009): 75.

42 Ibid., p. 76.

43 Fiedler, 'The Many Myths of Henry Roth', p. 26.

44 Altenbernd, 'An American Messiah', p. 683.

45 Hana Wirth-Nesher reads the scene slightly differently, arguing that 'David's thoughts about the crack between the car tracks where he seeks a spiritual rebirth through contact with a masculine God also evoke his desire to return to the womb, to the mother and the source of that oceanic oneness that he now seeks in a sublimated form.' Hana Wirth-Nesher, 'Between Mother Tongue and Native Language in *Call It Sleep*', Afterword to *Call It Sleep* (New York: Farrar, Straus and Giroux, 1991/1996), p. 457.

46 Roth, *A Diving Rock*, p. 401.

47 Leslie Fiedler describes this scene briefly as David's 'introjection of the father' when 'in an excess of blind rage he strikes down another boy in the street'. See Fiedler, 'The Many Myths of Henry Roth', p. 26.

CHAPTER 8

Robeson Agonistes

James Donald

One day in 1932, C. L. R. James was on his way to the British Museum, in Bloomsbury, when he saw the 'magnificent figure' of Paul Robeson, the singer, actor and scholar, walking towards him. They stopped to talk. James regarded Robeson as 'a man not only of great gentleness but of great command: he was never upset about anything.' On this day, however, clearly bothered, he asked James whether he had heard the gossip 'about a coloured singer and a member of the British Royal Family'. 'It's not me, James', Robeson declared 'passionately'. 'It's not me.' To Robeson's indignation, his friend laughed: 'What is there to laugh at? I don't see anything to laugh at.' James explained that, as 'a Negro from the United States' living in England, there was no disgrace in being linked 'to a member of the British Royal Family'. Hence his reaction: 'I laugh because you seem so upset about it. That is very funny.' Robeson was unmoved. 'They got the wrong Nigger in the woodpile, this time James,' he protested. 'It's not me – Hutch maybe – but not me!'[1]

Whether or not Paul Robeson had slept with Lady Edwina Mountbatten is less significant than the *intensity* of his response, the 'passionate denial' that James could not get out of his mind. Most men he knew would have been secretly flattered by the rumour of 'an illicit relationship with a member of the British Royal Family', reflected James. 'But for some reason or other, which I cannot go into here but which I think should be remembered about Paul, is his passionate statement: *"James, it isn't me."*

Although, pragmatically, Robeson may have been worried about damage to his career, that would not explain the *passion* of his response. One cause may have been Robeson's realisation that the rumour reinforced the dull, relentless habits of mind that rendered him always and only the embodiment of black, masculine sexuality. He had left Harlem in 1927, in part, because he had been hurt by accusations of endorsing white perceptions of black sexuality when he appeared in Eugene O'Neill's play about a disastrous mixed-race marriage, *All God's Chillun' Got Wings*. Now, in

London, in a different national cultural context, he was being ensnared once again by familiar, demeaning tropes and assumptions. And, although it 'wasn't him' this time, Robeson knew the dangers posed by what his biographer Martin Duberman calls his 'unconventional erotic history' – a history with its own idiosyncratic integrity, perhaps, but one that was vulnerable to being stereotyped in terms of the sexually voracious black man. There was an exhausting tension between public expectations of Robeson not just as a performer and a star, but also as a man of destiny and a leader of 'the race', and the affective reality of his inner life. At this point in his career, having been, to some degree, seduced by English society, he was all too conscious of the subjective costs of this precarious double life. As a result, Robeson experienced any hint of intolerance or rejection not just as a personal slight but as an injustice.

Eros

In 1930, Eslanda Robeson had published a biography of her husband. *Paul Robeson: Negro* is a curious book, not least because its purpose, as she confided to their New York friend, Carl Van Vechten, was to 'work out exactly the picture of Paul I want people to have.' The early chapters depict Robeson as the embodiment of the aspirations of the 'New Negro' movement in 1920s Harlem. 'Paul Robeson was a hero' in the sense that 'he fulfilled the ideal of nearly every class of Negro.' This heroic status was bound up with the way that he represented universal or at least collective cultural virtues. It was not just that he was an exceptional athlete and an emerging intellectual, it was that he played those roles as a modern black man with a particular style. 'Everyone was glad that he was so typically Negroid in appearance, colour, and features,' wrote Essie; 'everyone was glad that he was taking up the dignified profession of the law.' There is an edge to her portrait of Robeson as 'Harlem's special favourite', however, as she appears to remind her celebrated, and perhaps now overly cosmopolitan, London-based husband of where he came from and how much he owed her. 'When Paul Robeson had been in New York one year he had become part and parcel of Harlem, and was affectionately regarded as her favourite and most beloved son,' she asserts. 'When, a year later, he married a Harlem girl, he became still more closely bound to the community.'[2]

Essie's portrait of Robeson in Harlem brings out his function both as a symbol of modern black America and as a figure in a redemptive narrative of oppression, achievement, racial vindication and self-determination that called 'American Negroes' into being as a recognisable community. This was a 'Romance', in the sense that Hayden White defines the genre; that is, as 'a drama of self-identification'. The 'New Negro' narrative postulated a primordial Negro identity, in order to authorise the rights and political aspirations of modern black Americans. The generic logic and narrative drive of such a Romance are condensed in the person and actions of the masculine hero. Collective self-identification is 'symbolized by the hero's transcendence of the world of experience, his victory over it, and his final liberation from it.'[3] That is why the burdensome ideological mantle of 'New Negro' came to be draped across Robeson's broad shoulders. 'Unlike most moderns, Paul Robeson is not half a dozen men in one torn and striving body,' observed an astute *New Republic* journalist in 1926. 'The sureness of essential being takes him across the concert stage, as it did across the football field, with the fine, free movement of his strong athletic body, which is the reflection in action of an inward goal. Paul Robeson knows where he is bound.'[4]

This aura of heroic masculinity clung to Robeson throughout his life, despite the trials and setbacks he would suffer in later years. In 1949, for example, the Howard University sociologist E. Franklin Frazier praised Robeson for 'representing the negro man in the masculine role as a fearless and independent thinker.'[5] Two great American fighters also recognised his heroism. 'There are some people who don't like the way Paul Robeson fights for my people,' said the heavyweight Joe Louis in 1948. 'Well, I say that Paul is fighting for what all of us want, and that's freedom to be a man.' 'For me you have played a great part in my life,' wrote the light-heavyweight Archie Moore in 1958. 'I have followed many years and I always believed in your fighting spirit. I am not a hero worshipper by a long shot, but there are men I admire and you are one of the few.'

The bulk of Eslanda's biography deals with a more intimate aspect of Robeson's odyssey: their move to London in 1927 and Paul's apparent sense of finding a home there. The last part of the book, however, heads off in a new direction. It recounts a fictionalised conversation, structured around a walk on Hampstead Heath and a fireside heart-to-heart, in which Essie acknowledges and forgives Paul's sexual 'lapses', and he responds 'with eyes full of tears, and full of immense relief.'[6] In reality, their negotiations about their marriage were less easily resolved than this fanciful account allowed. (Another reason for Robeson's discomfort outside the British Museum, perhaps.) Shortly after the publication of her book, Essie had opened a love letter to Paul from Peggy Ashcroft, who was playing Desdemona to his Othello in the West End. 'I feel now that he is just one more Negro musician, pursuing white meat', she seethed in her diary. 'I suppose it's a curse on the race.' Although the two remained friends, Robeson's affair with Peggy Ashcroft did not last long. More threatening to Essie was Paul's relationship with a less distinguished actress named Yolande Jackson, whom he met in 1930. She was the daughter of a barrister, who had been head of the bar in Calcutta but now lived in a small villa on the outskirts of Worthing, in Sussex, on England's south coast.

In 1932, Robeson took Yolande with him to New York, for a revival of *Show Boat*, the musical he stole every time he sang 'Ol' Man River'. At a press conference, he acknowledged that he and Essie had been separated for a couple of years, that he had been seeing an Englishwoman, whom he hoped to marry, that she was neither Nancy Cunard nor Peggy Ashcroft and that he would quit the United States forever if the relationship stirred up any racist abuse. 'I desire above all things,' Robeson told a reporter, 'to maintain my personal dignity.'[7] When he returned to Europe, towards the end of 1932, expecting to go through with the divorce and then remarry, Robeson found that Yolande had bolted. The reasons are not wholly clear but Essie, for one, reckoned that 'it would be too risky an experiment to give up all her friends and stupid, social life to marry Paul.'[8] Within weeks, Yolande had married an aristocratic White Russian émigré, although she apparently continued to yearn forlornly after Robeson over the years. Despite being devastated, Robeson honoured his public engagements with good grace.

Over time, Robeson reframed this traumatic story, presenting himself as instigator of the break-up and its cause as his abhorrence of injustice. He had turned against Yolande, he would explain, after she had propositioned him in the back of a chauffeur-driven car and then scoffed when he protested that the driver might be embarrassed. After the war, Robeson inflated the incident into a class parable, as well as a metaphor for his falling out of love with England. It was in that car, he told Nancy Wills, a young Australian he met in London in the 1940s, at the moment when 'Lady So-and-so' treated her chauffeur as a menial of no account, that he comprehended 'the affinity between working men and women the world over, that, black and white, we all had a great deal in common.'[9]

In terms of Paul and Essie's relationship, the end of the affair with Yolande and the decision not to divorce were the prelude to an expedient but enduring marriage. Essie wanted to remain Mrs Paul Robeson, and so she accepted – or suffered – his other relationships and adventures. From now on, however, Paul's affection and respect for Essie would be tempered by a cold and implacable anger. Their son dates the origin of his father's

resentment to the publication of Essie's book in 1930. Although the infantilising treatment in her fantasy conversation about their marriage would
have been galling enough, Paul Robeson Jr. identifies its final paragraph
as the unforgivable offence. Here, Essie harks back to her earlier portrayal
of Paul strolling through the streets of Harlem, but now describes him as
a man universally recognised 'when he strolls down the main streets of
the large cities of the world.' The trouble lay in her choice of words. 'He
leaves a trail of friendliness wherever he goes, this Paul Robeson, Negro',
wrote Essie, 'who, with his typical Negro qualities – his appearance, his
voice, his genial smile, his laziness, his child-like simplicity – is carving
his place as a citizen of the world, a place which would most certainly
have made his slave father proud.' In this portrait, according to his son,
Robeson could see only 'a package of negative racial stereotypes of the
black male.' That ending confirmed how disastrously inappropriate publication of the book was as a means of communicating with a very private
man, 'whose way of dealing with trouble was to avoid it if possible, but to
strike the first blow without warning if conflict was unavoidable.' Nor was
Robeson a man to negotiate under threat. Instead, he quietly determined
to dismantle Essie's 'sense of ownership of him' and to 'free himself from
his dependency on her'. Although, outwardly, Robeson would 'remain his
genial self', the iron had entered his soul: 'Paul's silence on this subject
lasted a lifetime, but Essie's public humiliation of him in cold print was
beyond his tolerance.'[10]

Although these various stories all involve Paul Robeson's erotic adventures, something other than desire seems to have been driving him, that
enigmatic 'some reason or other,' which C. L. R. James would not, or
could not, name. The nature of this 'reason' might be inferred from the
'family resemblance' between the issues about which Robeson felt vehemently: a concern for reputation, a prickly defensiveness about his dignity, the courage to fight for his own freedom and the interests of others,
a quickness to take offence at perceived injustice, a sense of himself as
an instrument of history, and a capacity for intense and sustained anger.
One way of characterising the affinity between them might be through
the classical concept of *thymos*.

Thymos

In Plato's psychology, *thymos* refers to 'spiritedness', a third motivating
aspect of the masculine soul, which interacted with the rational, or calcu-
lating, dimension of personality and the more instinctual human desires

and appetites. *Thymos* connotes a man's will to achieve fame, the ambition to do great deeds and to be recognised for them, and, by no means least, a capacity for anger, if he is dealt with unjustly, and for shame, when he falls short of his own self-evaluation.[11] *Thymos* thus stands as a lost opposite to both *apathy* and *melancholy*, pointing to a realm of 'impassioned, energetic, interested, active liveliness'.[12]

In his book *Rage and Time*, Peter Sloterdijk identifies some 'thymotic energies' that echo both Paul Robeson's inner passions and his public reputation as a hero, a fighter and a free man: 'human pride, courage, stout-heartedness, craving for recognition, drive for justice, sense of dignity and honour, indignation, militant and vengeful energies.' Sloterdijk lists these characteristics in order to highlight a blind spot in mainstream academic psychoanalysis, which, he complains, has tended to treat Eros as the *only* motivation for human behaviour, without paying 'equally vivid attention' to the thymotic impulses.[13] The implication is that *anger* should be reinstated, alongside desire and love, as a fundamental and often positive motive for human behaviour. This reconfiguration of the human psyche offers an apposite paradigm for understanding Paul Robeson's later career. It provides a key to the intricate, subterranean consonance between his political commitments and a growing and self-destructive anger.

For Sloterdijk, the Socratic-Platonic interpretation of *thymos* as the capacity to control as well as to experience well-founded anger, already represents a curtailment or dilution of the 'quasi-divine Homeric *menis*' conjured up in the opening lines of the *Illiad*: 'Rage [menis] – Goddess, sing the rage of Peleus' son Achilles, / murderous, doomed, that cost the Achaeans countless losses.' The Socratic-Platonic adaptation marks a halfway point between the Homeric epos, with its conflation of hero with passion and action, and the Stoics' revisioinist emphasis on the affective and ethical management of the passions (now morphing into 'feelings' or 'emotional states') as key to the formation of a new understanding of selfhood. The Stoics thus developed a psychology based on the privacy and opacity of inner feelings. The inexpressive Stoic exterior (or 'reasonableness') denies others the expression of the passionate self. As a result, the self can never be fully visible. The signs of passion – a face contorted in rage, uncontrollable sobs of grief, wide-eyed surprise or jaw-dropping wonderment – are erased from the surface, and the urgent experience of passion is relocated within.[14]

This account may help to explain why Baudelaire, in his essay 'The Painter of Modern Life', proclaimed that nineteenth-century dandyism, which he saw as 'the last flicker of heroism in decadent ages', in some ways 'comes close to' Stoicism. Dandyism shares with Stoicism a heroism that is drained of the energy and passion of *thymos* and is filled instead with its antithesis. Like the setting sun, modern heroism is 'without heat and full of melancholy'. In the etiolated epic of modern life, masculine rage resurfaces as style. The modern hero is not a warrior, but the modern artist, a 'solitary mortal endowed with an active imagination, always roaming the great desert of men.' Rather than slaughtering his enemies in rage, his quest is 'to extract from fashion the poetry that resides in its historical envelope, to distil the eternal from the transitory.' To the world, says Baudelaire, this modern hero turns a Stoic or, to use Simmel's term, a blasé face: 'The specific beauty of the dandy consists particularly in that cold exterior resulting from the unshakeable determination to remain unmoved; one is reminded of a latent fire, whose existence is merely suspected, and which, if it wanted to, but it does not, could burst forth in all its brightness.'

In Henry James's *The Ambassadors*, the self-consciously unheroic American, Lambert Strether, is sent to France to chaperone a friend's son. He counsels his charge to 'live all you can', in a way that he feels he has not. Little Bilham is still young and energetic enough for adventure: 'you don't strike me as in danger of missing the train.' In Strether's own case, passion and action have been paralysed by a timidity born of Stoic reflection. 'It's too late', he laments. 'And it's as if the train had fairly waited at the station for me without my having had the gumption to know it was there. Now I hear its faint receding whistle miles and miles down the line.' Strether's regret at his own lack of 'gumption' – a kind of democratised and disenchanted *thymos* – has a broader resonance, beyond his own passing up of opportunities. It is 'too late' historically for heroism. All that remains for modern man is 'the illusion of freedom'; or, rather, 'the memory of that illusion'.[15] Like Baudelaire, James stoically records the hidden injuries inflicted by modernity's systematic repression of the classical masculine passions. Thymotic spiritedness gives way to a melancholy ethic of indifference, concealed behind Baudelaire's 'cold exterior'.

Against the modernist grain of Baudelaire, James and Simmel, a resuscitated conception of *thymos* might inaugurate an uncool version of modern heroism and modern masculinity. Taking Hegel as its first point of reference, this history would start from modernity's overriding concern, philosophically and existentially, with the creation and conduct of the masculine Self: the question of the subject. Insofar as it not just a 'given', and in order to be able to take a point of view on itself, the Hegelian subject has to be somehow separable from itself. Still incorporating the psychic divisions of Stoicism, this version of subjectivity is *achieved* in such a way that it is reflectively accessible to itself.[16] Whereas the wise Stoic was supposed to be satisfied with *self*-respect, the Hegelian subject is not only 'critically reflexive and self-conscious', but also 'capable of acting on norms, coordinating actions with others on the basis of such norms, capable of evaluating truth claims on the basis of rational (universal, publicly accessible and publicly defensible) norms'.[17] This relational, outward-looking characteristic of the Hegelian subject – its thymotic legacy – is a condition of its freedom. Its very existence is dependent on its ability to achieve recognition by others, and so it follows that modern heroism – and modern masculinity more broadly – will always be, and be experienced as, a performance.[18]

For Walter Benjamin, this performative dimension was the essence of Baudelaire's modernism: 'Flaneur, apache, dandy and ragpicker were so many roles to him. For the modern hero is no hero; he is a portrayer of heroes.'[19] The proposition that heroes are necessarily actors, it has been suggested, in effect reframes their heroism as both inherently aesthetic and uniquely modern. There thus appears to be a tripartite division within modern heroism, between the man, a socially designated role, and the man's performance of the role. Having once taken on such a role, the masculine protagonist can find it difficult to escape from the script, and so may come to perform it with ever-diminishing conviction.[20]

Paul Robeson had never felt wholly comfortable as the exemplary New Negro. Equally, however, he did feel the need for a social and historical persona that would enable him to achieve his political ambitions. The role would have to be one in which he felt comfortable, but one that also provided a focus and outlet for his thymotic spirit. This need to play the hero provides one way of explaining why from the mid-1930s onwards, under the mentorship of W. E. B. Du Bois, whose own political odyssey had a similar trajectory, Robeson took on the role not only of anti-fascist, anti-racist and anti-colonialist activist but also of Soviet sympathiser. By his own account, the event that emblematised Robeson's explicit political affiliation – his new role – was a rally in support of Republican Spain, held on 24 June 1937, at London's Royal Albert Hall. Robeson was due to be in Moscow that night, and he had prepared a contribution to be transmitted by radio. When the Albert Hall authorities threatened to jam the link, he dashed to London by plane, swept majestically onto the platform and delivered his speech. 'Every artist, every scientist, must decide *now* where he stands', he proclaimed. 'He has no alternative.' Robeson linked 'the struggle for Negro rights' to the 'wider anti-fascist struggle', and insisted that every artist 'must elect to fight for Freedom or for Slavery'.

'I have made my choice', he declared. 'I had no alternative.'[21] When, at a follow-up rally, Robeson sang 'Ol' Man River', he changed the Broadway showstopper from a pastiche spiritual into a song of protest and defiance. Whereas Oscar Hammerstein's lyrics evoked exhaustion and fear of death at the song's climax, Robeson's new words said: 'I must keep fighting / Until I'm dying.'

'I had no alternative', said Robeson. 'I must keep fighting.' These heroic words are often taken to represent a moment of self-transformation or even redemption. In what might be called a romantic-republican reading, the Albert Hall speech is cited as evidence of how Robeson found and fulfilled himself through political commitment. Thus Jeffrey C. Stewart argues that it was only in Europe, in the 1930s, that Robeson finally broke away from 'the black modernist nationalism of the 1920s and the white primitivist modernism of Greenwich Village'[22] and found his true, ambassadorial role as 'an international New Negro rebel'.[23] For Hazel Carby, the 'unwavering commitment to an international politics of social transformation' enabled Robeson to wrench his body 'away from performative associations with modernist strategies of inwardness' – modernist explorations of masculinity like Nikolas Muray's photographs of Robeson, O'Neill's play *The Emperor Jones* and Kenneth Macpherson's film *Borderline* – and to act 'in defiance of all cultural aesthetics that denied or disguised their political implications'.[24] Subjectively, according to Sheila Tully Boyle and Andrew Bunie's biography, the new single-mindedness displayed at the Albert Hall allowed Robeson to transcend 'years of self-doubt and floundering' and to find 'a clear-cut moral and ethical direction, a passion that satisfied his need for a higher calling, a passion that added a new and compelling spiritual dimension to his life'.[25]

The problem with such interpretations is that Robeson's apparently heroic disavowal of alternatives in effect locked him into one particular historical narrative and one particular language of moral-political vision, from which he would never thereafter escape. Over time, as a result, there appeared to be a growing disconnection between his chosen political role and his agency or selfhood. The novelist Doris Lessing spotted this when she met Paul and Eslanda at a Soviet Embassy reception in London in the late 1950s. The Robesons were 'stupid', she decided, because they spoke entirely in the 'communist jargon'. It is a harsh judgement, explicable in part by the fact that Lessing was not a disinterested observer – she was losing her own communist faith at the time. 'Not one word was said in normal speech', recalls Lessing, citing phrases she was coming to despise: 'capitalist lies, fascist imperialists, running dogs, democratic socialism (the Soviet Union), peace-loving peoples'. She enters an important caveat, however. At the time, Lessing admits, she had not grasped the extent to which such language might be used as a shield or camouflage. This appears to have been Robeson's situation. He played the role and used the language of a fellow traveller because, beset by enemies at home and dependent on the goodwill of his manipulative Soviet hosts, he had no alternative. Now that he no longer *embodied* universal aspirations as he had once done, he could offer only an unconvincing *performance* of heroic commitment. 'When politics and public life become as polarized as they were then', concludes Doris Lessing, 'then people may seem stupid.'[26]

The difficulty – or impossibility – of heroism in modern times lay at the heart of Hegel's aesthetics. In mythical or violent times, the Epic hero had the capacity to transform the commonplace by embodying artistically the unity between individuality and universality. The modern, bourgeois world had become, for the most part, prosaically unheroic. *Thymos* had become an anachronism, its violence appeared psychotic, and the world knew that heroes have feet of clay.[27] It was, therefore, perhaps inevitable that Paul Robeson failed to achieve the generic resolution ascribed to the hero of a Romance. He did not triumph over 'the world of experience', and he failed to achieve 'final liberation from it'. As Hegel might have predicted, his heroic 'confrontation with the old world' played out not as Epic or Romance, but as Tragedy.

Whereas Romance promises overcoming and redemption, explains Hayden White, Tragedy offers 'intimations of states of division among men more terrible than that which incited the tragic agon at the beginning of the drama'. That tragic realisation does not lead to despair, however. Rather, 'the fall of the protagonist and the shaking of the world he inhabits at the end of the Tragic play are not regarded as totally threatening to those who survive the agonistic test.' So, if not redemption, tragedy delivers at least 'a gain in consciousness for the spectators of the contest'. The form the 'gain' takes is this: 'the epiphany of the law governing human existence which the protagonist's exertions against the world have brought to pass'.[28] In Hegel's terms, likewise, the tragic hero is both protagonist and victim. The individual embodying a new and universally valid ethical principle may have to die, but the principle, and thus the universal, survives and becomes successfully established.[29]

Again, this perspective reinforces the view that Robeson's decision to foreclose alternatives, existentially as well as politically, is best understood as an instance of modern tragedy, whose modernity lies, according to Raymond Williams, in 'the loss of hope; the slowly settling loss of any acceptable future'. To trace the fall of Paul Robeson in terms of Tragedy requires more than a description of the nature and costs of the 'agonistic tests' to which he was subjected. It means asking how he 'shook' the world he inhabited and confronted, and whether any ethical principle might be derived from his fall and disintegration.

Agonism

Just as heroism is classically linked to *thymos*, so *thymos* presupposes the importance of *anger* or *rage* in the structure of subjectivity and the dynamics of agency. Within this paradigm, which also recognises anger as a proper response to injustice, Aristotle defined 'anger' as 'an impulse accompanied by distress, to a conspicuous slight directed without justification towards what concerns one-self or towards what concerns one's friends'.[30] Understanding the experience of *distress* as integral to the *impulse* of anger, as Aristotle does, not only helps to explain the various ways in which Paul Robeson's political commitment was tested but also provides a clue to their psychological costs. Today, the patterns of behaviour associated with Robeson's overwhelming anger would probably be diagnosed as bipolar depression, but words like 'pride', 'shame', 'self-doubt', 'hopelessness' and 'melancholy' describe his distress just as well.

In 1936, Paul and Eslanda sent their son to the Soviet Model School in Moscow, where his classmates included Stalin's daughter and Molotov's son. Although only nine years old, Pauli picked up on his fellow pupils' anxiety about Stalin's purges. By 1938, he had been transferred to a school in London for the children of Soviet diplomats. One day, after a schoolmate became distraught at the news that her parents were being recalled to Moscow, Pauli mentioned to his father that he had recognised the name of a Russian family friend in a list of people shot during the current purge, and asked 'whether something major had gone wrong under Stalin's rule.' Robeson first ignored and then dismissed the question. 'We all knew he was innocent,' young Paul remembers yelling, 'and you never said a word.' Without meeting his son's eye, Robeson told him to keep quiet, 'his voice a barely audible low rumble.' Pauli was about to argue, when his father looked up: 'The look in his eyes – an intense rage mixed with hurt – stopped me cold. I got up and left.' A few days later, Robeson dispassionately justified Stalin's executions to his son, on the grounds that 'great injustices may be inflicted on the minority when the majority is in the pursuit of a great and just cause.'[31] What is compelling is less Robeson's expediency, than that look of *intense rage mixed with hurt*. This is like the *passion* evident in his denial to C. L. R. James. There is a rupture between public performance and intrusive inner conflict. In this instance, Robeson maintains his role as unquestioning champion of the Soviet experiment, even to his son, despite the unbidden physical evidence of self-questioning, conflict and conscience.

In 1956, Robeson was at a low ebb. The State Department confiscated his passport in 1950, and the inability to tour overseas made it hard to earn a living. *Freedom* magazine and the Council on African Affairs, projects near to his heart, both collapsed in 1955. In March 1956, *The New York Times* published news of Kruschev's denunciation of Stalin to the Twentieth Congress of the Communist Party of the USSR. Robeson was physically unwell, suffering a recurrent urinary-tract infection and undergoing surgery for prostate cancer. He was also depressed. Early in the year, an obsession with the pentatonic scale as the universal key to all music signalled a manic episode. In mid-May, as he was slipping into a depressive phase, Robeson received a subpoena to appear before the House Committee on Un-American Activities in Washington, DC.[32] On the day of the hearing, 12 June, he appeared so listless that his lawyers, family and supporters feared he might collapse under the strain.[33]

Although the hearing was ostensibly to discuss his passport, that issue was mentioned only once, in passing. The Committee's aim was to goad Robeson into admitting that he was a member of the Communist Party. Having parried the members' familiar opening accusations, Robeson adroitly shifted the terms of the interrogation from Communism to race. Was the Chairman, Francis Walter, author of proposed legislation that would 'keep all kinds of decent people out of the country'? No, Walter replied, 'only your kind'. Robeson pounced: 'Colored people like myself.' When HUAC Counsel quoted a Soviet article in which he had written that 'only here, in the Soviet Union, did I feel that I was a real man with a capital "M"', Robeson responded with a familiar line: 'In Russia I felt for the first time like a full human being. No color prejudice like in Mississippi, no color prejudice like in Washington.' 'Why do you not stay in Russia?' interjected one of the Committee. 'Because my father was a slave, and my people died to build this country, and I am going to stay here, and have a part of it just like you,' retorted Robeson. Pressed on the question of Soviet slave camps, Robeson equivocated, refusing as always to denounce Stalin, and saying that it was for the Soviet Union to deal with its own problems and shortcomings. 'I am interested in the place I am in, the country where I can do something about it,' he declared, and crashed his fist down on the table so angrily that his lawyer feared he would smash it.[34] When Robeson denounced the Committee as the true 'un-Americans, and you ought to be ashamed of yourselves,' the apoplectic chairman adjourned the hearing. Robeson had the final word: 'You should adjourn this forever, that is what I say.'

On this occasion Robeson's rage reinvigorated both his spirits and his reputation, especially among the sceptical leaders of the nascent black civil rights movement.[35] But such outbursts had diminishing returns. By the time of his final overseas tour, to Australia and New Zealand in November 1960 – his passport had been returned in 1958 and he and Essie were again based in London – anger seems to have become his habitual disposition, not just a response to specific provocations or injustices.

The baiting at his first press conference in Australia did not help. Asked if he was 'bitter' about his treatment by the U.S. government, Robeson sarcastically echoed the word and launched into what the newspapers called an 'emotional outburst' or a 'nauseating tirade'. 'If someone did something bad to me I wouldn't be bitter – I'd just knock him down and put my foot into his face,' he told the reporters, stamping his foot on the floor. He was then quoted as saying that the Russians would 'hammer out the brains' of any country, including America, who took arms against them. In the event of such a war, he would side with Russia. Robeson's anger at this time, comments his most observant biographer, 'reflected not the momentary logic of events but stored-up griefs, a nature unravelling.' Behind the reporters' hostile but all-too-familiar questions, speculates Martin Duberman, Robeson may have heard their 'smug, unspoken subtext: "Come on, Robeson, *confess*, confess that your hopes have run aground, confess that human beings *stink*, confess that the rest of us have always been right, that we're perfectly entitled to go on leading the narrow, hardened, opportunistic lives you silly idealists once so righteously scorned."'[36]

As usual, there were good external grounds for Robeson's anger. On 10 November, the day after his impromptu performance of 'Ol' Man River' and 'Joe Hill' for construction workers at the half-built Sydney Opera House, one of his hosts, the activist Faith Bandler, screened a number of films about Indigenous Australians for him at his hotel, including a short documentary exposing living conditions in the Warburton Ranges. As he watched the film, Bandler recalled thirty years later, 'the tears came to his eyes and when the film finished he stood up and he pulled his cap off and he threw it in his rage on the floor and trod on it.' For the first time in years, he demanded a cigarette. 'He was so angry,' according to Bandler, that he promised her: 'I'll go away now, but when I come back I'll give you a hand.'[37] Writing to their friend Freda Diamond, Essie fretted that it was not just injustices like this that enraged Robeson. Paul had become 'angrier than ever' during this tour: 'It makes me shudder, because he is so often angry at the wrong people, and so often unnecessarily angry.' Robeson admitted to Nancy Wills that he was afraid to walk the streets in Australia: 'He didn't believe that the people here loved him.' When Essie, in Nancy's presence, suggested that they might spend a few days in the Philippines on their way to London, Paul raged that U.S. agents would kill him if he ever set foot there. 'It was frightening', Wills remembered, 'to see and hear anyone so distraught, so angry.'

This episode was followed by an apparent suicide attempt during a visit to Moscow in March 1961 and, in September that year, a catastrophic collapse in London. On that occasion, when the car taking him to a private psychiatric hospital passed the Soviet Embassy, Robeson showed signs of genuine terror. At the hospital, he was subjected to a regime of electric shock therapy and drugs, from which he never really recovered.

Home

In the masculine register of Epic, the impulse to achievement and fame – *thymos* – drives the hero restlessly from adventure to adventure, test to test, struggle to struggle. Finally, having survived them all, he returns home. The homecoming marks the maturity of the hero, insofar as 'home' represents the place where the active Self and the scrutinising Self are reintegrated, where the 'I' is undivided. In Paul Robeson's case, his political odyssey was also an existential search for 'home'. 'He felt even more at home in London than he had in America,' wrote Essie in 1930, and twenty-five years later, in *Here I Stand*, Paul confirmed that he had 'found in London a congenial and stimulating intellectual atmosphere in which I felt at home.' The 'discovery' of Africa in the imperial metropolis, however, 'made it clear that I would not live out my life as an adopted Englishman.' Robeson 'came to consider that I was an African,' and fantasised about setting up home in Africa. Then he discovered the Soviet Union; or the Soviet Union targeted him as a potential fellow traveller. 'This is home to me', he announced, during his first visit, although he would soon add, during his anti-fascist activism, that: 'To me Spain is another homeland.' In the end, neither London, Africa, the Soviet Union nor Spain proved to be *enough* of a home to make him feel he belonged there. It was Spain, he wrote, that brought him back to America: 'For another year I remained in Britain, and the more I became part of the Labour movement the more I came to realize that my home should be in America.' Back in Harlem in the 1950s, he rejoiced in 'the press of all that is around me where I live, at home among my people.'³⁸

In the psychoanalytic story, such an intense desire for 'home', which is also the longing for an end to struggle, for absolute security and silence, and so, in effect, for the relentlessness of life to stop, might be conceptualised in terms of the 'death instinct'. If Eros is 'the instinct to preserve living substance and to join it into ever larger units,' Freud speculated late in his career, then the death instinct is the impulse within the organism 'to dissolve those units and to bring them back to their primaeval, inorganic state.'³⁹ As it enters into the external world, however, the death instinct ceases to operate as a force for silent self-dissolution, but manifests itself instead as 'aggressiveness and destructiveness'.

This duality between a longing for inner stillness and aggressive behaviour begins to make sense of the coexistence of Paul Robeson's repeated invocation of 'home' with his constant subterranean anger and occasional outbursts of violent rage. Both dimensions can be discerned in an interview he gave to the *Daily Worker* during his first visit to the Soviet Union, in 1935. 'From what I have already seen of the workings of the Soviet Government,' Robeson is quoted as saying, 'I can only say that anybody who lifts his hand against it ought to be shot!' Then, immediately, as if in justification, he switches from the language of violence to a rhetoric of belonging. 'I already regard myself at home here,' he went on. 'I feel more kinship to the Russian people under their new society than I ever felt anywhere else.'⁴⁰ The tension between the *thymos* expressed as public political commitment and the desire to be subjectively 'at home' produced, in Robeson, the collateral damage of anger, grief, shame and terror that Paul Jr. saw in his father's eyes: '*intense rage mixed with hurt*'.

What made Paul Robeson heroic, from this perspective, was less his role in a redemptive political Romance, in which he leads the way towards a good society, always just over the horizon, always promised but never reached, than the generic logic of tragedy. Although, for Hegel, tragic heroes may be destroyed by the forces they oppose – they 'individually find their doom' – they nonetheless bequeath a *principle*, which 'penetrates, albeit in another guise, undermining that which existed previously.'⁴¹ Against the dominant view (which he would have shared) that Paul Robeson represented an *eschatological* principle, here the argument is that the decision he took in terms of his political commitment to Soviet internationalism trapped him within an anachronistic political paradigm and dragged him into ambiguity, compromise and bad faith. The alternative is to focus on Robeson's actual restlessness and his impatience with convention, and to infer from them a partial, disavowed and thwarted *cosmopolitan* principle. This may appear perverse, as this was not a political option that Robeson could consciously or publicly embrace. After the Second World War, 'cosmopolitanism' had been banished from the Soviet political lexicon as 'a reactionary theory that preaches indifference to the fatherland, to national traditions and to national culture' and a threat to a Soviet-led 'proletarian internationalism'.[42] Even if 'cosmopolitanism' was simply not available to him as a term of art, in his life Robeson enacted many of its principles. He took a sceptical distance from the apparent normality and inevitability of the present, and he worked through, often painfully, the political and existential reality of indeterminacy, indefiniteness and unpredictability. Cosmopolitanism insists that, contrary to what Robeson said, there *are* always alternatives, ethically and existentially as well as politically. It is the principle of uncertainty at the heart of cosmopolitanism that holds open the possibility that things will be otherwise and can be better.

What links Paul Robeson's passionate denial to C. L. R. James in Bloomsbury (*'It isn't me!'*) to his Albert Hall statement of political commitment (*'Here I stand!'*) is an anxiety that defined modern masculinity: the bifurcation of the acting male Self, which was once understood in terms of *thymos*, from a judging male Self, paralysed by its mistrust of unconscious motives, mortgaged to received and normative ideologies, and haunted by the loss of the illusion of freedom. Whereas eschatological politics and the fantasy of home both promise, vainly, to heal the split, cosmopolitanism acknowledges and embraces this homelessness and this non-identity. Paul Robeson's modernism lay in the extent to which he was a man who experimented with the possibility of a cosmopolitan life, even though, from where he took his stand, he could not see it for what it was.

Notes

1 This is the version of the anecdote published in *Black World* 20 (November 1970), quoted in Sheila Tully Boyle and Andrew Bunie, *Paul Robeson: The Years of Promise and Achievement* (Amherst: University of Massachusetts Press, 2001), p. 261. A later, more guarded, version records Robeson saying, 'Well, maybe there is something in what you say, but you know who it is.' 'Yes, I know who it is, and I know it isn't you, Paul', James replies, 'but nevertheless it is very funny.' C. L. R. James, 'Paul Robeson: Black Star', in *Spheres of Existence: Selected Writings* (London, Allison and Busby, 1980), pp. 263–264. Hutch was the pianist and singer Leslie Hutchinson.

2 Eslanda to Van Vechten, quoted in Boyle and Bunie, *Paul Robeson*, p. 230. Eslanda Goode Robeson, *Paul Robeson: Negro* (London: Victor Gollancz, 1930), p. 69.

3 Hayden White, *Metahistory: The Historical Imagination in Nineteenth-Century Europe* (Baltimore: Johns Hopkins University Press, 1975), pp. 8–9; discussed in David Scott, *Conscripts of Modernity* (Durham: Duke University Press, 2004), p. 47.

4 Elizabeth Shepley Sergeant, 'The Man with His Home in a Rock', *New Republic*, 3 March 1926; quoted in Hazel V. Carby, *Race Men* (New Haven: Harvard University Press, 2000), p. 48.

5 Paul Robeson, Jr., *The Undiscovered Paul Robeson: Quest for Freedom, 1939– 1976* (New York: Wiley, 2010), p. 182.

6 Martin Duberman, *Paul Robeson: A Biography* (New York: New Press, 1995), p. 140.

7 Duberman, *Paul Robeson* p. 160

8 Linda Grant, 'The Other Woman,' *The Guardian*, 9 October 2006.

9 Duberman, *Paul Robeson*, p. 164.

10 Eslanda Goode Robeson, *Paul Robeson: Negro* (London: Victor Gollancz, 1930), pp. 144–145; Robeson, Jr., *Quest for Freedom*, p. 173.

11 Robert Pippin, *Hollywood Westerns and American Myth* (New Haven: Yale University Press, 2010), pp. 47–48.

12 Philip Fisher, *The Vehement Passions* (Princeton: Princeton University Press, 2002), p. 228.

13 Peter Sloterdijk, *Rage and Time: A Psychopolitical Investigation* (New York: Columbia University Press, 2010), pp. 13, 14.

14 Fisher, *Vehement Passions*, p. 50.

15 Henry James, *The Ambassadors*, (London: Penguin, 1995), p. 215.

16 Pippin, *Modernism as a Philosophical Problem: On the Dissatisfactions of European High Culture* (Malden, MA: Blackwell, 1999), p. xv; *Hegel's Practical Philosophy: Rational Agency as Ethical Life* (Cambridge: Cambridge University Press, 2008), p. 215.

17 Peter Sloterdijk, *Rage and Time*, p. 24; Pippin, *Modernism as a Philosophical Problem*, p. xv.

18 Pippin, *Hegel's Practical Philosophy: Rational Agency as Ethical Life* (Cambridge: Cambridge University Press, 2008), p. 215.

19 Quoted in Josef Früchtl, *The Impertinent Self: A Heroic History of Modernity* (Stanford: Stanford University Press, 2009), p. 157.

20 Früchtl, *Impertinent Self*, p. 156.

21 *Here I Stand*, p. 60. The report in the *Sunday Worker*, on 14 November, has a slightly, but significantly, different version. 'The history of this era' becomes the 'history of the capitalist era', and there is an interpolation that gives a different gloss to the latter part of the sentence: 'despoiled of their lands, their culture destroyed, they are *in every country, save one*, denied equal protection of the law' ('Paul Robeson Speaks for His People and All Humanity', *Sunday Worker*, 14 November 1937, p. 11; quoted in Carby, *Race Men*, p. 83.)

158 Donald

22 Jeffrey C. Stewart, 'Paul Robeson and the Problem of Modernism', in *Rhapsodies in Black: Art of the Harlem Renaissance* (London: Hayward Gallery, 1997), pp. 99–100.
23 Jeffrey C. Stewart, 'The New Negro as Citizen', in George Hutchinson (ed.), *The Cambridge Companion to the Harlem Renaissance* (Cambridge: Cambridge University Press, 2007), pp. 21–22.
24 Carby, *Race Men*, p. 83.
25 Boyle and Bunie, *Paul Robeson*, pp. 377–378.
26 Doris Lessing, *Walking in the Shade, 1949–1962* (New York: Harper Perennial, 1998), p. 166.
27 Früchtl, *Impertinent Self*, pp. 36, 156.
28 Scott, *Conscripts of Modernity*, pp. 47–48.
29 See Früchtl, *The Impertinent Self*, p. 41.
30 *Rhetoric* 2.2, quoted and discussed in Paul Rabinow, *Marking Time: On the Anthropology of the Contemporary* (Princeton: Princeton University Press, 2007), pp. 92–93.
31 Robeson, Jr., *Quest for Freedom*, pp. 305–306.
32 Duberman, *Paul Robeson*, pp. 437–438. Duberman's diagnosis is challenged by Tony Perucci, *Paul Robeson and the Cold War Performance Complex: Race, Madness, Activism* (Ann Arbor, University of Michigan Press, 2012), p. 175.
33 Robeson, Jr., *Quest for Freedom*, p. 249; Duberman, *Paul Robeson*, pp. 439–440.
34 Duberman, *Paul Robeson*, pp. 441–442.
35 Duberman, *Paul Robeson*, p. 443. Robeson, Jr., *Quest for Freedom*, p. 255.
36 Duberman, *Paul Robeson*, pp. 487–488.
37 Faith Bandler, interviewed for *Australian Biography*, ABC Television (25 March 1993); quoted in Ann Curthoys (2011), 'Paul Robeson's visit to Australia and Aboriginal activism, 1960', in Frances-Peters Little, Ann Curthoys and John Docker (eds.) *Passionate Histories: Myth, Memory and Indigenous Australia*, ANU E Press, accessed 7 May 2011: http://epress.anu.edu.au/apps/bookworm/view/Passionate+Histories%3A+Myth%2C+Memory+and+Indigenous+Australia/1271/ch08.xhtml#toc-anchor.
38 Paul Robeson, *Here I Stand* (London: Dennis Dobson, 1958), pp. 40–41; "'I Am at Home' Says Robeson at Reception in Soviet Union', Interview by Vern Smith, *Daily Worker* (15 January 1935); Boyle and Bunie, *Paul Robeson*, p. 385, quoting *Daily Worker* 24 July 1938; Marie Seton, *Paul Robeson* (London: Dennis Dobson, 1958), p. 94; Robeson, *Here I Stand*, 53–54.
39 'Civilization and its Discontents (1930 [1929])', in *The Pelican Freud Library*, vol. 14, *Civilization, Society and Religion*, ed. Albert Dickson, (Harmondsworth: Penguin, 1985), pp. 309–310.
40 "'I Am at Home' Says Robeson at Reception in Soviet Union', Interview by Vern Smith, *Daily Worker* (15 January 1935).
41 Früchtl, *The Impertinent Self*, p. 41.
42 See Robert Fine and Robin Cohen, 'Four Cosmopolitan Moments' in Steven Vertovec and Robin Cohen (eds.), *Conceiving Cosmopolitanism: Theory, Context and Practice* (Oxford: Oxford University Press), p. 146.

CHAPTER 9

The Figure of Crusoe

David Marriott

Figure: from Old French *figure* (noun), *figurer* (verb), from Latin *figura* 'shape, figure, form'; related to *fingere* 'form, contrive'.

– Oxford English Dictionary

One way of talking about Caribbean writers and modernism is to try to understand the relation between margin and centre, the perhaps historical or more broadly 'cultural' question of imperial tradition and native talent.[1] Very different stories have been told, of course, about how Caribbean literature and culture comes to be modern, but they all share a common structure of *belatedness*: that is, the moment in which the colony, in its otherwise undeveloped form, is founded or grounded by the presence of a 'discoverer', whose presence is not really originary at all, but the secondary effect of how the imperial centre comes to project itself *as* origin from a retrojective saying or naming of the colony as inaugural New World. As retold by Caribbean writers, such stories were never simply about origins but about the imperial centre's ability to institute itself as origin, and in ways that simultaneously called forth much anxiety and ambivalence on the margins as well as a (more or less desperate) search for a more native tradition, whose genealogy was never simply absent, or somehow present in its absence, and where the consequences of 'discovery' start from rupture, trauma or loss, rather than from the redemptive state of an imperial legacy or inheritance. This complication of discovery, derived here from a sense of belatedness, gives rise to counter-stories of both resistance *and* haunting, in which a kind of radical or absolute refusal gives way oftentimes, and occasionally in the same work, to a kind of historical or critical melancholia where the search is always for something more originary than the origin that imperialism both founds and disrupts. This archaeo-revisionist schema is in fact definitive of Caribbean modernism in general, and of its cultural politics in particular (where the thematics of innovation-dispossession often appear in highly gendered and racial forms).

These points are now no doubt familiar but, however familiar the terms of this search for a Caribbean decolonial identity, what remains striking in this context are the ways in which the resistance to colonial history – and, consequently, the desire for a more liberatory narrative of both time and self – often has recourse to a language of gender that is marked from the start by asymmetry, separation, disavowal and *ressentiment*. For example, it seems to be no accident that the imperial margins are often read as, exclusively and exhaustively, the overcoming of the tradition (of the master), on the basis of a new (and henceforth independent) national-political identity. Artistic integrity is reclaimed by a new generation of writers who must purge themselves of the colonial fetish or idol in order to practise their new roles in crafting the emerging nation. Today, more than fifty years after Bandung, these anti-colonial nationalist visions of modernity are receiving new scrutiny and address: to the extent that they rely on 'highly masculine definitions' of freedom and sovereignty, say, or entail gendered narratives of liberation, tradition and art in the struggle for new forms of authority, recent critics of black modernisms have started to ask why these masculine imaginaries, connected to ideas of race and nation, have been rarely questioned.[2] To respond to this thinking of identity and of our ability to come to terms with the hegemony of certain assumptions about Caribbean men, by once again addressing how the response to the centre by the margins in general and by black men in particular is 'gendered', and to resume once more the search for identities otherwise disqualified by discourses of racial-national unity is, perhaps, to overlook the much more disturbing possibility that it may be the very exclusion of various 'others' from the dilemma of tradition in the colony that confirms the value and effectiveness of black revolutionary desire for nationhood. In both the world of anti-colonial politics and black intellectual world, there seems to be a low tolerance of sexual equivocation. The result of this intolerance and unease is a reproduction of gendered ways of thinking and of formulating ethical and aesthetic liberation. *Parri passu*, in politics and art, across the political spectrum, there is a consensus that attributes the insufficiencies of colonial culture of the post-war period to the absence of black male sovereignty. This kind of indictment, which seems to be essentially related to the fact (if not quite the event) of empire, appears to be fundamentally an account of emasculation, and wants, post-colony, to have political and aesthetic form reflect the trace of that loss, or perhaps lose the loss as loss, and so have history literally emerge from the terrain of male empowerment, via a peculiarly masculine form of mourning. Why is it that the unsparing rejection of the imperial centre and the rush to espouse the formerly degraded margin, whether in revolutionary or conservative writings, should perpetuate dualisms in which all the undesirable features of domination are reinforced and reappear in the ostensibly newly revealed and valoried form of black male identity? You would expect the outcome of independence to require a thorough embrace or rejection of the centre, so that the strengths and shortcomings of colonial culture may be revised or modified in the light of struggle. But sovereignty, in its political or critical-aesthetic form, is ultimately conserving of identity regardless of the contingencies affecting its meaning and employment. Sovereign loss (and not just the loss of sovereignty) may well be the affective state of diaspora, affecting the desire to belong as well as the fantasy of being cast out (as such, both would be desires for change marked from the start by a mourning that returns obsessively to what is felt to be already lost: a masculine ego or identity disavowed as such).

Let us say that this is just one way of approaching Caribbean modernisms and black masculinities. One way of understanding this approach is in terms of a double bind. Broadly speaking, the issue is this: Caribbean modernisms, in their perennial struggles with the imperial centre (as structure and authority), can neither claim an escape from colonial domination nor avoid reviving, as it were, the very forms of prescriptive sociality and traditional rationality they claim to overthrow.[3] During the anti-colonial and black power debates of the 1960s and after, I would be tempted to say, black male writers and intellectuals could neither forget nor neutralise the paradox, which translates at its extremes into a sort of authoritarian attenuation that leaves traditional forms of sovereignty intact, and so indirectly legitimates tradition's power by excluding other 'identities' (sexual and racial) from revolutionary social change. One hears echoes of the debate in twentieth-century Caribbean poets, over the nature of linguistic authenticity: whether verse form or diction constitutes the polity or disavows it, or whether the organic community rests on poetry's ability to name history, territory, language and custom, or whether poetry can ever be separated from power and retain its institutional and cultural consequences as the legislator of the New World. One thing that seems to be certain is that representation acquires a different resonance and rationale when the issue of sovereignty, homelessness and exile is at stake. In this vein, I propose a study of a key trope of Caribbean male modernist writing: the place of the white male 'discoverer' in the symbolics and semiotics of identity. This situation, which raises questions of race and gender, is already a problem of domination and power,

which is thus also one of empowerment and community, however much
it may continue to be confused with the warring engagements of black
masculinity.

In his 1965 lecture 'The Figure of Crusoe', the St Lucian poet Derek
Walcott associates Crusoe with Adam, while characterising West Indian
poetry as 'in the position of Crusoe, the namer'.[4] For example, he
announces that for West Indian poets, nouns, 'when written, are as fresh,
as truly textured, as when Crusoe sets them down in the first West Indian
novel' (FC: 36), and adds (in the name of another comparison, which will
return to haunt us) that inherent in the power to name there is a 'strength',
a baptism, a law-making fire in which 'all is combustible', a fire in which
creaturely life, set in language and deserted by God, is no longer fallen
but born anew (FC: 36). Crusoe 'is Adam because he is the first inhabit-
ant of this second paradise' (FC: 37): 'He does not possess the island he
inhabits', 'He is alone, he is a craftsman, his beginnings are humble', 'He
acts, not by authority, but by conscience.' Understood as creation rather
than possession ('craftsman' being perhaps the crucial word here …),
Crusoe's naming defines a condition of purity without precedent, and we
might imagine that it is as a symbol of a newly created world that Crusoe's
anguish and isolation comes to define West Indian poetry, he is a symbol
of an island culture that is unfallen. In any case, this symbolism, which is
not solely theological, is then related to the creation of a 'profane Genesis',
to the extent that Crusoe's arrival in the new world does not lead to the
lamentation of exile, but, on the contrary, the recovery of strength as the
prose of the natural world is replaced by the communicability and revelation of 'poetry's surprise', as mute nature, now named by Crusoe, finds
itself startled (FC: 37):

> out of such timbers
> came our first book, our profane Genesis
>   whose Adam speaks that prose
> which, blessing some sea-rock, startles itself
>   with poetry's surprise,
> in a green world, one without metaphors. ('Crusoe's Journal')[5]

(This is, incidentally, the point at which what Walcott calls 'tradition' looks
surprisingly like a homosocial account of social and political institutions,
which legitimises poetic domination as male authority and which, as such,
can only confirm its 'genesis' in the absence of Eve (indeed, I want to say
that it is the exclusion of her difference from 'our first book' *that gives
man, the poetic namer, the power to name*). The purity of naming is man's
sovereignty, but that sovereignty is *nothing* (least of all an institution)

unless it can legitimate and maintain itself against mute nature, and here the very formation of selfhood seems apparently to secure itself in opposition to sexual difference in order to be sovereign. But this is a legislation that appears to be, from the first, ungrounded by its very desire to have a ground – is this the story of what happens when 'nature' succumbs to metaphor and 'man' is no longer identical to himself? And why is this ability to 'name' a green world, precisely conceived here as what neutralises alterity in the interests of identity, why does it present that identity as essentially corruptible, made fragile by this wish to name an entire world?) Having gathered up names like remnants from a shipwreck, Crusoe then succumbs to the madness of his own 'anonymity' (FC: 38). The naming word has become, with sinister irony, the instrument of the most undifferentiated, narcissistic expression of Crusoe's loss of the world and, from the point of view of things, a reflection of language's impotence and decay. 'It is only when Friday arrives that Crusoe again withdraws into himself', Walcott adds. That is, by encountering the sight of the other, Crusoe rediscovers himself, but this is a self-discovery defined by self-alienation, dread and violence. Or as Walcott puts it, using almost Rousseauistic terms to describe the shift from natural man to man of culture:

> [Crusoe] withdraws into himself. He learns the fear of another. Now he stops becoming a writer, hermit, saint, and becomes by necessity, a master. He reverts to what he was taught and becomes self-righteous on such subjects as God, civilization, art and human nakedness. And, of course, race. He returns to a commonplace sanity, to the Puritanism that he had abandoned, when, unlike most men, he once really understood nothing. (FC: 38)

Walcott's purport would then be to show that Friday's conversion and servitude is, if one can put it like this, *made possible* by the abandonment and even the deconstruction of a language of names, but that, following the complex logic of Crusoe as symbol, missionary imperialism itself becomes a sign of this loss of immediacy as language falls into law and judgment, and the creaturely world becomes the measure of Crusoe's homelessness. Yet, if the colonial self usurps the sovereignty of true sovereignty, and leads to the eventual ruin of named nature, this is a version that disowns the political implications of legitimated violence for thinking difference per se. The aporia or gap that opens up is thus intrinsically ironic: the natural violence that founds poetry's power is not violent in its necessary rightness, for it is only with the appearance of difference (the black other) that sovereignty ceases to be sovereign empowerment and becomes, instead, law and suppression. Or, the lamented loss of nature is not aware of itself as loss until the self is reminded of its own alterity owing to 'fear of another', the recovery from which involves law and power. Following the complex logic of loss and gain, if shipwreck has led to the island's discovery and a new language of creation, then Crusoe, having undertaken, still less succeeded in, the severe task of naming the created world, has, like Adam, reverted to law, abstraction, mediation and judgement in his encounter with another. 'Confrontation with Friday, with Friday's barbarism and limited knowledge of language and its graces creates homesickness in Crusoe. He has made the island his own home, but now he sees its "shortcomings"' (FC: 38). Friday becomes the emblem of what disturbs Crusoe's writing, in that with his arrival Crusoe 'stops becoming a writer' and remembers 'the old order of things': including sovereign power, self-righteousness, Christianity, nakedness, imperialism and – let us not forget – race (but presumably not gender) (ibid.).

Schematically: there would be, apparently, a relation between Crusoe's new found mastery, and poetry in that naming (or at least its onto-theological phantasy) would manifest itself as sovereignty, or that sovereignty – or its concept – would push towards language as what guarantees its legislative novelty. Friday's *difference* as such would be linked with naming as an essential component of sovereignty, and sovereignty (or its metaphysical phantasy) would be none other, in the end, than the homesickness of the subject (individual or collective) for an autonomous and free existence. The point for Walcott would be to call on West Indian poetry to rethink – or think better – these relations, and especially to think better its own (novel, exilic) complicity with this legislation. This call is also a call to a certain conflagration, which would itself lead poetry to rethink the imperial concept itself, and its homesickness or 'ingratitude', as Walcott calls it. The lecture indeed begins with the injunction that West Indian poets should make a 'bonfire' of tradition by becoming a 'pure flame', '*un semplice lume!*' (FC: 34). After the fall of Crusoe into imperialism, it is up to Crusoe and Friday's descendants, the West Indian poets, to gather up the implements of Crusoe's words and refashion a new postcolonial present.

This is a legacy or inheritance, then, whose patriarchal legislation can only affirm the legitimacy of its institution in the absence of women, and whose violent founding act *itself* is neither white nor black, but the repetition of a violence that both founds the colony (out of nature) and confirms the legality of its power by confining nature to the mute 'essence' of language and the political as such; a legacy, in brief, that suggests without the 'union' of white and black men there would be no legitimacy of tradition or of language, just a corrupting power constantly subject to contestation, modification and violent overthrow. This striking juxtaposition of Crusoe and Friday may seem surprising, not only in that it is not common, so far as I know, but also in that the language of exile in question is not, apparently, of the same order in each case. Walcott's distinctions between language, dominance and servitude, indicates several specific challenges to recent readings of Crusoe. 'If we read the commentary of exiles, we will think that my position which is that of Crusoe or Friday, or more truly, a mixture of their imagined progeny, has been defensive when it is in fact logical' (FC: 39). The concept of imagined progeny itself seems quite dialectical, in that it seems that West Indian male poets can be original in different ways: here we are tempted to say that Crusoe and Friday (as poetic symbols) are not undergoing the same isolation and survival: not necessarily that one would be *less* exiled than the other, but that the homesickness is not the same in each case, and so neither is the bonfire they might hope to light. The West Indian male poet – white or black – can recreate the world by moving from the melancholy of loss to its acknowledgment and acceptance, but the choice is no longer between the original purity of names or the law–preserving violence of colonialism. Language has irredeemably withered into the condition of exile – that is, fallen, violent and unredeemable – but the poem remains the homeland, and poetry the expression of what it means to have legitimate power. Walcott's linking of these two figures would be the more dialectical because of this. But to describe this dialectic in terms of the imagined progeny of two men suggests that there is a homosocial logic to these dualisms of power and otherness. Maybe it would not be much of an exaggeration to say that what the Caribbean poet inherits is the desire for an identity (white *and* black) that consists of a fantasy (homosexual *and* interracial) that can be faithful to Crusoe's legacy only by re-inseminating a colonial model of patrilinear descent. This is why, among other things, a Caribbean modernist tradition can be to seen to persist or even emerge from an act of homosexual miscegenation, whereby the violence of colonialism can be burnt up or at least be utterly consumed by the founding act of a name that transfers the founding contract of the colony to one between language and the state of nature from which it supposedly emerged, and where the legacy bequeathed to 'us' marks a break from historical events to a mythical, newly discovered landscape, whereby black masculine authority can institute or even reimagine itself as the *repetition* of the 'essence' of sovereignty as such, via a return to the father's *first* word.

If the concept of the poem as homeland remains obscure, this is not immediately for want of analysis in the tradition (unlike with contemporary

West Indian poetry). Clearly it is out of the question for me to produce a genealogy (even a summary one) of this concept in the history of aesthetics, from Heidegger onwards: my point will be (perhaps in another figure of nomination) to bring out in the concept of exile as given to us by the tradition, resources that resist precisely its historical convergence with the concept of the subject and the associated values of autonomy, liberty, heroism and so on. We can begin to do this by recalling that 'before' being pulled towards history and tradition, exile, for Walcott, is an attempt to name exactly the opposite ('We must not commit that heresy of thinking that because we "have no past," we have no future' (FC: 39)): by this definition, which still calls to us, the true sovereignty of Crusoe (Walcott calls it a 'triumph of the will', FC: 40) is to have attempted to name the West Indian present as *anything but* 'absence', lack, 'ruins, in short, no civilization' (FC: 39, 40). Rather, what defines Crusoe's language of exile – the novel-being of the New World subject – transcends history by being opposed to its concept. We can find this opposition between homeland and historicism repeated in Walcott's 1992 Nobel Lecture, 'The Antilles: Fragments of Epic Memory': 'visual surprise is natural in the Caribbean; it comes with the landscape, and faced with its beauty, the sigh of History dissolves. We make too much of that long groan that underlines the past. ... The sigh of History rises over ruins, not over landscapes, and in the Antilles there are few ruins to sigh over.'[6] No sighing in St Lucia then, at least over the ruins of history, even if the surprising language of landscape has become, unsurprisingly, absolutely historical and commercialised. I invoke 'The Antilles: Fragments of Epic Memory' not to claim any particular kind of priority of homeland over the historical; but to show how Walcott continues to figure the relationship between the Old and New Worlds via the figure of Crusoe, whose foundational naming of the island remains the example through which the West Indian poet can resist and reinvent tradition by refuting its anachronistic view of the Antillean past. The West Indian poet must learn to make his own tools like Crusoe, Walcott suggests, by 'assembling nouns from necessity', rather than from disenchantment or decay (*WTS*: 70). For, as he explains, such acts of nomination answer

> those critics who complain that there is nothing here, no art, no history, no architecture, by which they mean ruins, in short, no civilization, it is 'O happy desert!' We live not only on happy, but on fertile deserts, and we draw our strength, like Adam, like all hermits, all dedicated craftsmen, from that rich irony of our history. It is what feeds the bonfire. We contemplate our spirit by the detritus of the past. (FC: 40)

This comment of Walcott's contains just about all the terms that matter to us here, and gives an outline of what it means for West Indian (male) poetry to redeem its heterogeneous origin.

We might also need to turn to Walter Benjamin if we wish to specify the history of the opposition of landscape to history, starting perhaps with a passage from *Origin of the German Tragic Drama*, in which Benjamin resituates the opposition as one between symbol and allegory: 'Whereas in the symbol destruction is idealized and the transfigured face of nature is fleetingly revealed in the light of redemption, in allegory the observer is confronted with *facies hippocratica* of history as a petrified, primordial landscape.'[7] We would have to reread Walcott's 1965 lecture on Crusoe, especially around the metaphors of ruin and fire, and the notion of nature independent of history and culture, through precisely these opposed terms. And if Crusoe is a 'symbol' invoking loss and epiphany, the secular apotheosis of thing and creature, then we should also remember that it is as a symbol that Walcott distinguishes his Crusoe from what he calls the modern secular allegory of the 'fashionable, Marxist method' – a method in which Friday is always the victim of history, a subject always exiled in the representation of his exile. And Crusoe always the possessing, self-possessed victor. It is this resistance to a reading of Crusoe and Friday as emblems that leads Walcott to define Crusoe-Friday as a conjoined symbol for West Indian aesthetic culture. I would suggest that this is not a debate over the permissible limits of allegory, but one turning on the 'irony' of modern ethical life: in which the very idea of a sacred landscape has become a major selling point for tourist boards and the operations of capital, and 'ethnic' nationalisms have fought to disqualify multiracialism from the actualities of culture and authority.[8]

This classic distinction between symbol and allegory, as it is posited by Benjamin – this distinction between nature and history, which found both its periodic confirmation and its negation in the Baroque and the epochs that followed – continues to pose questions for us, obscure questions, beyond all the restorations that came after. My hypothesis is that by searching in this obscurity, feeling or groping around the ruins (of history, as Walcott often puts it, always deprecatingly) that we can hope obviously not to *re-establish* anything, and certainly not a supposedly original sense of the named word (the one Crusoe had in mind, for example, after landing), but to find ourselves in the general area of what Walcott calls, much later in his text, 'homesickness', necessarily instituted on the basis of the *hetero-nomy* that appears with Friday's *appearing*. It remains to be seen whether in so doing we will find ourselves beyond exile, and if we can understand, or at least hear, what Walcott, just before announcing that Crusoe 'becomes by necessity, a master' (FC: 38), calls the 'anguish of authority' (FC: 36), the thought of which would somewhere demand an idea of sovereignty that we would clearly need to distinguish – or exile – from the fall of nature into history in allegory and the exile that precedes it, the fall of language from symbolic immanence into mere sign and signification, and the fall of man into difference.

From Crusoe as 'symbol' we move naturally enough to Friday as 'allegory', and from there to exile and homesickness. 'Allegories are, in the realm of thoughts, what ruins are in the realm of things', suggests Benjamin (OGTD: 177–178). I would like to argue that the sight of Friday's single, isolated 'footprint' can indeed not be thought without allegory, as an emblem of ruin and interruption, which resists any attempt to figure that interruption in terms of continuity or flux. Insofar as the footprint interrupts the seamless correspondence between language and landscape, and from there also mimics the indifference of nouns to the objects they reproduce or represent, Friday's footprint itself designates a faultline in Walcott's argument between novelty and ruin, insofar as the timeless novelty of nature cannot be thought or represented without a thought of time, of the temporality of time, which cannot be figured other than in terms of transience, dispersal and loss. Before immediacy or opportune surprise, Friday's footprint suggests novelty can be a moment of fear and doubt, precisely, the instant not as it flows continuously into a future without a past, but as it interrupts or breaks into that continuity with a cannibalising presence, or the moment in which the perfected immanence of the symbol is about to be consumed by the temporality of allegory. Before being a symbol or a stable referent, the footprint confronts Crusoe as pure anteriority, the unexpected that befalls, the discontinuous that makes its mark. Isolation gets its initial moment of negativity in this interruptive cut. Let us say for short that the footprint inscribes the coming of the other insofar as nothing can prepare for it, insofar as it surprises even the most careful preparation, and that in this sense, despite a whole (romantic?) tradition that would have the other appear without renunciation or loss, the other *never* comes at the right moment, or it is part of the *a priori* structure of the *symbol* to be thus figured only *after the event*. Following a structure that could no doubt be generalised to the most everyday experience of time, there is an effort before and after the event to integrate the event into the course of works and days, thus blunting or denying the cut of the event as such. Now it seems that allegory, be it thought by Benjamin or De Man, Hegel or Pascal, holds in the obscurity of its conceptual nucleus a constitutive relation to the *ruination* thought in this way, and that this relation gives rise to what appears regularly as a paradox or aporia essential to the concept of history, and that could even be called its essential *ruin*: insofar as it is always an allegory of the present, history never in fact manages to get hold of time, nor thereby of itself. (As an aside, this could also be the irony of history).

This 'ruin' of history is to be found most clearly stated by Benjamin. 'In the ruin history has physically merged into the setting. And in this guise history does not assume the form of the process of an eternal life so much as that of irresistible decay. ... Allegories are, in the realm of thoughts, what ruins are in the realm of things' (*OGTD*: 177–178). The only ruining on the island is the experience of the decay of nature into history, that is, an experience that allows Crusoe to escape his servility to nature only by obliterating it as a naïve and rude symbol. In spite of the sentiments of belonging to *place*, Crusoe's homesickness, in which the island territory itself becomes emblematic of emptiness, in which the textured reality of the landscape no longer offers an integrity of experience, means that the experience of locale is no longer one of plenitude, a simple presence to what dwells. The concept of history, in its imperial guise, can never know the island as a presence, but only as absence and loss (and, as a result, unworthy of political and historical recognition). In Defoe's novel, Crusoe's loss of home never leads to a loss of manners or language, his authority may be anguished but he never loses that sentiment of self that comes with being an historical subject (even after an isolation of more than twenty-five years).

To be in history – rather than nature – is always to make an effort, to work, to make nature servile to law and time, indefinitely continued, indefinitely repeated. In Defoe's novel, the experience of exile is redeemed by productive labor. In Walcott's reading, it is Crusoe's *aesthetic* labor – the making of the earthenware pots, for example – that results in a new shaping of time and nature, and a new relation to locality and finitude.[9] What are we to make of this difference in response to loss and homelessness? Here are some lines from Walcott's poem, 'Crusoe's Journal', from the 1965 collection, *The Castaway and Other Poems*:

> So time, that makes us objects, multiplies
>   our natural loneliness.
> For the hermetic skill, that from earth's clays
>   shapes something without use,
> and, separate from itself, lives somewhere else,
>   sharing with every beach

a longing for those gulls that cloud the cays
  with raw, mimetic cries,
never surrender wholly, for it knows
  it needs another's praise
like hoar, half-cracked Benn Gunn, until it cries
  at last, 'O happy desert!'
and learns again the self-creating peace
  of islands. ('Crusoe's Journal': 52)

Once again time and creation come together in the contradictory emotions aroused by bereavement. Historicism sets our nature against ourselves by multiplying our loneliness. We become aware of our separateness
and our transience, as we long for a nature whose significance is no longer
our own. Labour and convention may shape the profane world by raising
it to meaning, but as soon as it does so, nature itself has become allegorical, that is, robbed of its immanence it falls into a series of 'mimetic cries'
to which we can 'never surrender wholly'. We may associate knowledge
with assigning things meaning, but we know nothing, absolutely, of what
is not in representation, hence the modality of our servile being, subordi-
nated to the future, to its linking in time. We know nothing, absolutely, of
the truth that is form. Like Adam, we use names, like symbols, to translate
the otherness of the world into meaning, but thereby reduce the world to
the abstract mediation of signs. Form remains our only access to this truth
'separate from itself', short of or beyond all knowing. But this hermetic
work requires a disclosedness that proceeds 'without use'. In a word, we
know nothing of the dwelling place of truth, *of what forms the self-creating
peace of the island*. The operation that historical knowledge is stops when
the sovereignty of form is its object (and just because 'form' is a sovereign
act or event, it is not as such totally graspable or repeatable by mimesis or
history). Historical knowledge is never sovereign: in order to be *sovereign*,
it would have to grasp itself as a pure present, as a kind of pastless time
or zero point in history. In this way we shape things, always aware that in
doing so we multiply our natural loneliness. Perhaps this is what Walcott
means when he says: 'we draw our strength, like Adam, like all hermits,
all dedicated craftsmen, from that rich irony of our history'. (This is, incidentally, the point at which what Walcott calls 'mastery' defines tradition
as a power that creates itself ex nihilo, and whose genuinely decisive act is
the power to authorise itself as both foundation and origin. The authority
of that tradition cannot ever be quite understood outside of this logic of a
self-founding act whose advent is masculine emancipation from alterity.)
On this account, the strength of 'our' sovereignty cannot begin without

the phantasy of a newly mended world, a phantasy that has to forget the violence of its own foundation, without which there would be no concept or intuition of a *fall* to be raised up or reversed by the power of poetry.

Whence the idea of the poem as a 'conflagration' of tradition (even if 'language' is still a problem here, and already a problem for Walcott, who writes that the 'original language dissolves from the exhaustion of distance like fog trying to cross an ocean' (*WTS*: 70)), a conflagration that is only truly such, only truly sovereign insofar as it is utterly consuming, 'a pure flame' in which we 'dissolve in burning' (FC: 34). 'All becomes pure flame, all is combustible, and by that light, which is separate from him, he contemplates himself' (ibid.). Now this self-burning moment which, as we have said, cannot be that of a plenitude, is essentially consciousness of language as an obliteration of *the world's separateness*: for Walcott links it to the following 'That given a virgin world, a paradise, any sound, any act of naming something, like Adam's baptizing the creatures ... such a sound is not really prose, but poetry, is not simile, but metaphor', which is why 'the poets and prose writers who are West Indians, despite the contaminations around us, are in the position of Crusoe, the namer' (FC: 36). It is no accident that Walcott systematically links this burning instant not only to the sacred, but even to the *miracle* of creation (the poet's miraculous reign and conversion of things into names is compared to a baptism and a sacrifice (FC: 35): 'When he is tried and returns into himself, then he has performed some kind of sacrifice, some ritual'), and even, explicitly, to imperialism, in a strange echo of Crusoe's conversion and reign over Friday, which not only confirms (did we need confirmation?) how profoundly gendered Walcott's analysis of exile remains, but which brings us back to a certain sovereign instant in naming (for, as he says elsewhere, to name is to make 'a bonfire of tradition'), in writing, and more especially the writing of poetry, language, memory and experience all get burned up, turned to smoke and ash, that is, disfigured beyond ruins. Here then is the point at which poetry transforms the ruins of history into a symbol of its own ruination *and* rebirth.

In spite of the trauma, the marks of separation introduced by the history of imperialism to these islands, this experience of exile is not to be lamented as a condition of *impotence*. On the contrary, the fragments, shards, echoes of New World culture are the strongest thing: they are the recovery of strength because they are a refusal, whence its paradox, of history as decay or ruin; they are not merely an allegory of exile but a symbol in which the concept of ruin is itself obliterated. Consequently, Walcott is careful not to make a clear separation between Crusoe and Friday and thus confirm their opposition, but, in the name of a generalised (even 'democratic') New World, where everyone is homeless, in exile, no longer held back in adoration of the places they left, he insists that one of the legacies of the colonial encounter should be inaugurated mourning rather than aberrated mourning.[10] If the latter remains trapped in melancholia, the former is able to confront and bear the agony of loss, work through and be educated by it, and through restitution see the world afresh. What these Fridays are waiting for is the miraculous moment when the representation of exile becomes the exile of representation, when the poet, 'making his own tools like Crusoe ... assembl[es] nouns from necessity' (*WTS*: 70). The outcome of this inaugural process is, however, a return to a ('natural') violence formed to guard against the constitutive 'impotence' of the unnamed, the feminine, the historical: all those corrupting fragilities against which the strength of sovereignty is necessarily opposed, but which remain the only measure of sovereignty in its claims to have converted heteronomy into the logos of a first paternal word.

In developing in this way the figure of Crusoe into its aesthetic and political consequences, has Walcott made an incision, some kind of cut in the fabric of tradition? Can we read in these texts the trace of a miraculous moment at which Crusoe, or at least the figure of modern West Indian culture, would be set free from everything that binds it servilely to the tradition? It seems clear that we must reply 'no' to this question, and the perplexity that this reply should also leave us in itself forms part – such at least is my hypothesis – of the complexity in which we are groping here. This *resistance* of the traditional fabric (and let us remember that Walcott regularly defines West Indian poetry via its resistance to history and allegory) is not only betrayed by the explicit reference to Crusoe as origin, but in the fact that Walcott is no doubt doing nothing other than developing (and thus rendering more legible) invariable features of *Robinson Crusoe* in its most classical determinations.[11] In Defoe's novel, Crusoe himself relates his shipwreck to a moment of *absolute* ruination, which, or so it would seem, has the same formal properties as those posited, albeit negatively, by Walcott – for example in one of the first journal entries, where he says that 'I, poor miserable Robinson Crusoe, being shipwrecked, during a dreadful storm, in the offing, came on shore on this dismal unfortunate island, which I called the Island of Despair, all the rest of the ship's company being drowned, and my self almost dead'; or again, in a fragment after the discovery of the cannibal feast, 'and then recovering my self, I looked up with the utmost affection of my soul, and with a flood of tears in my eyes, gave God thanks that had cast my first lot in a part of the world where I was distinguished from such dreadful creatures as these' (*RC*: 172). As I have tried to show elsewhere from a different point of view, this discontinuous loss and recovery renders the male self curiously but essentially precarious, and it is this that gives rise to the history and politics of colonialism as such. This fear of exposure appears to flow directly, as it were, from the fear of being unprotected: having landed on the island and undergoing a crisis of dissolution, Crusoe finds himself in a situation in which he *is not yet other* to the islands' subjects, while introducing him to the fear that his self-defences are what define him precisely as *other*. But, *being* constantly exposed, and in fear of constant exposure, his isolation can never *secure* its sovereignty by imposing any law on itself: even within the walls of his fortification, his self-presence, secured in recollection, is made indistinguishable from a fear of being unfounded. Being sovereign only in the instant of its pure will, Crusoe's self-perpetuating fear is that he *does not exist*; he cancels himself in the very attempt to grasp his sovereignty, and is therefore mastered and never master. As Walcott also sees in his way (and we could here read 'the self is dread' motif as laid out in, for example, 'Crusoe's Island', in which Crusoe's 'crazed' identity seems to flow from the realisation that he learns 'nothing ... / From art or loneliness'), his view of Crusoe is existentialist (but not Marxist), and indeed this is its only strength and its only value. In Defoe, we can show easily that *colonial sovereignty has already lost its head, is already crazy*, and therefore, as Crusoe says, his first duty is to recover and defend the self, which is why he will need various supplements (legislator, executioner, educator, merchant and priest) that can only confirm the precarity, or at least his unfree capture, as a self. As Walcott says very rapidly in 'Crusoe's Island', what startles Crusoe is his first exposure to the otherness of himself: 'As startling as his shadow / Grows to the castaway' (p. 69), and one could doubtless extend this logic to the analyses of Crusoe's encounter with Friday proposed by Walcott.

We could confirm this comedy of the concept of mastery, a comedy we might be tempted to call self-referential, if Crusoe himself had not already named it as such, 'I likewise taught him to say Master, and then let him know, that was to be my name' (*RC*: 209). In response to this named gift, Friday, we are told, 'made all the signs to me of subjection, servitude, and submission imaginable' (*RC*: 209). I have tried to show how Walcott's entire aesthetic thought is organised around the numinous connection between being and language, but also that this triumph of spirit and the loss of nature it entails is inscribed in the very act of the sovereign who names, even in order to affirm its paternal legitimacy. We could go so far

as to say that the very fact of naming the master as master already begins
the loss of sovereignty to recognition and judgement (this would be why
Friday needs to be told the meaning of mastery, and presumably also why
he needs to communicate all the signs imaginable of what it means to be a
slave). Naming mastery as such, as mastery, would thus really be the most
servile outcome of representation – and the most comic – in that this
name already relinquishes what sovereignty is in itself. And this would be
the ironic lesson of history, according to which the strength of the New
World must explicitly identify with the slavish mastery that founds it.
(And this would be the only chance of Crusoe's and Friday's 'progeny'; but
it is precisely against exposure to such institutionality that Walcott defines
his account of a Caribbean modernist tradition.) We might recast this
now by saying that the future authority of that mastery, as it were, can be
affirmed – as language, as symbol – only insofar as naming, in its purity,
can master the history of male subjection, servitude and submission, and
so convert prostration into presence, and so make virility the inherited
concept of tradition for the adamic poet in his – queer and interracial –
masculine faith.

One might think that Walcott would provide a rigorous rethinking of
this self-representation and its ironic result. By linking Crusoe to a 'triumph of will' in the 1965 lecture ('I have tried to show that Crusoe's survival
is not purely physical … but a triumph of will', FC: 40), Walcott elides
the anxiety and fragility which, as such, contrasts with Crusoe's imperious
nature. The notion of existential triumph has no means to understand, or
even to recognise, what underpins this romantic individualism; the vicissitudes that expose the metaphysics of the subject as benevolent sovereign,
whose rights over others and over himself can only be asserted violently,
allegorically, and has failure built into it. Crusoe's relation to difference is
radical: he lives only by foreseeing what he cannot foresee, the invisible
enemies whose difference is there to be eliminated. Here we see again the
allegorical elements we have picked out: Crusoe's sovereign decision (but
we would have to say that any decision worthy of the name is sovereign
in this sense) is 'triumphant' only if we forget the groundlessness from
which it begins. 'Crusoe's triumph', writes Walcott, 'lies in that despairing
cry which he utters when a current takes his dugout canoe further and
further away from the island that, like all of us uprooted souls, he had
made his home, and it is the cynical answer we must make to those critics
who complain that there is nothing here, no art, no history, no architec-
ture, by which they mean ruins' (FC: 40). Walcott does not claim that
this cry is triumphant because it is cynical and despairing, but precisely

because it is at this moment of loss and finitude that Crusoe undergoes a transformation of his initial identity. If sovereignty is a moment of surprise, of crisis and unanticipated happening, a moment when substantial life is in collision with itself, then its truth must lie in what exceeds meaning and representation, and its form must be prior to the first name and first man. Crusoe's sovereignty would then derive not from colonising but from relinquishing and exposure, as well as grasping his freedom at a moment of destruction. And it is important to understand that, even if the question of sovereignty (and therefore, for Walcott, of the novelty of the new world) requires the extreme existential case in which the very existence of the subject is threatened, it is no less the case that it is at this moment that Crusoe is forced to break through meaning and representation, and that his cry results in him speaking ontologically, in a reversion to the muteness before names. (I will not pursue here, with Benjamin, the consequences of this ontological speech as regards allegory or symbol, except to suggest that the cry is perhaps irreducible to the name as symbol of revelation, and that in its ruination it offers neither the story of language's fall nor one of language's salvation, and indeed no horizon at all, and consequently can hardly be thought even within the messianic terms of our distance from God or presence within time.)

In spite of our efforts to bring out and accentuate the paradoxical and even impossible components of Crusoe, it might still reasonably be objected that, in spite of some appearances, all these ways of reading him remain under the aegis of a metaphysics of male subjectivity. This metaphysics (this would be its 'modernity') would stem precisely from the abolition of the clear distinction between power and representation, history and aesthetics. The non-subjected triumph Walcott talks about would be none other, in sum, than the *aestheticisation of the political* via this appeal to an originary moment that escapes the 'contaminations' (his word) of power. The occlusion of the violent predation of Defoe's novel, which we could track in Crusoe's affirmation of capital accumulation as a sign of moral benevolence without once connecting his survival to the real slaves who support him, would merely confirm this objection, even as it accentuates the occlusions that are our concern here. And, so the objection would go, what we have tried to draw from the *figure* of Crusoe with its emphasis on the unforeseeable, discontinuity and precariousness would simply come back to a thought of masculine presence, but in fact the apparently simple transformations set up by Walcott's myth of origins do not (and cannot) remain simple, and symptoms of this failure or impossibility can be read in the text. Almost inevitably, Crusoe's shadow looms large here to the extent that, in Walcott's reading, it is he who defines blackness as abjection: and yet it is Crusoe's legacy that nonetheless comes to embody the black modernist attempt to move beyond the desire to abjure or surpass the abjected (a desire that Walcott, again not unproblematically, assigns to the black man's failure to fully recognise the sovereign *uses* of abjection, uses that undermine or act against racist domination and impotency. To return to Walcott's gesture in the text that has guided us here, we would need to try to think beyond fire or ruin as resources for West Indian poetry, which, however rich and fascinating, would be too traditional (that is to say, too servile in their institutionality or institutionalisation of tradition)).

It seems to me that that would be a simplification that would miss the sense of Walcott's text and his appeal to a certain configuration of tradition and meaning. Everything we have learned from Walcott about the relationship between imperialist tradition and its deconstruction leads us to believe that the 'figure' of Crusoe cannot simply be posited beyond the political. Recall that his wish is for a *third truth* (p. 39, my emphases), which might be third only by not being either exile or homesickness. Refusing V. S. Naipaul's choice of exile ('I knew Trinidad to be unimportant, uncreative, cynical', *The Middle Passage*), and George Lamming's reluctance to return ('no one would feel secure in his decision to return', *The Pleasures of Exile*), Walcott makes the laconic comment: 'To each his own terror, to each his own isolation' (FC: 40). 'To each his own terror, to each his own isolation' would not simply be a call for one to choose between them, except insofar as exile or return would be a gesture of reading the opposition between colonialism and freedom, and thus leaves a certain legibility to the 'postcolonial' thus marked. Walcott's decision to stay and write in the West Indies cannot here simply be derived from a security of decision (as if the desire for cosmopolitan exile could ever be secure, and would even, on Lamming's construal, be coterminous with resentment). Any representation of exile owes it to itself to remember the homeland, on pain of seeing itself condemned to repeat the exile, and be in exile from the exile that allows the self to be [aestheticised as] reborn elsewhere, that we use Naipaul and Lamming to illustrate here. We would need to avoid this romanticist lure (its *ressentiment*) of claiming to cut ourselves once and for all from Crusoe's legacy. 'We' would need to let this tradition burn utterly: a bonfire of loss that turns all loss into profit, or at least the residue of newly imagined progeny, a rebirth always between men, but men haunted by their own precarious institutionality.

Notes

Earlier versions of this paper were presented at The Ward-Phillips Annual Lecture, University of Notre Dame, 13 October 2009; the University at Buffalo, SUNY, Dept. of Comparative Literature, Capen Seminar, 26 October 2010; and at Lutecium: a non-school of Lacanian Psychoanalysis, Winter Immersion seminar, 2010. My thanks to these audiences for their comments and criticism, and, in particular, I am grateful to Maud Ellmann, John Wilkinson, Rodolphe Gasché, John Sitter, David Johnson, Jorge Gracia, Steven Miller, Jacques Siboni, Robert Groome, and Ewa and Kryzstof Ziarek, for their generous support and engagement.

1 For canonic examples see Paul Gilroy, *The Black Atlantic: Modernity and Double Consciousness* (Cambridge, MA: Harvard University Press, 1993); and Edward Said, *Culture and Imperialism* (New York: Knopf, 1993).

2 Michelle Ann Stephens, *Black Empire. The Masculine Global Imaginary of Caribbean Intellectuals in the United States, 1914–1962* (Durham: Duke University Press, 2005), p. 15. See also Hazel V. Carby, *Race Men* (Cambridge, MA: Harvard University Press, 1998), pp. 5–6; David Marriott, *On Black Men* (New York: Columbia University Press, 2000); and David Scott, *Refashioning Futures: Criticism after Postcoloniality* (Princeton: Princeton University Press, 1999).

3 For an account of this 'double bind' see Wilson Harris, *Tradition, the Writer, and Society: Critical Essays* (London: New Beacon Publications, 1973); and Simon During, 'Waiting for the Post: Modernity, Colonization, and Writing', *Ariel: A Review of International English Literature* 20 (October 1989): 31.

4 Derek Walcott, 'The Figure of Crusoe', in Robert D. Hamner, ed., *Critical Perspectives on Derek Walcott* (Boulder: Lynne Rienner, Inc. 1997), pp. 33–41. Hereafter FC plus page no.

5 Derek Walcott, *Collected Poems* (London: Faber and Faber, 1992), p. 51. All citations of poems are from this edition.

6 Derek Walcott, *What the Twilight Says: Essays* (New York: Farrar, Straus, and Giroux, 1999), p. 68. Hereafter *WTS* plus page no.

7 Walter Benjamin, *The Origin of German Tragic Drama*, trans. John Osborne (London: Verso, 1998), p. 166. Hereafter *OGTD* plus page no.

8 '[I]n the drafts of his unpublished autobiography Walcott would try to express his conflicted feelings about the 1970 [black power influenced] revolt. At Woodford Square he listened to the orators screaming for power over their microphones and proclaiming that only pure black would be allowed to survive. He felt threatened and worried about his children's future in Trinidad. His first priority was the safety of his house, to which he returned by taxi. The driver warned him that the placard bearers, who were holding up traffic, were dangerous. Hearing shouts of "black is beautiful" Walcott thought about the implications; did it mean that he and his children were ugly?' Bruce King, *Derek Walcott: A Caribbean Life* (Oxford: Oxford University Press, 2000), p. 255.

9 For the relation between Walcott's notion of the artist as craftsman and that of Pound and Eliot, see Anita Patterson, *Race, American Literature and Transnational Modernisms* (Cambridge: Cambridge University Press, 2008), pp. 173–178.

10 See Gillian Rose, *Mourning Becomes the Law: Philosophy and Representation* (Cambridge: Cambridge University Press, 1996).

11 Daniel Defoe, *Robinson Crusoe* (New York: W.W. Norton & Co, 1993). Hereafter *RC* and page no.

CHAPTER 10

'What I don't seem to see at all is you': D. H. Lawrence's The Fox and the Politics of Masquerade

Thomas Strychacz

When D. H. Lawrence came to revise an earlier manuscript of *The Fox* (1923) in late 1921, he made one important change to this curious tale about Banford and March, two women who are attempting (rather poorly) to run a farm, when young Henry Grenfel arrives unexpectedly to disrupt their lives. In the later version Banford dies. Her death is significant, since it seems to underscore the shift Lawrence was making about this time to the so-called leadership phase of his career, marked by a 'new type of relationship to be established between men and women, in which women are to submit to men and relinquish their newly acquired independence'.[1] This 'new type' of relationship therefore returns to the very old: at worst, a 'worship of male power' and a 'doctrinaire masculinity'.[2] The most commonly rehearsed version of this argument holds that Lawrence adopts a language of archetypes and universals – the 'compulsion of a life-force ... and of a lord of life'[3] – as a way of countering the challenge World War I posed to a culturally approved notion of potent, self-possessed manhood: men were slaughtered by the millions in France, while associated social upheavals brought women's political power and newly prominent queer lifestyles into sharper focus. If men and women are to feel once more whole and fulfilled, Lawrence seems to urge, they need to return to a traditional, even pre-modern, state. Henry must assert his masculine prerogatives, while March must remove the manly breeches she wears to be the 'man about the place' and don a dress, so that each can pursue their "natural' bent, his to lead, hers to follow'.[4] Banford, the (perhaps) lesbian figure who stands inflexibly against Henry and March's moves to reclaim their natural positions, must die.

Looked at from this perspective, it is easy to see why Lawrence has been invoked so often in feminist and post-feminist critiques of literary modernism, which have worked against the grain of a story such as *The Fox*, while diminishing his reputation. As Sandra Gilbert mused in the 1990s,

'how can you be a feminist and a Lawrentian?'⁵ The story appears to celebrate Henry's coming into his own as a powerful man. New appraisals
of literary modernism turn that plot of male awakening on its head: it
signifies instead the attempt of (white) male writers to preserve or reinvig-
orate male cultural authority at a historical juncture when they 'feared
the loss of their own hegemony' and used their work to express 'alarm at
the feminist challenges to male privileges'.⁶ Representative not so much
of modernism as *masculinist* modernism, *The Fox* can be seen as part of a
widespread cultural movement to reimpose normative gender and sex roles
by writing women into their place – the grave or, in the case of March, the
marriage bed.

If there is any doubt in Lawrence's polemic, scholars have held, it
lies in the odd irresolution of the ending, which plunges the wedded
couple into unsettling frustration. 'To be fair', writes Hilary Simpson,
'*The Fox* does end on a question mark' so that it 'would be too simplistic to assume that Lawrence whole-heartedly endorses Henry's attitude'.⁷
Simpson's conclusion is itself so fraught with question marks – how are
we to tell with which part, or with how much, of his heart Lawrence
endorses Henry? – that it is worth asking how critics have unmasked the
writer's belated attempts to make his story more complex. One way is to
find the story 'artistically dishonest',⁸ either because Lawrence failed to
marshal his material well or because he succeeded only too well in mar-
shalling it didactically.⁹ From this perspective, the tale looks like a bom-
bastic account of gender roles put to rights, supplemented by a pose of
artistic dialogism. Another possibility – much more subtle because it is a
governing assumption about how Lawrence's fictions unfold rather than
an articulated experience of *The Fox* – is to bracket off the question mark,
to confine it to the shifty terrain of the last few pages. The story's half-
hearted conclusion looks forward to a doubtful future (for the characters) but it cannot unsettle interpretive decisions made earlier in the tale.
Interpretive decisions once ratified during the process of reading *The Fox*,
it seems, are ratified for good. Yet question marks in English mark the
difference between statement ('how foolish') and interrogative ('how are
we to tell?') by reaching back from the end of the utterance to the very
beginning, in an instantaneous transformation of every sign: they resist
the assumption that an interpretive question mark cannot retrospect-
ively govern an entire text. Elsewhere I have argued that the experience of
reading *Women in Love* (1920) can take the form of 'doing a double-take':
a process of leading, of gulling the reader to make secure-seeming judgements that turn out to be provisional, so that one comes to expect as a

routine matter the activity of backtracking and un-settling.[10] Then why not work the logic of the interrogation mark back into the fabric of *The Fox*? Why not, fox-like, double back?

The event that frequently appears in the critical literature to prevent a critical doubling-back is the termination of March's masquerade. At the moment that March abandons her wartime breeches and tunic for a dress, Simpson argues, she reveals her 'true, "womanly" nature'; the story therefore 'implies that women's assumption of independence and responsibility is as superficial and temporary as their assumption of men's clothes'.[11] By the end of the tale, Sandra Gilbert and Susan Gubar agree, 'true rule has been reestablished, an order based upon male dominance-female submission recovered from transvestite disorder.'[12] For these critics, March's act of donning female dress necessarily signifies a series of irreversible shifts: from transvestism to appropriate dress; from disorder to an order based on 'natural' male/female roles; and therefore from a temporary to an enduring identity. The ending of March's masquerade seems to determine two interlinked interpretive directions: it establishes a linear thrust to the narrative and simultaneously enacts a symbolic retrogression whereby women are put back in their 'proper', pre-modern places. In what follows, I shall take issue with this interpretation of March's masquerade, showing that it signifies more credibly in terms of Lawrence's narrative embrace of theatricalised gender roles and a rhetoric of performance that remain resistant to a sequence of disorder followed by reconstruction and then (natural) order.[13]

But there are larger issues at stake. Of late, masquerading has enjoyed a generative role in structuring the discourse on literary modernism in its guise as a trope, perhaps *the* trope, for subversive modernist play. The 'hyperbolic, disruptive power'[14] of masquerade has come to seem crucial to understanding the early twentieth century, a historical moment when pyrotechnic narrative performances often seem to derive vigour from cultural sites of mask and masquerade, many inflected by a powerfully emergent mass culture: burlesque, drag, music hall, African masks, vaudeville, minstrelsy, cabaret. To many scholars, narrative styles organised around the trope of masquerade present a number of potent challenges to the social order, alienating the categories of nature and authenticity that grant coherence to hegemonic constructions of identity, class, nation, empire and masculinity. 'The effectivity of masquerade', writes Mary Ann Doane, 'lies precisely in its potential to manufacture a distance from the image, to generate a problematic within which the image is manipulable [and] producible.'[15]

This problematic also makes for a particularly fruitful interchange between historical studies and the current preoccupations of theorists of gender-as-performance. Masquerade can represent, as Suzanne Young argues, a 'specific instance of the general epistemological uncertainty of the modern age'[16] – and a powerful one since it dovetails neatly with theories of gender performances, where masquerade can function as the exterior sign of an ungrounded subjectivity constructed through its iterations. At such moments, Judith Butler insists, an 'abiding gendered self will then be shown to be structured by repeated acts that seek to approximate the ideal of a substantial ground of identity, but which, in their occasional discontinuity, reveal the temporal and contingent groundlessness of this "ground."'[17] Masquerade, in short, disrupts the assumption that there must be an authentic identity behind the mask by putting in question the relationship between the two. Humans are constantly constructing and re-performing their 'real' identities; masquerade merely makes that process evident.

Mary Ann Doane, however, adds a crucial caveat to her appraisal of masquerading: she insists that this problematic is only 'readable by ... women', since only female readers, disadvantaged by contemporary symbolic orders, can acquire the stance, the distance, to destabilise them. How then to read male modernists who write of and through masquerade but whose allegiance to the symbolic order presumably forces them to sacrifice its potential for manufacturing distance? Consistently, the trope of masquerade in works by male modernists has been described as a ruse of power. In this articulation, masquerade 'involves a distinction between the artificial and the real. Behind the façade of the mask lies the real face, to be revealed when the masquerade is over'.[18] That (male) face is usually thought to be an anxious one. Masks dramatise social changes menacing to male hegemony and compulsory heterosexuality; but the maskers yearn to remove the masks and resolve gender roles into their conventionally secure and authentic forms. To trouble the neat resolution of March's masquerade is therefore to contest – to double back on – the interpretive strategies that see order appearing out of transvestite disorder and begin to ask how ruling the dramatic and rhetorical registers of *The Fox* out of bounds might be generated by, and contribute to, an overly rigid account of the gender of modernism.

I

At one point early in the story, the dog-fox, otherwise 'so sly', emerges from cover to confront the 'spell-bound' March in a startling stare-down:

he 'looked into her eyes, and her soul failed her'.[19] That moment keys the story's near-obsession with spectatorship, articulated through an amazing variety of gazes that shape the characters' interactions with each other. The scene of Henry's arrival, for instance, recapitulates and enlarges upon the encounter with the fox. Henry 'stared brightly, very keenly from girl to girl' (14), while March 'stared at him spell-bound' and Banford shrunk away 'with half-averted head'. Soon March assumes Banford's role: she 'did not want to be noticed' (15), and so she 'shrank and shrank, trying not to be seen' (16). Despite her efforts, Henry obsessively seeks out the 'half-invisible woman' (18): 'ever his eyes came back to her, searching, unremitting' (16).

It is difficult not to construe these moves in terms of a scopic regime of power that Henry effortlessly dominates.[20] A predatory fox-male, his keen glance forces the two women into submissively averting their eyes; spell-bound, March can do nothing but cower 'still and soft in her corner like a passive creature in its cave' (18). 'Don't talk to me about Nature' (18), says Banford a few moments later; but this scene seems to manoeuvre, even to bully, us into seeing her statement as precisely the problem with the two women, who need to be forced into accepting the inevitable, because natural, prerogative of the male. We can therefore understand the force of Anne Smith's critique when she argues that at the end of *The Fox* March's 'semi-comatose acquiescent stupor ... presents woman as the "gentle domestic beast" so dear to the hearts of the Victorians' (45). The last scene of the story, like the first meeting, seems to put the anthropomorphising logic of the classic Aesopian beast-fable to brilliant use: so inevitable is Nature, so potent is the predatory stare of the dog-fox, that Henry breaks March out of her masculine masquerade just by looking at her!

There is no gainsaying Henry's desire to dominate the visual field or the fact that March and Banford fail to resist his predatory surveillance. What prevents the story's readers from having to succumb 'spell-bound' to Henry's mastering gaze is the pervasive and often lugubrious theatricality of his attempts to exercise power, which makes it possible for us to comprehend male power as a strategic performance rather than the natural outcome of being male – or, more disturbing, to comprehend the 'natural' being of being male in terms of a strategic performance. His decision to expropriate the farm by pursuing March, for example, plunges him immediately into a masquerade. Though a 'huntsman in spirit', he 'remained in appearance just the nice, odd stranger-youth, staying for a fortnight on the place' (24). From this vantage he stage-manages scene after scene of the novella. The seduction scene when he asks March to marry him is exactly that: a little drama in which Henry plays the part of the sincere lover, 'putting all the strange softness into his voice' (25). After coming back inside intent on angering Banford, his new opponent, Henry tries on a variety of masks. Perhaps 'you don't like me coming to tea without my coat' (27), needles Henry, posing as someone too natural to want to masquerade in conventional dress. A little later, sitting 'with his knees stuck wide apart' (28), he gives 'Banford's sitting-room the look of a lumber-camp'. Even after March changes into a dress, Henry displays his directing abilities: 'He had put her [March] in the corner, so that she should not look out and see the lighted window of the house' (53) and thus be reminded of Banford's presence. All of these stage-techniques are on display in the scene of Banford's death, where Henry watches her with 'intense bright eyes' (65) and cons her into standing still: 'the tone of his voice seemed to her to imply that he was only being falsely solicitous and trying to make her move because it was his will to move her' (65). Henry stage-manages her death skillfully, making a scrupulous fidelity to truth seem just fake enough to be interpretable as a masquerade and then mis-directing Banford to a faulty interpretation of it.

The unsettling implication here that the perception of truth owes every-thing to its staging also applies to the scene most critics see as a fairly unambiguous guarantee of Henry's masculine authority: his killing of the fox. Henry certainly presents himself as a powerful hunter. He is the man who did what March could not. He puts into practice the near-mythic 'supreme act of volition' (24), which the narrative attributes to the hunter's power over its prey, and perhaps assumes the power of the fox. Scholars have been suitably impressed: responses vary, but prominent among them are those which see Henry absorbing the primal energies of the fox, his 'psychic avatar' (Renner 258), and those which see Henry superseding the fox that once held March's attention, in which case the 'scene of trophy-display' terminates the 'imposition by March of a false identity for Henry' (Balbert 221). No one has yet remarked that the fox cannot signify Henry's manhood in any way until he has created and tried to command a thea-tre of self-dramatisation. '[H]olding up the warm, dead brute' (40) for inspection in the dark yard, Henry suddenly realises '"[y]ou can't see, can you? Wait a minute." And he took his flash-light from his pocket, and flashed it on to the dead animal.' Trophies, Henry recognises, must be staged appropriately if their meanings are to be read correctly. Once spot-lighted, the dead fox serves to underscore the hunter's prowess; 'He will make you a lovely fur' (40) he tells March, inviting her to make the fox signify his ability to provide for her. But whatever decision March or we readers come to about Henry's manhood must be contingent on the self-dramatisations – staging the fox and Banford's death, acting like a lumber-jack, dressing down for tea – that occur prior to whatever interpretations of them March (or we) can make.

The graver problem, which again plays no part in critical analyses of this story, is that Henry's heterogeneous performances are of indeterminate scope and extent. On what ground, for example, could we determine the truth of Henry's 'I mean what I say' (26) during the scene where he asks March to marry him? The scene could be construed as an unending performance: Henry works on her 'putting all the strange softness into his voice'; he 'sounded hurt'; he waits, 'watchful' (25–26) for the right moment to touch her. March's accusation of 'tomfoolery' (25) seems correct: he does not really mean what he says; his 'sounded hurt' is a sham. Or does his subsequent feeling of 'great exultance' (26) signal a shift – the moment when love breaks through the pose? Perhaps then it is possible after all to believe that Henry 'sounded hurt' because he was hurt? Or does his elation mean that he realises his pose is working? The point is that we cannot tell when, if ever, he 'really' wants to marry March and when, if ever, he really means what he says. There is therefore much justice in March's lament in her rejection letter, '[w]hat I don't seem to see at all is you' (57) – not simply because Henry's performances continue to suggest a 'false identity' but because the 'you' the narrative defines is (or I am arguing should be) a matter of conjecture, debate and contest.

It is worth pausing here to consider two clearly marked positions in the critical literature on *The Fox* that seem designed to overcome such an objection to a regimen of natural, even primal, identities. The first is to build on the logic that Henry is a 'huntsman in spirit' (24) and thus naturally inclined to hunt from cover; or remaining 'in appearance just the nice, odd stranger-youth' might be what the hunter-fox wears, trickster-like, in order to get into the hen-house. Henry's stagings might then be interpreted as appropriate actions for killer-males (fox or human). The second, keeping in mind the story's constant references to his boyishness and with a nod to its enigmatic conclusion, asserts exactly the opposite: Henry may not be old enough, not enough of a hunting *man*, to accomplish his purpose. Now Henry's penchant for self-dramatisation can be understood as a sign of the gap that separates him from self-sufficient manhood. So to Peter Balbert, Henry cannot emerge 'from youth into manhood' until the 'false identity' March has made between him and the fox can be erased and his adolescent obsession with 'voyeurism and melo-dramatic fantasy' starts to crumble.[21] Both positions are plausible. But we should note that both derive from and in turn secure a structural link between manly self-sufficiency and boyish copies. When Henry spotlights the dead fox in tribute to his hunting prowess, the critical literature has taken up two interlinked positions, which generate each other: if man, not boy; if boy, not man. Either Henry, a man, deploys the stratagems signifying his male power so that the trophy-fox simply 'means what it says', or Henry, a boy, possesses a gauche theatricality, which implies by contrast a self-possessed manhood that needs no trophy/trope to represent it. In so doing, these positions rule out of bounds a third possibility: masquerades of indeterminate extent, the consequence of which is to place the signifying function of the trophy-as-trope under scrutiny and to stage the problematic of a manhood that has to 'say what it means' if it is to mean anything at all.

What should really give us pause in attempting to establish once and for all the male 'you' behind Henry's poses is the extravagantly strange scene critics have tapped to delineate the end of the story's gender confusions: when March for the first time wears a dress, allegedly putting to rights transvestite disorder and her false masculine pose, while Henry awakens into manhood. Perceiving March as 'another being' (49), knowing her 'soft and accessible in her dress', seeing her 'much more subdued' (50), Henry 'suddenly ... felt a man' (49). The scene, as Gilbert and Gubar put it in the most complete consideration of masquerading in *The Fox*, 'definitively transforms the two of them into the true male and true female each had been all along' (338).[22] Most scholars, overtly or not, concur: March's dress authenticates her (and by extension Henry's) 'real self' (Draper 246) and in the process discloses the inauthentic poses that must have defined them prior to this moment. In preparation for revisiting the issue of masquerade in this scene, I want first to unpack some of the surprisingly complex manoeuvres that lead scholars to this simple assumption. For any reading insisting that Lawrence uses female dress to confirm the 'truly female' confronts what appears to be an intractable problem: Banford, who does wear 'soft blouses and chiffon dresses' (48) but whom Henry thinks of as possessing 'tiny iron breasts'. To him she seems scarcely a woman at all. Gilbert and Gubar corroborate Henry's conclusion when they argue that the scene displays the 'unwomanliness' of Banford, who becomes a 'sort of absurd female impersonator'.[23]

Gilbert and Gubar's solution – and again it is a determination many critics have made – is to organise Lawrence's masquerades around his privileging of heterosexuality. Dresses cannot establish Banford's true female nature because she is a lesbian.[24] Hence the 'tiny iron breasts': she is sexed but (to Henry) non-sexual. That is why she challenges Henry, why she must die and why she is a female impersonator: she is not a real – that is to say, heterosexual – woman. And that is why she casts conventional signs awry. While March temporarily masquerades in man's clothing, Banford's wearing of a dress seems to empty 'proper' (48) female attire of all meaning. A dress has no power to transform a fake (lesbian) woman into a woman. Oddly, though, a true woman such as March *must* wear a dress in order to display her hidden essence as a heterosexual woman to Henry's approving gaze. The logic of a 'female impersonator' implies that Lawrence, puzzlingly, must be working with not one but two foundational and near-contradictory expressions of womanhood. On the one hand, Lawrence organises his sense of the 'true female' around heterosexuality; the outward signs of Banford's inner being could betray her as a masquerader in no other way. Here dress codes may be revealing but are not constitutive of womanhood. On the other, since Henry seems unable to read March's heterosexuality until she wears a dress, Lawrence must view womanhood as a *correlation*, a bringing into harmony of attributes whose disordered relation to each other once defined the trouble with March's identity. Here dress codes are in fact constitutive of womanhood, since March could not come to full womanhood without them. To put this perplexing situation another way: Banford's masquerade cannot hide her true being, but March's true being cannot be recognised until she comes out of masquerade.

We should note, however, that applying a logic of correlation to the story requires a theory of heterosexual origins for the true female subject, if the more puzzling aspects of this approach are not to surface. For Banford most disorders the harmony of conventional and biological female attributes by appearing to correlate them perfectly. She possesses a female-sexed body, surpasses her culture's expectations about dress codes for women by wearing soft blouses and chiffon dresses, has an appropriately domestic demeanour, and maintains throughout the female weakness that in the end gets her squashed by a phallic tree. Looked at like this, the assumption that Banford is a lesbian becomes more than simply a plausible interpretation of the story: it is mandatory if one is to safeguard the ability to distinguish between a true 'transvestite disorder', March's temporary transvestism, and the sort of masquerade that has Banford emptying out cultural constructions of femininity by wearing them so well. To insist on Banford's lesbianism preserves the trope of masquerade as a tool for settling the sort of gender confusion that could arise were we to find no difference between the story's representations of March and Banford.

The history of Lawrence scholarship therefore poses a problem for any attempt to interpret Banford as an impersonator of authentic womanhood, since most readers accusing Lawrence of trying to reassert normative gender roles perceive Banford in a dress as a *woman*!

In one sense this divergence does not matter since virtually everyone reading the sartorial play in the story – March in breeches, Banford masquerading (or not) in a dress – employ some variant of Gilbert and Gubar's wonderful sleight-of-hand manoeuvre whereby March changes into the true female she 'had been all along'. To those who begin reading with the assumption that an idealised construction of obedient, heterosexual womanhood governs *The Fox*, March's change of dress must be inconsequential. It never signifies as a problematic transformation to be negotiated because the story has never permitted true transvestite disorder in the first place. One consequence is that the question I begin to raise above – how is it possible for different readers to perceive a woman in a dress as wholly in masquerade, or wholly out of it? – never arises because readers secure in their sense that stable gender categories govern the story from its first words all concur that whatever faces are thought to exist behind whatever masks they are thought to inhabit are effortlessly legible.

But the supposition that *The Fox* never embraces the disorienting energies of masquerade jibes awkwardly with the cascade of incongruities that appear in the scene when March first dons a dress, and a weirdly flippant, playfully disorienting narrative voice begins to dominate the supposedly happy occasion of her coming-out as a 'true female'. Henry, for one, seems completely bewildered. Unlike critics who read March's masquerade as being empty from the start, Henry seems unable to recognise what a properly subdued female self looks like until he has had his fill of compulsively staring at the dress. It upends his interpretive world. Far from imposing his gaze, he is mesmerised: he was 'unable to take his eyes off her' (48); 'he looked her up and down, up and down.' He exercises his scrutiny with lugubrious insistence – at one point he 'simply stared at March, while he ate his bread and margarine in huge mouthfuls' (49). And he exercises it with erotic insistence, so that the scene takes on overtones of a burlesque as he gapes at her fetishised form, seeing her 'legs move soft within her moderately short skirt' and noting her 'black silk stockings' (49).

The fact that this is a very eccentric burlesque engineered by March's putting the 'proper' clothes back *on* should, however, alert us to further discordances. March, having claimed what scholars like to consider her true self, feels 'unpeeled and rather exposed' (50), 'almost improper', and like a 'pink monkey' (49). Henry, supposedly responsible for returning

March to the way she 'had been all along', could not have been more surprised if 'she had suddenly grown a moustache' (48). Nothing here matches up. The narrative overdetermines the mastering and eroticising gaze that allows Henry to suddenly feel 'a man' by placing it amid a veritable avalanche of gazes. Everywhere we look Henry is looking, staring, mesmerised while he wolfs his food, slurps his tea and 'shove[s] his nose in his teacup' (49). Underscoring the fetishising male gaze so vehemently, the scene makes it minutely scrutable. We have our noses shoved in its machinations, its functioning and effects. For her part, March wears the correct clothes and acts in a more subdued manner – but also feels like a pink monkey and 'unpeeled' (like a banana?). And the narrative voice continues to emphasise the perversely farcical effects of this return to gender norms by situating the three characters amid a jumble of public ceremonies – a 'wedding' (49), a 'funeral', the 'last supper' (50) and, hilariously, the Mad Tea-Party from Lewis Carroll's *Alice's Adventures in Wonderland* (1865). 'March was suspicious as a hare' (24) the narrator informs us at one point, and no wonder: the 'everlasting tea' she serves matches the 'never-ending meal' the March Hare enjoys to the 'distant sobs of the miserable Mock Turtle'[25] – Banford, who 'turtle[s] up' (51) in this scene before she bursts into a 'spasm of sobs'. And Henry, curiously, curiously at least for critics who have pondered his totemic attributes as the fox, suddenly appears in wholly new guise as the Dormouse with 'a little hot tea upon its nose' (59) and as the (head of the) Cheshire Cat with a 'rather wide, cat-shaped face', and again, a face 'wider' and 'cat-like' (50).

The scene marking the end March's transvestism re-positions her as a woman – and immediately launches a sort of music-hall variety show. She becomes a pink monkey, a banana, the March Hare, a bride, a corpse, a woman wearing a moustache, perhaps a prostitute.[26] Farcical, burlesque, lugubrious, full of 'tomfoolery', the scene embraces a disorderly array of theatrical registers, posing the 'heaviness of male destiny' (49) against a serio-comic send-up of a gaping male burlesque audience and placing the woman who impersonated a man back into female dress, whereupon the narrative proceeds to imagine Henry's bewildered apprehension of March as a sort of female female impersonator: a woman with a moustache impersonating a (wo)man! Unsurprisingly, *The Fox* draws to an end with Henry's confusion unresolved and the narrative still working through the enigmatic procedures of the rhetorical double-back. As the couple waits to depart for Canada, Henry feels that March, once she submitted, 'would not be a man any more, an independent woman with a man's responsibility' (70). Beginning in complete illogic (March would not be a man *any more*?!), the sentence attempts to backtrack by supplying a clause in apposition whose meaning turns out to be in opposition: 'A man, woman'. But this floundering question mark of a sentence, this stab at suturing incompatible elements together, this aporia, is in perfect keeping with the pivotal scene where March and Henry attempt to align their future with conventional gender norms and succeed only in unleashing a barrage of shifting impersonations.

II

The supposed termination of March's 'transvestite disorder' in the scene which seems most obviously responsible for hammering home Lawrence's reassertion of traditional gender roles underscores instead the destabilising power of masquerade. March's proper/almost improper dress fractures into an array of masks; humans don hare- and pink monkey- and cat-fur; and the end of the tale teases us with the possibility that March, far from being the woman she had been all along, becomes once more the 'man' she never was. In turn, Lawrence's costume changes and rhetorical tomfoolery draw attention to the way in which exegeses of the story have tended to erase its illogic and buffoonery, its staginess, its hints of identities remaining prob-lematically in masquerade, and in so doing have enforced the traditional gender roles that scholars have simply assumed underpinned the story. But what makes it possible for so many scholars to close down the story's theatrical registers? What is at stake in enforcing traditional gender roles in a narrative that seems intent on confusing them utterly? I conclude this essay by sketching the outline of an answer to these questions.

In part, the concept of masquerade has risen to prominence because of its viability as a critical tool. Masquerade appears virtually synonymous with a critique of the symbolic order; its fluidity distances and alienates truth, ontology, heterosexuality, cultural constructions of gender, dress codes, aesthetic codes and more. But for many scholars of the gender of modernism, the potential of masquerade can be secured only by female modernists (and, as Mary Ann Doane writes, by female interpreters) who have 'more invested in changing the gender restrictions signaled by cos-tume'.[27] High modernists such as Lawrence, Pound, Eliot, Yeats and Joyce, whatever purchase their works have on masquerade, aim at an 'essentializ-ing view' of a 'fixed and readily identifiable truth'[28] which underpins their attempts to 'excavate an ontological link between biological sexuality and the traditional sexual ideologies whose disintegration they found so dis-turbing'.[29] Narrative (and poetic) form participates in this recuperation of a substantial ground of identity. As Suzanne Young puts it, to male modernists '[o]rnament and artifice were the enemies of the artistic order in the same way that 'unnatural' or 'deviant' sexuality was the enemy of the naturalized order constructed around heterosexual pairing.'[30]

Modernist studies in fact tend to deploy masquerade as a reversible figure equally adept at exploding gender categories or enforcing them. Once the strategies male modernists use to curb its subversive play are exposed – once we concede that Lawrence putting March back into a dress reserves masculinity for Henry alone – the category of masculinist writing can be identified, and identified moreover as an act of narrative coercion. Upon that foundation literary historians confidently demarcate a High male modernism in opposition to the female or queer. And, since masquerade incorporates the 'uncertainty of the modern age'[31] and thus exemplifies the subversive potential of modernity, the masculinist move to shut it down serves to displace High masculine modernism from the privilege that has often been claimed for its superior powers of historical representation. More subtly, studies of the gender of modernism consistently depend on one particular element of the discourse on male masquerade to structure and secure their arguments: the assumption that male modernists were impelled by anxiety over the threatened loss of their social power and cultural prerogatives. The anxiety hypothesis comprehends the emergence of tropes of masking in male modernist writing as the product of a historical moment when men could no longer take masculinity at its ontological face value; it comprehends the closing down of those tropes as a yearning for the full presence of some authentic male self supposedly revealed once the mask comes off.

But in a story where March's wearing a dress reminds Henry of a woman sporting a moustache, and where March becomes a woman while somehow remaining 'a man' – where, in short, the boundaries defining masculinity remain permeable and mutable – it is legitimate to inquire whether the anxiety hypothesis explains everything and/or nothing. It runs the danger of enacting a wholly circular argument: Lawrence's anxieties lead him to write about March and Henry in masquerade, and their masquerades are how we know Lawrence must be anxious. Within that logic it is impossible to know, in fact impossible even to inquire, whether the narrative might represent masculinity as being *in play* rather than (or as well as) under threat, since every hint of 'play' has already been grasped as anxious self-display. To assert that transvestite disorder persists in the duplicitous rhetorical double-backs of *The Fox*, a story so often thought to celebrate male leadership and authority, therefore poses a challenge on numerous levels to literary histories built around the concept of anxious masculinist masquerades. It disrupts the anxious mask/true face dyad so common in scholarly analyses of this story by intimating that the 'you' behind the mask might not only be masked but capable of reproducing itself in a panoply of further masks. It suggests that the concept of masquerade cannot be employed securely to determine a category of masculinist modernism. And it raises the possibility that the attempt to do so is itself an anxious defense of the ability to determine gender categories at a historical moment, nearly a century after the publication of *The Fox*, when an emphasis on gender as performance is beginning to upset faith in such determinations – and favour the sort of confusion that positions March as 'a man … an independent woman'. It still sounds illogical to say that we cannot 'see at all' Lawrence's true male or female behind the costume changes. But who would have thought that March would come to her true self as a pink monkey? Or that when speaking to the March (Hare) Henry 'I mean what I say' Grenfel could, for a time, impersonate Alice in Wonderland?[32]

Notes

1 Hilary Simpson, *D. H. Lawrence and Feminism* (DeKalb: Northern Illinois University Press, 1982), p. 72. F. R. Leavis set this tone early with his comment that *The Fox* is a 'study of human mating; of the attraction between a man and a woman that expresses the profound needs of each and has its meaning in a permanent union'; see F. R. Leavis, *D. H. Lawrence: Novelist* (London: Chatto & Windus, 1955), p. 260. More scholars have taken the harder stance represented by Judith Ruderman's claim that for Lawrence 'male lordship must be encouraged as a necessary correction to female domination', Judith Ruderman, '*The Fox* and the "Devouring Mother,"' *The D. H. Lawrence Review* 10, 3 (Autumn 1977): 265.

2 Cynthia Lewiecki-Wilson, *Writing Against the Family: Gender in Lawrence and Joyce* (Carbondale and Edwardsville: Southern Illinois University Press, 1994), p. 108; Robert Burden, *Radicalizing Lawrence: Critical Interventions in the Reading and Reception of D. H. Lawrence's Narrative Fiction* (Amsterdam: Rodopi, 2000), p. 284.

3 H. M. Daleski, 'Aphrodite of the Foam and "The Ladybird" Tales', in Harold Bloom, ed., *Modern Critical Views: D. H. Lawrence* (New York: Chelsea House, 1986), p. 212.

4 Janice Hubbard Harris, *The Short Fiction of D. H. Lawrence* (New Brunswick: Rutgers University Press, 1984), p. 153.

5 Quoted in Cornelia Schulze, *The Battle of the Sexes in D. H. Lawrence's Prose, Poetry, and Paintings* (Heidelberg: C. Winter, 2002), p. 4.

6 Marianne DeKoven, *Rich and Strange: Gender, History, Modernism* (Princeton: Princeton University Press, 1991), p. 20; Claire Kahane, *Passions of the Voice: Hysteria, Narrative, and the Figure of the Speaking Woman, 1850–1915* (Baltimore: Johns Hopkins University Press, 1995), p. 64.

7 Hilary Simpson, *D. H. Lawrence and Feminism* (DeKalb: Northern Illinois University Press, 1982), p. 72. Having March 'not quite accepting her submergence' is a 'saving grace' of the story for H. M. Daleski, 'Aphrodite of the Foam', p. 212; and P. T. Whelan argues that one cannot make a 'clear-cut judgment about the last pages of *The Fox*', which in its 'inconclusiveness and its note of disharmony ... refrains from asking us to accept the total surrender of a lively woman to the mindless, phallic Pan-power of her lover', in 'The Hunting Metaphor in *The Fox* and Other Works', *The D. H. Lawrence Review* 21, 3 (1989): 285. Recently, Ronald Granofsky has followed the same logic: the story is typically Lawrentian in its concern that a woman 'must submit her will to the man in a heterosexual relationship' but unusual in that it ends with 'uncertainty, a groping', in *D. H. Lawrence and Survival: Darwinism in the Fiction of the Transitional Period* (Montreal & Kingston: McGill-Queen's University Press, 2003), p. 43.

8 Ian Gregor, '*The Fox*: A Caveat', *Essays in Criticism* 9 (1959): 10.

9 E. F. Shields considers that the ending makes for a 'seriously flawed' piece of work, in 'Broken Vision in Lawrence's "The Fox,"' *Studies in Short Fiction* 9 (1972): 363; and many have agreed.

10 Thomas Strychacz, *Dangerous Masculinities: Conrad, Hemingway, Lawrence* (University of Florida Press, 2007), pp. 176–188. The classic instance is the final statement of the novel, which in effect invites us to begin reading again in light of 'I don't believe that'.

11 Simpson, *D. H. Lawrence and Feminism*, p. 73.

12 Sandra Gilbert and Susan Gubar, *No Man's Land: The Place of the Woman Writer in the Twentieth Century, Vol. 2: Sexchanges* (New Haven: Yale University Press, 1989), p. 338. See also R. P. Draper, 'The Defeat of Feminism: D. H. Lawrence's *The Fox* and "The Woman Who Rode Away,"' *Studies in Short Fiction* 3 (1966): 186–188.

13 Although I take a very different route to this conclusion, I agree with David Seelow's point, in his brief reading of *The Fox*, that the novella 'eludes any stable alignment of sex-gender roles', *Radical Modernism and Sexuality: Freud/ Reich/D.H. Lawrence and Beyond* (New York: Palgrave/Macmillan, 2005), p. 94. I have also been influenced by Anne Fernald's argument that Lawrence's rhetoric always asks us to 'examine our own ideas and learn to fight back', '"Out of it": Alienation and Coercion in D. H. Lawrence', *Modern Fiction Studies* 49 (Summer, 2003): 188; and Paul Eggert's claim that Lawrence's prose is 'more chameleon, mercurial ... than has been recognised', 'Comedy and Provisionality: Lawrence's Address to his Audience and Material in his Australian Novels', in Paul Eggert and John Worthen, eds., *Lawrence and Comedy* (Cambridge: Cambridge University Press, 1996), p. 135.

14 Terry Castle, *Masquerade and Civilization: The Carnivalesque in Eighteenth-Century English Culture and Fiction* (Stanford, CA: Stanford University Press, 1986), p. 86.

15 Mary Ann Doane, *The Desire to Desire: The Woman's Film of the 1940s* (Bloomington: Indiana University Press, 1987), p. 32.

16 Suzanne Young, 'The Unnatural Object of Modernist Aesthetics: Artifice in Woolf's *Orlando*', in Elizabeth Jane Harrison and Shirley Peterson, eds., *Unmanning Modernism: Gendered Re-Readings* (Knoxville: University of Tennessee Press, 1997), p. 173.

17 Judith Butler, *Gender Trouble: Feminism and the Subversion of Identity* (New York: Routledge, 1990), p. 25.

18 Harry Brod, 'Masculinity as Masquerade', *The Masculine Masquerade: Masculinity and Representation* (Cambridge, MA: MIT Press, 1995), p. 17.

19 D. H. Lawrence, *The Fox, The Captain's Doll, The Ladybird*, ed. Dieter Mehl (Cambridge: Cambridge University Press, 1992), pp. 9, 10. Further references contained in text.

20 So authoritative is Henry's gaze that Linda Ruth Williams sees *The Fox* as a prominent exception to Lawrence's typical interest in the voyeuristic female gaze. See her *D. H. Lawrence* (Jackson: University of Mississippi Press, 1997).

21 Peter Balbert, 'Freud, Frazer, and Lawrence's Palimpsestic Novella: Dreams and The Heaviness of Male Destiny in *The Fox*', *Studies in the Novel* 38, 2 (Summer 2006): 225, 223.

22 Gilbert and Gubar, *No Man's Land*, p. 338.

23 Ibid.

24 As early as 1972 Leo Gurko noted that one of Henry's main obstacles 'is of course Banford, with whom March has a lesbian relationship', 'D. H. Lawrence's Greatest Collection of Short Stories: What Holds It Together', *Modern Fiction Studies* 18 (1972–73): 180. Lillian Faderman puts the same case more strongly, arguing that Lawrence 'teaches that lesbians are morbid and must be either killed or captured', *Surpassing the Love of Men* (New York: Quill, 1981), p. 350. More recently, Justin D. Edwards has argued that Lawrence adopts a more ambiguous approach to lesbianism; but he too accepts without question that March and Banford are lovers, 'At the End of *The Rainbow*: Reading Lesbian Identities in D. H. Lawrence's Fiction', *The International Fiction Review* 27, 1–2 (2000): 60–67.

25 Lewis Carroll, *Alice's Adventures in Wonderland and Through the Looking Glass* (London: J. M. Dent, 1981), p. 109.

26 Although I disagree with Claude Sinzelle's likening March to a prostitute (since Lawrence was supposed to have deemed crape dresses 'prostitutey' [168]), I appreciate the possibility that this is one more costume change for March. See her 'Skinning the Fox: A Masochist's Delight', in Peter Hoare and James T. Boulton, eds., *D. H. Lawrence and the Modern World* (Cambridge University Press, 1989), pp. 161–179.

27 Suzanne Young, 'Unnatural Object', p. 195.

28 Ibid., p. 176.

29 Gilbert and Gubar, *No Man's Land*, p. 326.

30 See Ben Knights, *Writing Masculinities: Male Narratives in Twentieth-Century Fiction* (London, Macmillan, 1999), p. 180. Knights' chapter on male impersonation in twentieth-century narrative argues against returning to an 'essentialist notion of gender' (136) but nonetheless perceives male authors writing in masquerade (here, in a female role) as an 'act of colonisation' (138).

31 Suzanne Young, 'Unnatural Object', p. 173.

32 Both Henry (to March) and Alice (to the March Hare) say 'I mean what I say' (Carroll *Alice*, 58; Lawrence, *Fox*, 26).

PART IV

Masculine Form

CHAPTER II

Engendering Adorno: On Time and Masculinity in Modernist Music

Tyrus Miller

I

Consideration of Theodor Adorno's theoretical and critical writings from the point of view of gender studies has been, to date, limited, although increasing as more of his texts have been made available in English translation and his ideas have found wide dissemination in current literary, artistic, musical and cultural studies. In 2006, for example, a collection of essays appeared in the Penn State Press's 'Re-reading the Canon' series under the title *Feminist Interpretations of Theodor Adorno*, which surveyed previously published and new writings on Adorno from a gender-critical and feminist perspective.[1] Similarly, feminist philosophers and critics in the German-speaking academy, where Frankfurt School 'critical theory' has been broadly incorporated into the cultural and social sciences, have also discussed Adorno, with attention to the gendered elements and implications of his conceptual repertoire.[2] Especial attention has been given to Adorno's social psychology, his theory of mass culture and 'culture industry', his philosophy of nature, and his 'negative dialectics' as a critical theory of difference, with affinities to, but also crucial divergences from, feminist and queer theories of sexual difference.

The present essay is indebted to that broad rereading of Adorno in progress, but approaches the 'engendering' of Adorno's thought with a couple of distinct restrictions on my field of inquiry. I am concerned specifically with Adorno's aesthetics of radical modernism – an indeed crucial and representative node of Adorno's thought, but by no means an exclusive one in the multifaceted, multidisciplinary investigations that compose his larger corpus of writings. Moreover, within this general topic of Adorno's modernist aesthetics, I will focus my discussion on a set of key texts dealing with musical modernism. This narrowing of scope is not, however, just a necessary pragmatic decision to control the mass of texts to deal with in a short number of pages. Modernist artworks and the aesthetics that Adorno derived from them fulfil, I would argue, important conceptual imperatives of his thought, providing models and examples of alternative modes of experience, organisation and action with relevance to extra-artistic domains of life as well. Moreover, my experience as a modernist scholar working with Frankfurt School theory suggests that despite Adorno's vast culture and the sweep of his writings across music, literature, theatre and to some extent visual arts, his most articulate consideration of modernism as a distinct historical formation of the arts is to be found in his musicological writings. Thus, by extension, if instances of artistic modernism furnished Adorno with diagnostic models of more encompassing social contradictions and figurative examples of alternative social forms, then the musical writings provide favourable passage into his labyrinthine and often bewilderingly complicated philosophical oeuvre.

At the centre of the Frankfurt School's theoretical account of aesthetic modernism – above all, in the work of Walter Benjamin and Theodor Adorno – was the question of modern temporal experience in the epoch of high capitalism and metropolitan urbanism. To what extent, they asked, did the artistic innovations of the later nineteenth and early twentieth century, beginning with Baudelaire and Wagner and continuing with futurist, expressionist, surrealist, and constructivist avant-gardes, reflect a new social structuring of experienced time? To what degree did this new time-sense confront artists and thinkers with new problems of writing narrative, interpreting history, creating coherence in temporally developed form, or representing the interweaving of objective and subjective temporalities in a complex fabric of lived time? To what extent does modernity, as a temporal complex, impact the ability of artworks to refer to history, to serve as indices of 'modern times'? And finally, is it possible to see within modern artworks new models of temporal experience or historical coherence that might serve as heuristics for new political, social, even scientific practice?

Both Benjamin and Adorno moreover consistently tied this concern with modernism's temporal dimensions to social and historical questions of artistic *comportment* and stance. Thus, for example, as expressions of the accelerating tempo of modern urban life, Benjamin singled out Baudelaire's regular changes of residence, his habit of writing in public places while standing up, his affirmation of the sudden *trouvé* snatched from the urban welter, and his self-reflexive image of the poet as fencer

parrying the shocks of the crowd. Deploying a new rhetorical and thematic armature, Benjamin argued, Baudelaire translated into specific
poetic expressive means and types the rapidly changing rhythms of fashion and obsolescence, the ebbs and flows of crowds in city streets, and the
disintegration of enduring habits under the pressure of novelty and sensation. Benjamin observes the same consistent disintegration of temporal
duration in the specifically sexual and gendered aspects of Baudelaire's
modernity: his fascination with prostitutes and lesbians (as images of
female sexuality separated from marriage and procreation), his sexual
impotence, his insistent imagery of male submission and erotic damna-
tion. Benjamin suggests that 'infertility and impotence are the decisive
factors' in Baudelaire's sexuality, and they must be understood in their
specifically negative relationship to the temporal durations established by
the institution of the family.[3] Baudelaire's 'erotology of the damned' is a
strongly gender-marked comportment towards a more general fractured
and accelerated temporality of the modern.

Adorno, I would suggest, identified an analogously altered artistic comportment as the complement of aesthetic modernity in musical
works that he valued as the most significant in modern music: the compositions of Richard Wagner, Gustav Mahler, Arnold Schoenberg, Igor
Stravinsky, Alban Berg, Anton von Webern, Karlheinz Stockhausen,
Pierre Boulez and John Cage. Yet, I will suggest, his emblematic image
of this comportment is not, first and foremost, a biographical figure like
Benjamin's Baudelaire, but rather a literary character: Homer's cunning
hero, Odysseus. Put in apposition to the canon of male modernist composers from Wagner to Cage, Odysseus becomes for Adorno a prism
through which to consider the problem of the modern artist's appropriate comportment towards the condition of modernity. Thinking through
the Odyssean predicament, Adorno thus poses key questions for the
modernist composer: How can a modern composer engage in artistically productive dialogue with psychically archaic and historically anterior
material, while avoiding the twin dangers of regression and repression?
What 'stance' must be adopted towards the past and future to achieve
this result? As I have already suggested with Benjamin's Baudelaire, this
question of comportment and stance in turn expresses itself in gendered
characteristics of the male artists from whom Adorno's aesthetic canon is
constituted. The critical modernism that Adorno champions is not simply, I would argue, a new way of making artworks; it is also, implicitly, a
different way of being male.

II

A key starting point for considering the role of sexual difference in
Adorno's thought is the 'excursus' on Homer's Odyssey in Adorno's collaborative text with Max Horkheimer, *Dialectic of Enlightenment*. This chapter has formed a nodal point for critical discussions of Adorno's sexual
politics, including important essays by Rebecca Comay, Andrew Hewitt,
and Sabine Wilke and Heidi Schlipphacke.[4] Adorno and Horkheimer
explore in *Dialectic of Enlightenment* a formative dialectic of 'error /
errancy' and 'proof' in the long history of the bourgeois subject, and
accordingly, their textual 'excursus' on antiquity lies squarely at the centre
of their critique of contemporary subjectivity as the final exasperation of
humanity's 'domination of nature'. Odysseus's dalliances with Circe and
Nausicaa, his reconciliation with his faithful wife Penelope, and his cunning disarming of the Sirens' seductive but fatal song were key to Adorno
and Horkheimer's genealogy, which interweaves Nietzschean, Weberian
and Freudian notions of how sexual repression, ascetic renunciation and
the marginalisation of bodily experience shape our conception of modern,
enlightened 'man'. Their excursus already explicitly engages with issues of
male and female gender roles, the gendered division of labour and of pleasure, and the psychological dispositions related to patriarchal mastery and
subjugated femininity. Feminist critics thus to some extent are retracing
the lineaments of a gender critique already threaded through Adorno and
Horkheimer's account of bourgeois subject formation, but they also render this critique of gender more explicit and consistent, expose its limits
and blind spots, and extend it to other facets of Adorno and Horkheimer's
complex interdisciplinary melange of sources.

For my purpose, however, the most pivotal of the Homeric episodes treated in *Dialectic of Enlightenment* is that of the Sirens, which
is discussed in Adorno and Horkheimer's first chapter, 'The Concept of
Enlightenment'. Adorno and Horkheimer interpret the episode allegorically, to explicate how enlightenment separates present experience from the
historical past, allowing the past to provide material for practical, instrumental goals but disarming it of any substantial challenge to the present
order of things. They suggest that one of the burdens of Odysseus's wandering is precisely to organise the identity of life in relation to a coherent structure of time that breaks with the mythic structures of recurrence
or archaic timelessness. As the protagonist of epic, Odysseus's life itself
is subjected to the unfolding and organised recursions of narrative time.
A key effect of this temporal reorganisation, however, is to reconstitute

the past as experiential 'material', available for disposal and application in present circumstances, rather than appearing as the effective force of the archaic – for instance, the threatening primordiality personified by the cave-dwelling cattle herder Polyphemos:

> What Odysseus left behind him entered into the nether world; for the self is still so close to prehistoric myth, from whose womb it tore itself, that its very own experienced past becomes mythic prehistory. And it seeks to encounter that myth through the fixed order of time. The three-fold schema
> [past / present / future – T.M.] is intended to free the present moment from
> the power of the past by referring that power behind the absolute barrier of
> the unrepeatable and placing it at the disposal of the present as practicable knowledge.[5]

But the real goal of this discussion for Adorno and Horkheimer is to discern the original sin of art in its anthropogenesis out of the world of myth. Accordingly, they situate art's birth in Odysseus's cunning evasion of the mythical allure of the Sirens' song. Not only does Odysseus's victory over myth put the present out of the reach of the mythic forces of the archaic past; it also generates a new way for the past to return, as disenchanted myth: as art, or more precisely, as *music*.

In their discussion of this episode, Adorno and Horkheimer attend to the specific 'technology' of Odysseus's cunning ruse for defeating the Sirens: his stopping the ears of his oarsmen, while having himself bound to the mast to allow him to hear the Sirens' song without fatal consequences. What they discern in the Homeric episode is nothing less than what would come to full fruition in the total concert-hall experience of nineteenth-century Bayreuth, or the radio apparatus that disseminated music to a mass audience beginning in the later 1920s, or the sports arena spectacle of a contemporary rock concert. In Odysseus's technical arrangement of his passage by the Sirens' rock, there are arrayed the manual labourers who are excluded from the enjoyment of the Sirens' song, while at the centre of the staging is fixed the ship's sovereign master, who may enjoy the song's full sensuous force. Yet this privilege of enjoyment is purchased only at the cost of quarantining music from the experience of labour and its reception in a state of immobilisation and willed passivity: '[Odysseus] listens, but while bound impotently to the mast; the greater the temptation the more he has his bonds tightened' (34). For Adorno and

Horkheimer, this division underlies the incapacity of music to transform the domain of present-day social practice, despite presenting an experientially coherent corrective to its insufficiencies:

> The bonds with which [Odysseus] has irremediably tied himself to practice, also keep the Sirens away from practice: their temptation is neutralized and becomes a mere object of contemplation – becomes art. The prisoner is present at a concert, an inactive eavesdropper like later concertgoers, and his spirited call for liberation fades like applause. (34)

The master's passive consumption of the sensuous pleasures of art is the antithetical complement of his mastery over the instrumental force of manual labour. The division between these two severed realms is mutually constitutive and mutually reinforcing – an ever-deepening division that Adorno and Horkheimer believe paralyses social change rather than providing it with the motive force of dialectical antagonism.

Within this paradoxical scenario of Odysseus's masterful submission to the Sirens, Adorno and Horkheimer also discern the gendered polarity implied by the male epic hero's confrontation with feminine voices emanating out of the mythic world. The Sirens' song speaks of the deep past, as well as the more recent historical past, in ways that threaten the achieved masculine subjectivity of the epic hero:

> The Sirens' song has not yet been rendered powerless by reduction to the condition of art. ... While they directly evoke the recent past, with the irresistible promise of pleasure as which their song is heard, they threaten the patriarchal order which renders to each man his life only in return for his full measure of time. ... Even though the Sirens know all that has happened, they demand the future as the price of that knowledge. (32–33)

Just as in his encounter with the Cyclops Odysseus sacrifices his nominal identity ('Udeis' as 'No-Man') to survive his encounter with mythic forces, in his withstanding the test of the Sirens' song, Odysseus sacrifices his virility to conquer an overwhelming feminine power pulling him into the recurrent temporality of the archaic past. Bound to the mast and crying out, he paradoxically achieves a victory of male power that allows him to return to his place on the throne at Ithaca and in the bed of Penelope. As Adorno and Horkheimer suggest:

> It is impossible to hear the Sirens and not succumb to them; therefore he does not try to defy their power. ... Odysseus does not try to take another route that would enable him to escape sailing past the Sirens. And he does not try, say, to presume on the superiority of his knowledge and to listen freely to the temptresses, imagining that his freedom will be protection

enough. He abases himself. ... He keeps to the contract of his thraldom and struggles in his bonds at the mast, trying to cast himself in the destroyers' arms. ... Odysseus recognizes the archaic superior power of the song even when, as a technically enlightened man, he has himself bound. He listens to the song of pleasure and thwarts it as he seeks to thwart death. (58–59)

The sexualised agon of Odysseus and the Sirens is concluded in favour of a new, bourgeois pact of male hegemony, the marriage contract through which both male and female are unequally subjugated. The defeat of the Sirens, which in a sense comes at the expense of Odysseus's own virility, is decisive for the subsequent fate of music. 'Since Odysseus' successful-unsuccessful encounter with the Sirens all songs have been affected', they write, 'and Western music as a whole suffers from the contradiction of song in civilization – song which nevertheless proclaims the emotional power of all art music' (59–60). Art music hereafter hovers ambiguously and irresolutely between two possibilities: between the unsublimated, eroticised pleasure of the Sirens song, and inert sonorous material bereft of any affective force.

III

Adorno and Horkheimer's discussion of the Sirens in *Dialectic of Enlightenment* has generally been connected to Adorno's concerns with 'the regression of listening' in his writings on radio, recording technology and the culture industry. In this interpretation of the allegory, characteristic of *Dialectic of Enlightenment*'s paradoxical historical anthropology, the very first experience of listening would also be the very first instance of the regression of listening. Odysseus is already, *in nuce*, the avid radio listener and record collector. This is clearly on the surface of Adorno and Horkheimer's concern and key to their diagnostic of the present as that moment in which the dialectic of enlightenment has entered a final self-destructive or redemptive self-transcending phase. Despite this critical and largely 'negative' deployment of Odysseus and his cunning self-consciousness, however, I want also to suggest that there is another face of this figure, more positively turned towards artistic modernism.

Going beyond the more obvious allegory equating Odysseus and the musical listener, we might ask: what if Odysseus were also potentially a depiction of the modern *composer* and the Sirens episode a parable about compositional method? In that case, we would see Odysseus's predicament no longer primarily as a matter of a forbidden pleasure that can be experienced only at the cost of its neutralisation, but rather as that of modernism's delicate artistic compromise struck between raw, archaic affects and abstract, intellectualising formalism, a dynamic compromise negotiated through singular, specific, cunningly desperate acts of composition. In other words, implicit in Odysseus's sly ploy with the Sirens may reside a more positive exemplar for the modern composer, who is fraught by the twin dangers of primitivist regression and formalistic abstraction; Odysseus's stratagem in this context offers an image not of repression, but of successful artistic sublimation (which nevertheless, as Nietzsche and Freud remind us, is still a mode of repression transformed).[6] Moreover, this reinscription of the allegorical reference may also have revisionary implications for the gender implications that Adorno and Horkheimer discern in the Sirens episode. If the first interpretation would lead us to see the encounter with the Sirens as a desexualisation of both male and female, but under the sign of a domesticated male dominance in the marriage contract, the second would emphasise the utopian aspects of Odysseus's surrender of aggressive virility in favour of a heightened sensuous receptivity and intensity. Although in general this second interpretation is at best an undercurrent in *Dialectic of Enlightenment*, Adorno's musicological writings suggest that he was indeed willing to draw these more positive conclusions as well from the Sirens scenario, as they apply to the situation of the modernist composer.

Let us consider, for example, the following characterisation in Adorno's essay on Anton von Webern's *String Trio*:

> The trio is constructed down to its very last note, but has nothing constructed about it: the power of the shaping spirit and the nonviolence of an ear that simply listens passively to its own composition while composing come together in a single identity. An irrepressible mistrust toward the active intervention of the subject in his material, as a shaping presence, might well serve to define Webern's stance.[7]

Here the passive receptivity of Odysseus, cunningly defending himself against the fatality of mythic voices, has become a positive willingness to receive mimetic communication from the musical materials, to take on, as composing subject, the characteristics of the object rather than to impose subjective tastes, judgements and meanings upon it. Moreover, in this passivity and stance of non-violence, Adorno sees a gendered defence against patriarchal authority in the art world, a willingness to set aside heroic masculinity in favour of an ethically motivated practice of relinquishing power:

> It is the stance implied in his motivic micro-work in the first miniatures: its aim was the defense against the arbitrary, against caprice. The need for

security, a kind of wariness, is something he shared with his friend Berg. Possibly a response to the pressure exerted by Schoenberg's authority, it brought both of them in opposition to the dominating, patriarchal manner of his music. ... The authenticity of the impact he has made derives from such a lack of violence, from the absence of the composer as sovereign subject. (100–101)

With respect to Berg, Adorno goes still further, positively affirming the passive element in Odysseus's submission as a consistent compositional stance with implications for the formal principle of the musical works. Berg, he writes, 'unlike Schoenberg, had something passive about him'.[8] But he deployed this passivity to achieve internally coherent large-scale forms without the formal twelve-tone rows that Schoenberg saw as a necessary means to this end. 'The question of specific relevance to Berg', Adorno concludes, 'is how it can be possible for an act of constant yielding, listening, a gesture of gliding, of not asserting himself, to culminate in something like a large-scale form' (187). In his book-length study of Berg, Adorno similarly states that 'Evanescence, the revocation of one's own existence, is for Berg not the stuff of expression, not music's allegorical theme, but rather the law to which music submits.'[9]

Moreover, Berg's passivity is not simply an aesthetic stance towards his materials, it is also an ethical disposition towards their social significance. This is evident when Berg, like Gustav Mahler before him, 'carries along the lower, cast-off music, or rather reawakens it as subterranean folklore',[10] as he does in the lullaby that Marie sings to her child, in the military parade music, or in the tavern music that is incorporated in grotesque anamorphic projection in *Wozzeck*. The social valence of Berg's passivity is even more manifest in relation to his *dramatis personae* such as Marie and Franz in *Wozzeck*, or Lulu, Alwa, and Countess Geschwitz in *Lulu*. Here the Odyssean passivity of the composer's listening ear is the first step to a social, even political passion for the oppressed, in which Adorno saw the redemptive possibility to disarm inexorable – seemingly cosmic, mythic – fate. He concludes his early essay on *Wozzeck*, published in 1929, with the following words:

> The entire third act skirts the abyss; the music contracts and counts the minutes until death. Then it throws itself into the orchestral epilogue and is reflected as distantly, in the children's scene of the conclusion, as the blue of the sky appears at the bottom of a well. This reflex alone indicates hope in *Wozzeck*. ... It illuminates the character of the opera softly, and late. Its character is *Passion*. The music does not suffer within the human being, does not, itself, participate in his actions and emotions. It suffers over him.

... The music lays the suffering that is dictated by the stars above bodily onto the shoulders of the human being, the individual, Wozzeck. In wrapping him in suffering so that it touches him wholly, it may hope that he will be absolved of that which threatens ineluctably in the rigid eternity of the stars. (625)

Adorno's comments on Berg are consistent with the more general philosophical orientation he would articulate in later writings such as *Negative Dialectics*, *Aesthetic Theory*, and related essays, in which the accent falls on a certain subjective passivity – a disposition to suspend subjective mastery, allowing oneself to be 'affected' by the object, to experience it as a 'passion'. Thus, for example, in his late essay 'Subject and Object', Adorno writes of a 'fearless passivity' that is proper to the conduct of the negative dialectician:

The preponderant exertion of knowledge is destruction of its usual exertion, that of using violence against the object. Approaching knowledge of the object is the act in which the subject rends the veil it is weaving around the object. It can do this only where, fearlessly passive, it entrusts itself to its own experience. In places where subjective reason scents subjective contingency, the primacy of the object is shimmering through – whatever in the object is not a subjective admixture. The subject is the object's agent, not its constituent.[11]

Adorno suggests that appropriate to the dialectical thinker's stance – or to the dialectical artist, as he implies Berg should be characterised – is a certain submissiveness and humble servitude towards the material world, of which he is the only the facilitating 'agent' and not the originating creator. (One might also note here Adorno's deep appreciation and understanding of Samuel Beckett, whose imperative murmuring voices in the head are not only signs of schizophrenic dissociation, but also harkening recollections of the voice of Nature which, to the closed subjective reason of *Endgame*'s Hamm, is thought to have 'forgotten us'.)

In another essay on Berg, Adorno gives this stance of submission and servitude, this 'fearless passivity', a specific erotic accent. He thus explicitly connects Berg's embrace of passivity as a compositional method to the highly charged gendering of the dramatic situations in his operas. Not just passivity, but male erotic submission, Adorno suggests, characterises the composer's relation to his feminine love-objects in the operas *Wozzeck* and *Lulu*:

The degenerate, addicted aspect of Berg's music is not a feature of his own ego. It does not aim at narcissistic self-glorification. Rather, it is an erotic enslavement, the object of which is nothing other than beauty and which calls to mind a nature that has been oppressed and degraded by the taboos of culture. The two great operas, *Wozzeck* and *Lulu*, contain nothing heroic, and in them spirit puts on no airs. Instead their enslaved and lethal love attaches itself to the lower depths, to lost souls, to the half-demented and at the same time helplessly self-sacrificing soldier, to his beloved whose instincts rebel against him and whom he destroys together with himself. Later that love attaches itself to Lulu. ... This music gives not alms, but total identification; without reservation it throws itself away for the sake of others.[12]

With this passage in mind, we can almost discern in the bondage of Odysseus, tied to the mast and tormented by seductive female voices, an archaic anticipation of the 'lower depths' of Frank Wedekind's human circus world or Bertolt Brecht's underworld characters. The erotic enslavement gripping *Wozzeck*'s Franz or *Lulu*'s Alwa and Countess Geschwitz, or the 'sexuelle Hörigkeit' (sexual dependency) balladed by Mrs. Peachum in Brecht's *Three-Penny Opera*, paradoxically appears in a redemptive light. Male sexual servitude, Adorno suggests, is modernism's exacerbated figure of a still-latent, utopian masculinity, which, in sacrificing without reserve the last vestiges of heroic virility, discovers in submission a new expressive language of sympathy with the oppressed. Adorno renders the connection of Berg and Odysseus even more explicit, when he suggests that Berg is capable of listening with such sympathy to the voice of the past, that he is able to open himself to the seductive affections of kitsch, without himself making kitsch of these emotions:

> Such a tone was always part of Berg's spiritualized music. Stylistic purists imagine themselves superior to such things and talk about kitsch when it shocks them. They hope to protect themselves against the shock of the parental world and against a seductiveness that they feel as strongly as Berg, but they lack the strength to expose themselves to it while retaining their self-control. Thanks to this strength, Berg has something of what Wedekind, the author of *Lulu*, also possessed. Karl Kraus praised his *Pandora's Box* by saying that in it trashy poetry became the poetry of trash. ('Alban Berg', 79)

Adorno speaks of 'strength', but he means a specifically modern form of artistic *virtù* different from that possessed by the virile heroes of the past, or embodied by the brute muscularity of *Lulu*'s acrobat. He means a paradoxical having the strength to let go of power, having the capacity for a sympathy that approaches a traditionally feminine-coded weakness and sentimentality – yet which artistically merits the characteristic that Adorno identified in Berg as 'great-heartedness' ('Alban Berg', 72).

IV

As I have suggested, Adorno links musical form, historico-anthropological time (myth, history and utopia), and masculine erotic dispositions in a single critical constellation. As might be expected, this constellation comes into clear view in relation to Richard Wagner, who lies at the origin of Adorno's musicological corpus. Taking up an argument against Nietzsche's negative criticism of Wagner's decadence, Adorno revalues decadence as an estimable mode of passivity, a willed weakening of the artistic ego's domination of its material, which potentially facilitates a new alignment of the past with the future:

> There is not one decadent element in Wagner's work from which a productive mind could not extract the forces of the future. The weakening of the monad, which is no longer equal to its situation as monad and which therefore sinks back passively beneath the pressure of the totality, is not just representative of a doomed society. It also releases the forces that had previously grown up within itself.... There is more of the social process in the limp individuality of Wagner's work than in aesthetic personas more equal to the challenge posed by society and hence more resolute in meeting it.[13]

In ironic agreement with Nietzsche, who maliciously encapsulated the gendered implications of Wagner's decadence by arguing that the Ring operas and Flaubert's *Madame Bovary* were siblings of the same psychological impulse, Adorno likewise underscores the erotic aspect of decadence in Wagner, his masochism and resignation of heroic masculinity. But Adorno lends this ascription a positive accent:

Even the masochistic capitulation of the ego is more than just masochistic.

> It is doubtless true that subjectivity surrenders its happiness to death; but by the same token it acknowledges a dawning realization that it does not wholly belong to itself. The monad is 'sick', it is too impotent to enable its principle, that of isolated singularity, to prevail and to endure. It therefore surrenders itself. Its capitulation, however, does more than just help an evil society to victory over its own protest. (154)

In Adorno's view, the monadic individual – which we see in its formation with the Homeric hero Odysseus and in its dissolution amidst Wagner's 'twilight' – is a formation of both social relations of production and gendered relations of reproduction. For Odysseus, his ear-stopped sailors and his faithfully waiting wife were mutually constitutive facets of his subjectivity; so too the enslaved Niebelungen and the familial palace of Walhalla, built from their pilfered gold, are fatally intertwined for the doomed characters of Wagner's Ring. Surrender of heroic masculinity and submission to pleasure, even unto death, represents Wagner's protest against a world order in which love has been displaced by law, property and contract, and hence can be experienced only as fatal transgression:

> Ultimately, [capitulation] also smashes through the foundations of the evil isolation of the individual itself. To die in love means also to become conscious of the limits imposed on the power of the property system over man. It means also to discover that the claims of pleasure, where they were followed through, would burst asunder that concept of the person as an autonomous, self-possessed being that degrades its own life to that of a thing, and which deludes itself into believing that it will find pleasure in full possession of itself, whereas in reality that pleasure is frustrated by the act of self-possession. (154)

Love-death yields to the fatal voice of myth, calling the human to regress back to the elements of earth and water. Yet recurrently, in ever-diminishing amplitude, it also holds consciousness upright against this regressive descent. Masculinity is therefore not so much abandoned in this process as radically refigured; it is torn asunder and resutured by the passionate intermittence of pleasure in the rhythmic fading of the subject. Wagnerian passion is thus not simply enjoyment of self-induced inanition of the present and regression to the archaic past, Adorno suggests. In their passion, Wagner's heroes also catch sight of a future in which the delusion of self-sufficient masculinity stands clarified in the light of death and the historical end of a fate-imprisoned world.

In compositional terms, Adorno suggests, the formal problem of how to handle recurrence and repetition also becomes an intensive point of ethical-erotic reflection on masculinity for the modernist composer. The mediating link is the question of time and its articulation by the organised recurrences of music. Thus, for example, Adorno discusses the reiterated gestural motifs that substitute in Wagner's operas, he argues, for genuine development:

> Sonata and symphony both make time their subject; through the substance they impart to it, they force it to manifest itself. If in the symphony the passage of time is converted into a moment, then by contrast, Wagner's gesture is essentially immutable and atemporal. Impotently repeating itself, music abandons the struggle within the temporal framework it mastered in the symphony. (*In Search of Wagner*, 37)

In his use of these compositional means, Adorno judges, Wagner remains a subjectivistic technician of repetition rather than a compositional agent of time's authentic coming to expression. Adorno perceives in Wagner's kaleidoscopic plethora of musical forms and colours an underlying sameness:

'Whereas Wagner's music incessantly arouses the appearance, the expectation and the demand for novelty, strictly speaking nothing new takes place in it' (42). Similarly, in an essay from 1963 on 'Wagner's Relevance for Today', Adorno would reiterate this objection to Wagner, now further inflecting his judgment with the critique of identity thinking that he had advanced in *Negative Dialectics* and which, I have suggested, also implies the necessity of radical change in the nature of masculine subjectivity:

> In Wagner unceasing change … ends in constant sameness. … For chromaticism – the principle par excellence of dynamics, of unceasing transition, of going further – is in itself nonqualitative, undifferentiated. One chromatic step resembles another. To this extent, chromatic music always has an affinity with identity.[14]

The incapacity to invite and actualise non-identity in musical composition is not simply a technical shortcoming, however; it is an ethical shortcoming in the creative comportment of the composer towards his materials, an index of insufficient strength to let go of masculine defences and allow the voice of the other to manifest itself within his artistic process.

Even more than Wagner, however, it is Stravinsky who most invites the charge from Adorno of mechanical repetition and the dissociative spatialisation of musical time. In his notorious attack on Stravinsky in *Philosophy of New Music*, Adorno suggests that Stravinsky carried to an exasperated limit Wagner's 'suspension of musical time consciousness', which manifests the experience of a bourgeoisie, 'which, no longer seeing anything in front of itself, denies the process of history itself and seeks its own utopia through the revocation of time in space'.[15] In Stravinsky, Adorno suggests:

> Time is suspended, as if in a circus scene, and complexes of time are presented as if they were spatial. The trick surrenders power over the consciousness of duration, which emerges naked and heteronomous and gives the lie to the musical intention in the boredom that arises. Instead of carrying out the tension between music and time, Stravinsky merely makes a feint at the latter. For this reason, all of the forces shrivel that accrue to music when it absorbs time. (142–143)

In a later reconsideration of Stravinsky, Adorno would relate this dissociation of time to another characteristic aspect of Stravinsky's work, his penchant for parody of other music. Adorno modulated his earlier critique into a subtle diagnosis of a self-directed violence unleashed by the problem of time for Stravinsky:

> He is beset by the crisis of the timeless products of a time-based art which constantly pose the question of how to repeat something without

developing it and yet avoid monotony, or else to incorporate it integrally. The sections... may not be identical and yet may never be anything qualitatively different. This is why there is damage instead of development. The wounds are inflicted by time, something which identity finds offensive and which in truth does not allow identity to persist. This is the formal, unliterary significance of the parodic style in Stravinsky. The necessary damage to the form appears as mockery of it. What Stravinsky's music does to his stylistic models, it also does to itself. He permanently wrote music about music, because he wrote music against music. His own bowed freely to a principle which was not just alien to itself; it was hostile. It inscribes itself in the music in the form of repression.[16]

By extension, then, Adorno suggests that a comportment that sets time apart as an alien otherness returns in the form of a self-directed destructive impulse. The gendered aspect of the violence remains implicit in Adorno's account, but clearly enough of it derives from the defence of masculine creative sovereignty against the implication of temporal posteriority. Historical derivation conjures up the spectre of sexual difference in the compositional field, insofar as the myth of the male artist as modernist self-progenitor, forever 'making it new', confronts the historical anteriority of musical styles. Unable wholly to repel or repress the feminine voice of temporal difference that sounds through musical history, Stravinsky's artistic masculinity recoils upon its own derivative constitution, registering the self-inflicted damage as an unsparing parodic deformation of traditional musical idioms.

I will conclude by suggesting two positive examplars that Adorno affirms, indicating a future direction for composition in a historically unprecedented tolerance for 'planned disorganization' and 'informality'. The first is given by Alban Berg, who I have already discussed at length. However, it is notable that in his 1961 essay on Berg, Adorno identified Berg as a forerunner of a 'musique informelle' that he saw as a way forward for a 'new music' that was showing, by the 1950s, symptoms of 'aging' and technical reification. With reference to Berg's 'March' from *Three Pieces for Orchestra, Opus 6*, Adorno observed that Berg had discovered ways of composing 'large-scale musical prose', one of salient achievements of which was its ability to manage recurrence in a radical new fashion with respect to the flow of musical time. Referring back to an analysis he had already made of the piece in 1937, Adorno offers a self-corrective observation:

> I no longer think of the third, self-contained entry of the March as a recapitulation. In reality the piece simply moves forward inexorably, much as marches do, without looking back. It is as if Berg had been the first to

explore from within a large-scale work the fact that the irreversibility of time is in profound contradiction to the recurrence of an identical being.[17]

Notably, one could say as much of Gertrude Stein in the literary realm: her work, from *Three Lives* and *The Making of Americans* on, explored the tensions between recurrence and non-identity in time. Out of these temporal dimensions inherent to language, Stein unfolded her vast series of experiments in non-hierarchical, 'prose informelle'. We might, accordingly, put Stein and Berg together in another respect as well: as complementary instances of a new type of modernist gendered subjectivity.

The other positive compositional exemplar is only sketchily given in another essay of 1961, whose title indicates its prospective nature: 'Vers une musique informelle'.[18] Although related to developments in the new compositions of Stockhausen, Boulez, and Cage that Adorno had been encountering at recent festivals and on the German radio, in the essay he is not willing to nominate any of these individuals as the new Odysseus who can apprehend authentically 'informal' music. Instead, he offers his readers only the image of an anonymous ear, at once Beckettian in its reduced purity and Odyssean in its unreserved openness to the sound of the material world. To this ear, the composing subject's total control over the sonorous material would already have become indiscernible from total surrender to the murmur of material itself: 'It must become the ear's form of reaction that passively appropriates what might be termed the tendency inherent in the material. ... It is comparable to the assertion that someone has mastered a language, an assertation which only possesses a meaning worthy of mankind if he has the strength to allow himself to be mastered by that language' (319). The gender of this unnameable artistic master is likewise to date unknown, yet such ignorance with respect to its nominal identity and gender is not contingent but definitive of its utopian mastery, a mastery marked by its continuous abdication of sovereignty. For as Adorno concludes, 'The aim of every artistic utopia today is to make things in ignorance of what they are' (322). An emancipated humanity too would dwell within the powerless utopia that informal works adumbrate – learning to compose its experience collectively and freely, according to the example of uncoerced events of sound.

Notes

1 *Feminist Interpretations of Theodor Adorno*, ed. Renée Heberle (University Park: Pennsylvania State University Press, 2006).

2 See, for example, Sabine Wilke and Heidi Schlipphacke, 'Construction of a Gendered Subject: A Feminist Reading of Adorno's *Aesthetic Theory*' in Tom Huhn and Lambert Zuidervaart, eds., *The Semblance of Subjectivity: Essays on Adorno's Aesthetic Theory* (Cambridge, MA: The MIT Press, 1997), pp. 287–308; and *Zwielicht der Vernunft: Die Dialektik der Aufklärung aus der Sicht der Frauen*, ed. Christine Kulke and Elvira Scheich (Pfaffenweiler, Germany: Centaurus, 1992).

3 Walter Benjamin, 'J66a, 9' in *The Arcades Project*, trans. Howard Eiland and Kevin McLaughlin (Cambridge, MA: The Belknap Press of Harvard University Press, 1999), p. 347.

4 For Comay and Hewitt, see note 1; for Wilke and Schlipphacke, see note 2.

5 Max Horkheimer and Theodor W. Adorno, *Dialectic of Enlightenment*, trans. John Cumming (New York: Continuum, 1972), p. 32.

6 Further to this motif of sublimation in Adorno, cf. Joel Whitebook, 'Sublimation: A Frontier Concept', in *Perversion and Utopia: A Study of Psychoanalysis and Critical Theory* (Cambridge, MA: The MIT Press, 1995), pp. 217–262.

7 Theodor W. Adorno, 'Anton von Webern', in *Sound Figures*, trans. Rodney Livingstone (Stanford, California: Stanford University Press, 1999), p. 100.

8 Theodor W. Adorno, 'Berg's Discoveries in Compositional Technique', in *Quasi una fantasia: Essays on Modern Music*, trans. Rodney Livingstone (London: Verso, 1992), p. 187.

9 Theodor W. Adorno, *Alban Berg: Master of the Smallest Link*, trans. Juliane Brand and Christopher Hailey (Cambridge: Cambridge University Press, 1994), p. 2.

10 Theodor W. Adorno, 'The Opera *Wozzeck*', in Theodor W. Adorno, *Essays on Music*, ed. Richard Leppert (Berkeley and Los Angeles: University of California Press, 2002), p. 624.

11 Theodor W. Adorno, 'Subject and Object', in Andrew Arato and Eike Gebhardt, eds., *The Essential Frankfurt School Reader* (New York: Urizen Books, 1978), p. 504.

12 Theodor W. Adorno, 'Alban Berg', in *Sound Figures* 72.

13 Theodor Adorno, *In Search of Wagner*, trans. Rodney Livingstone (London: New Left Books, 1981), pp. 153–154.

14 Theodor W. Adorno, 'Wagner's Relevance for Today', in *Essays on Music*, p. 597.

15 Theodor W. Adorno, *Philosophy of New Music*, trans. Robert Hullot-Kentor (Minneapolis: University of Minnesota Press, 2006), p. 140.

16 Theodor W. Adorno, 'Stravinsky: A Dialectical Portrait', in *Quasi una fantasia*, pp. 153–154.

17 Theodor W. Adorno, 'Berg's Discoveries in Compositional Technique', p. 190.

18 Theodor W. Adorno, 'Vers une musique informelle', in *Quasi una fantasia*, pp. 269–322.

CHAPTER 12

Stag Party: Henri Gaudier-Brzeska and Vorticist Organicism

Jessica Burstein

On 16 March 1914, Ezra Pound employed the word 'snuggly', and not as a term of denigration. It is easy to miss. In *The Egoist*'s 'Exhibition at the Goupil Gallery', Pound was following through on an earlier encomium of the sculptures of Jacob Epstein and Henri Gaudier-Brzeska, dedicating the column's first half to their different approaches to animal life; and the second half of the column to painters, singling out names which would become familiar to *Blast* readers that summer: 'Wyndham Lewis is well represented', '[Frederick] Etchells has gained greatly in strength', and [Edward] Wadsworth's 'refractions' are 'brilliant' and 'interesting'.[1] On the whole, another typical touting of Pound's coterie du jour – but for that little adjective.

This chapter will argue that the received account of the masculine, associated critically with virility and the usual accompanying litany of heteronormative givens, is too reductive a lens for viewing the full scope of what was at play in the artist Henri Gaudier-Brzeska. Even as a familiar gender binary is manifested in how one strand of art history, represented here by Wilhelm Worringer, was taken up by later modernists – with a coolly masculine geometric abstraction on the one hand, and a feminine strain associated with empathy on the other – that binary collapses in Gaudier's case. The collapse is two-fold: first, in the case of a differentiated set of aesthetics; and second, in the case of a sex-gender system based on definition by difference. The two are linked, and the collapse is a telling one, for it allows us to acknowledge another paradigm for aesthetic form operative in early twentieth-century modernists. Sex-gender dynamics here emerge as far more fluid, challenging how we read artworks, even and especially as those works are embedded in surrounding rhetorics that seek to rigidify what we see. Taken as exemplar, Gaudier's work provides an instance of not simply art and its surrounding accounts as conflicted, but an aesthetic that emerges in terms of that confusion. That aesthetic encompasses forms of life in which sexuality figures as dynamic, empathetic, fluid and, above all, organic. More widely, we see in Gaudier how artworks can trouble the very systems designed to support them. Discernible and insistent as it is, masculinism is reshaped under Gaudier's hand to encompass an organicism that does not conform to the easy allocations of our critical histories.

Owing to recent exhibitions, Vorticism has returned to the public eye.[2] This follows a period of literary-critical shyness regarding its import, indexed by Lawrence Rainey's 1998 conclusion that (compared to Italian Futurism), '*Blast* was indeed a dull affair'[3] and ranging at least up until Miranda Hickman's strategic 2005 concession that 'I am certainly not prepared to argue that, contrary to popular belief, Vorticism was a weighty, thoughtful, groundbreaking movement of great import.'[4] (This alongside Hickman's perspicacious investment in its resonance.) Critical histories lope alongside and behind artistic ones; it is this chapter's purpose to call into question the efficacy of neat critical histories in general, in particular one aligning abstraction with technophilia with Vorticism with masculinism, and then having done with it. However historically specific, Vorticism is a blanket term that should emerge as a little less comfortable, if a little more frayed. Organicism is our warp, and Gaudier our woof. But first, snuggly.

'Brzeska is in a formative stage, he is abundant and pleasing. His animals have what one can only call a "snuggly," comfortable feeling, that might appeal to a child. A very young child might like them to play with if they were not stone and too heavy.' ('EGG', 109) One of the pieces Pound was describing was Gaudier's sculpture *Stags*, to which we shall return. For the moment we linger over the peculiarity of the writer associated with praising the clean line giving any non-vicious airtime for something – synonyms fail – snuggly. Even the reference to children could be squeaked in as continuous with the pedagogical impulse later resulting in *ABC of Reading* (1934), *ABC of Economics* (1933), 'How to Read' (1931), and the continued compulsion to disquisition. Pound's pronouncements could lead to strange syllabi, but the wobbling of mere facts is here beside the point: one need not know anatomy in order to appreciate the deep strangeness of his suggestion that the brain is a clot of semen.[5] And to this as well, alas or otherwise, we shall return.

In the same issue of *The Egoist*, Pound responded in a letter to the editor, Dora Marsden, to an earlier complaint made by a reader signing himself as 'Auceps' (Richard Aldington) concerning Pound's 16 February 1914 treatment of, among other things, the Greeks ('probably the most unpleasant set of people who ever existed').[6] With 'The New Sculpture', in the course of dispensing with the Greeks, 'realism in literature', the 'psycho-intellectual novel' and those members of 'modern civilization' with 'brains like those of rabbits', Pound would single out for his campaign 'this new wild sculpture' ('NS', 68). 'One therefore says that Epstein is the only sculptor in England. One hears whispers of a man called Gill. ... And more recently one has come into contact with the work of a young sculptor Gaudier-Brzeska.' ('NS', 68) Rabbit-brains aside, 'wild' resonates positively, evoking a world unfettered by modern civilisation. It is of a piece with Pound's vaunting 'Djinns, tribal gods, fetiches [*sic*], etc. [in] the arts' ('NS', 68). Lisa Tickner captures the double-edged quality of modernist primitivist rhetoric in pointing out that 'one of the apparent paradoxes of modernism is its recourse to the "primitive" in pursuit of the new'.[7] In Gaudier's case the confluence of modernism and primitivism took most memorable written form in the epithet of 'savage messiah' eponymously accorded the sculptor by his biographer H. S. Ede, but originally coined by Gaudier's lover and fellow artist, Zofia Zuzanna (Sophie) Brzeska.[8]

Pound's 1914 swiping at the Greeks was a far cry from his famous 1912 endorsement of H. D.'s 'Hermes of the Ways' as the slither-less 'straight talk – straight as the Greek!'[9] and the Imagist school of poetry, but it was not the result of diagnosing degrees of success in different media. In 'The New Sculpture', Greek modes of representation were contrasted directly with those of other cultures, and it mattered that Pound was holding Gaudier and Epstein up over an art-historical gold standard, even as 'Auceps' begged to differ. Pound would reply to 'this pother about the Greeks' by stating that 'Art is not particularly concerned with the caressable,' and that Greek art too had its ups and downs. '[O]ut of a lot of remnants and fragments there remain certain masterpieces to be set apart and compared with other masterpieces from Egypt and from India and from China, and possibly from the south seas and other districts equally remote from Victorian or Pateresque culture.'[10]

In his equation of Greek art and 'masterpieces' from non-Western cultures, Pound was responding to ideas imported by the critic T. E. Hulme. It wasn't the first time. Hulme, as critics have noted, had been responsible for importing Henri Bergson to English readers; his 'authorised translation' of Bergson's *An Introduction to Metaphysics* and his *Introduction to Bergson* headed the list of 'Swift's Compelling List of New Books' in 1912 advertisements featured in *The Egoist*'s precursor, *The Freewoman* (topping even the listings for Pound and Katherine Mansfield, compelling-wise).[11] Hulme also brought Georges Sorel to England's notice, translating the 1908 *Reflections on Violence* into English in 1914. He was, as Edward

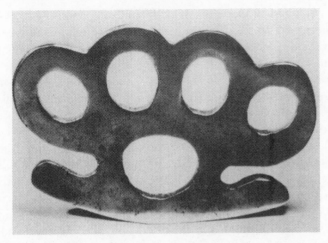

Figure 12.1. Henri Gaudier-Brzeska. *Knuckle-Duster.* 1914. Cut brass. 7.6 x 11.4 cm. (3 x 4.5 in.). Private collection.

Comentale and Andrzej Gasiorek put it, 'at the center of pre-war London's most advanced intellectual circles'.[12]

To his further credit, the man also wrote some rousingly dirty love letters to Kate Lechmere, a financial backer of the Rebel Arts Center and *Blast*. He addressed her as 'K. D.,' as in Knuckle-Duster (she did the same), named for the Gaudier 'toy' with which the two performed some mutually satisfying and unspeakable acts. Lechmere's explanation of Hulme's account of the object's design is helpful: 'The two pieces curving out sideways at the bottom are the woman's parted legs ... [T]he central hole is her vagina, and the four holes in a row at the top are the woman's head tossing and turning as she achieves [*sic*] orgasm.'[13] [Figure 12.1] O'Keeffe notes more chaste deployments as well: 'the philosopher liked to slip it on to his hand and playfully thump people on the arm to reinforce his arguments'.[14] (Hulme would fiddle with other of Gaudier's smaller sculptures 'while talking', according to Epstein, but scholarship has remained silent as to exactly how.[15]) At least two knuckle-dusters existed, and there is some imputation that the second was made for another of Lechmere's lovers, Wyndham Lewis.[16]

This is primitivism, at several levels. O'Keeffe casts Hulme's knuckle-duster as 'a fairly crude production' (229); the characterisation is right. Both knuckle-dusters are rather beautiful in their combination of metallic tactility and austerity, alongside the stilled kineticism of their fashioning – brass bent and whorled – and purpose(s). But snuggly, no. These are

'perfore', as Jonathan Wood notes: 'perforated' or 'pierced', 'a fact Gaudier
... was keen to detail ... in his list of works'.[17] A distinction need be drawn
between the organicism Gaudier would exhibit, and the aesthetic of violence and sex here brought to hand. Such objects were meant literally to
be grasped; *Knuckle-Duster* and objects Gaudier carved such as *Torpedo
Fish*, *Green Stone Charm* and *Ornament* are not intended to be observed
at remove. Whether primitivism connotes pre-modern, pre-industrial or
non-institutional art, the fact that Gaudier's toys were not all too heavy to
handle is key. Wood taxonomizes Gaudier's 'small-scale objects' in terms
of reflecting a Vorticist aesthetic that included 'not only the mechanised
objects and processes of technological modernity (the machine, the gun,
the drill), but also notions of craftsmanship (the artisan, the carver, the
worker), ideas of magic, animism and "primitive" agency (talismans,
charms, amulets and totemic animalia), physical violence and sport
(knuckledusters, boxing, wrestling) and erotica and sexual symbolism
(fertility symbols, genital imagery, sex toys)' ('O', 43).

However, Hulme's still critically underestimated effect in literary-critical accounts of Anglo-American modernism, despite the fine work of
Michael Levenson,[18] rests in importing the ideas of Wilhelm Worringer to
the English art scene. That Worringer reckoned with the aesthetic value of
non-Western art animated Pound's March 1914 references to non-Western
masterpieces and the concomitant idea that Epstein and Gaudier were not
just following in those footsteps but ahead of the English herd in doing so.
In this way, Hulme, via Worringer, drew a line from the past to the possibility of future art, and the implicit ratification of contemporary artists.

In the 16 February 1914 piece Pound began with an account of Hulme's
talk 'some nights ago', 'an almost wholly unintelligible lecture on
cubism and new art at large' ('NS', 67). Almost wholly unintelligible or
not, Pound was a quick study; Hulme's talk is clearly behind 'The New
Sculpture''s equation of Gaudier, Gill and Epstein with non-Western
art; and Worringer's *Abstraction and Empathy* is in turn behind, or more
accurately up front in, Hulme's lecture. A month earlier, on 22 January
1914, Hulme presented 'The New Art and Its Philosophy' to the London
Quest Society (the talk would transmute into the essay 'Modern Art and
Its Philosophy'), and his distillation of Worringer's ideas included one of
the artists Pound was championing: Hulme 'recognised this geometrical
character re-emerging in modern art. I am thinking particularly of certain pieces of sculpture I saw some years ago, of Mr. Epstein's.'[19] Hulme
presented Worringer's cleavage between two types of cultures. While
Vorticism is primarily associated with one of them, both by a number

of its members and subsequent critics, Gaudier is a vital exception to the proposition of mutual exclusivity.

In the tidy and popular 1908 account of aesthetics as the result of different cultures' responses to 'the phenomena of the outside world', *Abstraction and Empathy: A Contribution to the Psychology of Style* argues that

> the artistic volition of savage peoples, in so far as they possess any at all, then the artistic volition of all primitive epochs of art and, finally, the artistic volition of certain culturally developed Oriental peoples, exhibit [the] abstract tendency. Thus the urge to abstraction stands at the beginning of every art and in the case of certain peoples at a high level of culture remains the dominant tendency, whereas with the Greeks and other Occidental peoples, for example, it slowly recedes, making way for the urge to empathy.[20]

Worringer's general point was the need to 'pass beyond a narrowly European outlook' (*AE*, 135), and take non-Western art seriously; underlying this was the distinction between two ways of seeing the world[21] and their attendant aesthetics. The latter apparently divides neatly. The geometric is opposed to the vital; the abstract to the empathetic; the angular to the soft; the lifeless to the naturalistic. Organicism, with its vitalism and naturalistic modes of representation, was apparent in cultures and art like that of the Greeks, providing a prime example of empathetic art, which 'finds its gratification in the beauty of the organic' (*AE*, 4); while abstraction took the task of 'de-organicising the organic, i.e., of translating the mutable and conditional into values of unconditional necessity' (*AE*, 134). Abstraction is manifested through planar composition and the flattening of depth, while empathy manifests in artworks containing perspective and the representational. Oriental and Egyptian art is abstract, and Classical and Renaissance art displays empathy.

The distinction between abstraction and empathy would come to map neatly onto an art history that sought to preserve gender differences. Just as we saw Pound dismissing a 'pother about the Greeks', the planar and the abstract were to be vaunted for strength, clarity and masculinity.[22] Empathy's aesthetic, or what others might call institutionalised art, would be deployed in a rendering of a feminised art world that needed straightening up, literally. For Worringer and Hulme, the two aesthetics are in the end mutually exclusive. For Gaudier, they are not. Organicism is the key.

In order to get at this more fully, it is necessary to return to the dominant understanding of *Blast*. Vorticism is generally understood as a male endeavour.[23] Despite being obvious, the conclusion is accurate. Witness demographics: *Blast*'s female contributors – Rebecca West, Jessica Dismorr, Helen Saunders, Dorothy Shakespear – constitute the minority. Too, the organ edited by Wyndham Lewis is repeatedly represented in criticism as indicative of (some combination of) a masculinist and/or misogynist ethos. It is indeed difficult to get around the martial aspects of something called *Blast;* what Janet Lyon has identified as the 'anti-bourgeois alliance' between Vorticism and the English Suffragettes, with the latter fashioned by the former as 'avatars of political energy and therefore … *not* artists';[24] and Tickner's argument that Vorticism 'offered opportunities for a *feminist* repudiation of femininity' ('MW', 21–22). Even Miranda Hickman's argument that in the 1930s H. D. would '[enlist] a Vorticist geometric vocabulary' and that the 'geometric body offers possibilities for feminist emancipation' takes for granted the rigidification of the clean line and planar field as synonymous with Vorticist artists and writers, and an attendant 'struggle with the category of "effeminacy"' (*GM*, 138, xvi). The *Knuckle-Duster* we have just seen conforms readily to a heteromasculinist ethos, with its combination of austerity, violence and giddily bad intentions – all coming together with what it means to have a woman in the palm of your hand.

There is however another aspect of the Vorticist aesthetic represented by and found in the work of Gaudier. The term masculine opens toward it, but does not capture its vicissitudes and complexities. We see here an organicism that mixes abstraction with empathy, complicating the sexual politics of a heteromasculinist artistic ethos.

Despite Worringer arguing that '[T]he primal artistic impulse has nothing to do with the rendering of nature' (*AE*, 44), Gaudier partook of both ends of the spectrum. He was clearly marked as a primitive, as we have seen in the epithet of savage messiah, and his inclusion in *Blast* rests easily alongside its declarations that 'The Art-instinct is permanently primitive', that its makers are 'Primitive Mercenaries', and even the translated excerpts from Wassily Kandinsky's *Concerning the Spiritual in Art* that *Blast* ran: 'The more abstract the form, the more purely and therefore the more primitively it will resound.'[25]

At the same time, this was an artist who did not simply conform to straight masculinist mores. Gaudier's biography serves as background: the Frenchman hyphenated his surname with that of Sophie Brzeska. For legal reasons, they passed as brother and sister. For more complicated reasons, beginning but not ending with the fact of a twenty-some–year age difference, he wrote letters addressing her as mother, and signing them son. They never married. He met her in the reading room of the Bibliothèque Sainte-Geneviève in 1910 and had fallen in love; she told him (to his chagrin) there would be no sex, although they would live together. The celibacy lasted for two years, lapsing (if this is the word) in what appeared to be shared delight, and their partnership lasted until his death in the war at twenty-three.[26] He had sex with women, 'declar[ed] that he was homosexual, expecting us to be horrified',[27] wore a cape, and never stopped being grimy. Gaudier was 'a sort of shy, wild faun-like creature' for Frank Harris; John Middleton Murray had him as 'a panther, crouching to the ground, almost one with the earth, sensuous, swift and strong' and for Pound, the artist was 'a well-made young wolf or some soft-moving bright-eyed wild thing'.[28]

The recurrent image of Gaudier as animal, whether predatory or prey, is sensual, queer, organic and metonymic, in that panthers, fauns and other creatures served recurrently as subjects for both his sculpture and drawing. Even while his writing in the first *Blast*, 'Vortex. Gaudier Brzeska', hews closely to the emphasis on abstraction that we have seen traced earlier in this chapter, the same issue featured his sculpture *Stags*, a concertedly natural subject rendered so as to befuddle any clear distinction between the representational and the abstract.

Gaudier's first 'Vortex' is a whirlwind tour through art, history and geometry, beginning with the 'Paleolithic Vortex' and the 'decoration of the Dordogne caverns', moving through the 'Hamite Vortex', Egypt, and pyramids (*B1*, 155), the 'Shang and Chow dynasties' (*B1*, 157), and eventually 'WE the moderns' (*B1*, 158). Each culture is accorded a geometric object or quality: convex maturity, sphere, parallelogram, pointed cone; and the manifesto ends with the Vorticist symbol of the electrified, northward-pointing cone presaging storms to come.[29] 'Vortex' possesses the familiar cryptic bombast of manifestos, but it is notable for at least two things. First, even given the prominence accorded abstraction, there is an overture to exchange between aesthetics, between the 'fair Greek' and the 'Hamite Vortex' to which he is exposed; 'this influence [of Egypt]' percolates across civilisations – even if to no avail, for the 'fair Greek' fails to grasp it, and 'saw himself only. He petrified his own semblance' (*B1*, 155–6). (Gaudier had followed Pound in slamming the later Greeks [and 'Auceps'] in *The Egoist*.)[30]

Second, Gaudier's manifesto begins with the statement that 'Sculptural energy is the mountain' (*B1*, 155). Art begins with nature, and Gaudier located abstraction there. The manifesto's history of art and civilisation repeatedly casts the natural (bulls, lions, 'the spirits of the horse and of the land and the grain' [*B1*, 157]) alongside the geometric. 'Vortex' bristles with 'the sphere', 'the parallelogram' (*B1*, 155), 'the square' (157), 'the cube' (158), 'the truncated cone' (157) and 'the pointed cone' (158); as well as perspectival terms such as the 'convex' (155, 157), 'the horizontal' (156) and 'the vertical' (155). Life is organic; 'the earth [is] the sphere' (156), and any clear distinction between abstraction and nature's geometry is undone. In this he echoes a subtler reading of Worringer's own text.

Hulme and company tend to take the conjunction in *Abstraction and Empathy* as one signifying mutual exclusivity. This accords with Worringer's rhetorical use of them as separate 'poles' of artistic styles and psychologies ('This counter-pole to the need for empathy appears ... to be the urge to abstraction' [*AE*, 14]), but at another level of his reckoning, abstraction and empathy are, while distinct, contiguous. It is worth repeating Worringer's words quoted above: 'the urge to abstraction stands at the beginning of *every art*' (emphasis added). Abstraction for Worringer was not an eschewal of the natural world per se; it simply engaged that world differently than the empathetic impulse, 'suppress[ing] ... the representation of space' and depth (*AE*, 21). In bringing the natural world alongside that of the planar and the geometric, Gaudier's manifesto hints at what his artwork would speak even more loudly: the organic and the vital move alongside abstraction. Gaudier's rendering of the organic does not allow any segregation between abstraction and the natural world, and the imbrication allowed an interweaving of otherwise differentiated gender dynamics.

In medium, subject matter and style, *Stags*'s naturalism is at odds with the art elsewhere in *Blast:* Frederick Etchell's *Head*, Wadsworth's *March* or *Radiation*, Lewis's *Plan of War*, *Slow Attack*, or the human-being-as-solar-powered-parking-meter illustration *Enemy of the Stars*. *Stags* is a sculpture carved from red-veined alabaster. [Figure 12.2] The variegation of its veins is in exclusive accord with the material, bearing no relation to anatomy. It is about forty centimeters high, and slightly less in width. From approach it is difficult to pinpoint where the eye is to rest, because of the busy-ness of the striations, the combination of distinct planar surfaces, and compactness. That compactness is the effect of stilled action: *Stags* depicts two deer nestled extremely closely. It is a gentle piece, both in its featuring of a couple and in that nestling. The two most identifiable features of the sculpture are its eyes – typical for Gaudier: ovoid (regardless of species) and open – and the cloven hooves of the deer, which tip the gracefully bent legs tucked snugly beneath the animals. However satisfying *Stags* is to observe, it initially announces itself as immune to viewing; there is some sense in which the spectator is extraneous. At the same time however, even as we have seen Pound claim that 'Art is not particularly concerned with the caressable', there is something indisputably tactile about the object.

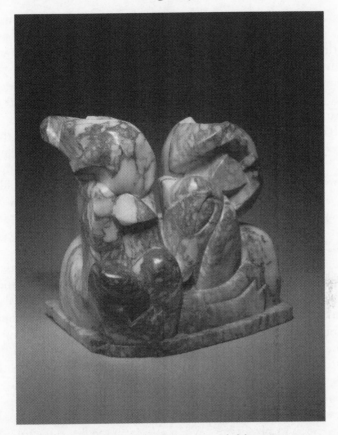

Figure 12.2. Henri Gaudier-Brzeska. *Stags.* 1914. Veined alabaster. 39.3 x 33 x 27.7 cm.
(13.5 x 13 x 10.75 in. [with base]). Gift of Samuel Lustgarten. 1953.22. The Art Institute of
Chicago. Photography © The Art Institute of Chicago.

One wonders how *Stags* feels, not in the emotive or psychological sense,
but literally.

This may be the result of the means of its making. Mark Antliff has
astutely charted the political and aesthetic importance of direct carving (as
opposed to casting from wax models, for example) for Gaudier,[31] and that
immediate encounter, of artist and chisel with matter, rhymes with *Stags*'s
emphasis on proximity. While Antliff remarks on the attraction Gaudier
had to the 'virility needed to carve into hard substances' ('SN', 56) – evident in the brass *Knuckle-Dusters* and even more so in the Pentelicon marble *Hieratic Head of Ezra Pound* – in *Stags*, the result is one of repose, even
as the subject is manifestly male.

'Manifestly' in that the title names the creatures as male. The maleness of the animals is as important as the sculpture's sexuality is made strange. The former is evident in its secondary sexual characteristics (there are antlers) but so of a piece with the creatures as a whole that the rigid determination of sex collapses because, if you will, their being keeps getting in the way. Somewhere between anatomy and ontology, the couple resists any easy partitioning of what it means to be sexed.

Here we move between what I am positing as the fluidity of the sex-gender system of *Stags* and the aesthetics of its modes of representation. Even as the antlers are evident, they are accorded far less detailing than the sculpture's lower quadrants. The antlers are exactly where space and body join and mingle most thoroughly, for their planar lines are massed contiguously against the marble from which they are carved. It is periodically difficult to discern where 'antler' stops and marble ('surround') begins. If abstraction is associated with a clean line or the need to suppress space, and empathy with the acknowledgement of and pleasure in depth, *Stags* has it both ways. Not only are the animals proximate to each other, the individual bodies are proximate to what we see as space, particularly in the surround of the antlers: all is carved in marble. While encompassing the homosocial or the homoerotic – for it remains immensely important that these are two male deer – the aesthetic is not exhausted by it, and the assignation of human sexuality to the piece in the clumsy terms of the pathetic fallacy risks whiting out the calm otherness of the piece.

I do not wish to downplay Gaudier's virile aesthetic. Not even a swift glance at his most famous sculpture, *Hieratic Head of Ezra Pound* (1914), could overlook its phallicism. 'When seen from the front, the viewer confronts Pound's totemic visage [the image appears in *Blast* 2], but when viewed from the back, the bust resolves into a brazen display of male sexual desire' ('SN', 52). As promised, we engage the brain as semen, in order to underscore the fact that Gaudier did partake of the masculinist aesthetic and ethos of his pack. The rhyme between thinking and heterosexual copulation has been remarked, by Pound via de Gourmont, and Gaudier's sculpture can be seen as a proactive commemoration of Pound's comment: 'There are traces of it in the symbolism of phallic religions, man really the phallus or spermatozoide charging, head-on, the female chaos. Integration of the male in the male organ. Even oneself has felt it, driving any new idea into the great passive vulva of London, a sensation analogous to the male feeling in copulation' ('TP', 207). *Hieratic Head* is a somewhat cumbersome form of play, conflating 'brain and spermataphore' ('TP', 207), and its stalwart phallicism must be seen as asserting the imperatives of sexual difference – or as remarking upon their rigidity. It is not much of a leap from a binary system of gender to heteronormative allocations regarding aesthetics and practices of art-making, and the rhetoric surrounding them. There is no denying the diminishing and at times outright loopy dynamics of modernists who conceive of art as a male or masculine endeavour, and females or femininity as a factor in an artistic economy that necessitates sanitising, naturalising, excision, inseminating, educating, reification, ignoring or silencing. The latter's obverse – females or femininity as demanding aesthetic announcement, inclusion, elevation, celebration – is in clear ways an improvement, but does not engage the system per se. The system is based on difference and distinction, and beyond that there is no budging. Valuable in Gaudier's work is ultimately not the fact that he obviates or erases difference, but the creative trouble emergent upon their collapse.

Stags partakes of the natural world and its own order of things, and the sculpture's otherness – its nonhumanism – is consonant with its maleness. The sculpture is at once an overture to coupling (these are two creatures) and reproof to pairing (these creatures are like each other, and they are not like you). As a reproof to pairing, the sculpture resists simile (deer are not like people) and thus resists any account of the natural world that rests on the pathetic fallacy. At the same time, in reshaping the couple so as to encompass a different kind of difference, not naturalised but natural, *Stags* does suggest a relation to its viewer. The fact of the coupling suggests an intimacy not only between the creatures depicted but also between what is being seen and who is seeing it. Abstraction and organicism have come together, the former in terms of the sculpture's nonhumanism and its mode of depiction, the latter in terms of the creatures as sculpture. The object's maleness, with its overture to being viewed – and even, I would say, touched – is an overture to the beholder and establishes some sort of return to the human world. In that sense the viewer cannot but see this maleness as kin to masculinity. Such masculinity partakes of the natural and the organic via the inorganic medium of alabaster and its play with abstraction, and two male deer can reflect what in another species' realm would be termed homosociality or homosexuality, for it is impossible to discern where one deer stops and the other begins. This is nonhumanism, but insofar as it accepts the terms of the natural world, it is not antihumanism.

The fact that the German word for empathy, *Einfühlung*, 'had been originally coined as an aesthetic term by Robert Vischer in 1873' and by the turn of the century came to encompass a 'method useful not only to aesthetics but for the psychological understanding of another person' is to the point.[32] Empathy's path from an aesthetic term to a means of negotiating other humans involved shifting the terms of alterity: from empathy as the projection of one's self into an object, to the projection of one's self into a subject. In looking at *Stags,* the process of empathetic art comes full circle. Its invitation to resemblance – it looks like two deer – is at one with a way of viewing that suggests there is something here which resembles us.

Blast 1 also included two drawings by Epstein of what Lewis described in *Blast* 2 as 'one of the best things he has done', the sculpture *Rock-Drill.*[33] The fully realised piece takes up the metonymic relation between penetration, creation and procreation, typing pregnancy as offspring of technophilia by marrying organic form to prosthetics. It suggests that creating extensions of oneself is inherently prosthetic, in which case a fetus-embryo, a drill and an artwork become of a piece. There is organicism here too, but as spectacular as *Rock-Drill* is, by literally containing its organicism within the mechanical (the fetus-embryo is embedded within the mechanical man), it accords with a familiar critical history of *Blast* and technophilic triumph.[34] This is not the full story, and not just because Epstein would not sign *Blast*'s manifesto. It would be useful to re-begin Epstein, starting with his 1913 series of marble mating birds, memorably characterised by Lord Drogheda, in terms both abusive and accurate, as 'those fucking doves' (*V,* 125).

Inasmuch as Epstein more clearly toes the Vorticist line – both in his technophilia and his irritation with Vorticists – it is Gaudier who demands further attention. The fact that he only partly fits the received aesthetic pushes us to refine our account it is of what we need to see. The artist was rife with contradiction. In linking Gaudier's direct carving aesthetic to his anarchist political affiliation, Antliff has explained how an antimilitarist who took loud joy in flouting compulsory military service could a few years later voluntarily enlist.[35] Wood has tracked the fact that Gaudier never quite fit the neat schism that emerged between the artists later affiliated with *Blast* and Omega Workshop artists following the 'Ideal Home Rumpus'. As Wood puts it, Gaudier 'maintained an association with both the Omega and the Vorticists up to his departure for the front. … His various affiliations and associations were seen as conflicting.'[36]

Gaudier specialised in differing – and a different sort of differing than the attraction/revulsion mode of someone like Lewis, in which aesthetic embrace would be followed by repudiation, or even the continual gadfly mode of someone like Pound, who would take pleasure in vaunting the overlooked or the unpopular. Gaudier's mode was more akin to that of Mina Loy, someone who did not ever quite fit in with groups, whether Futurist, Dadaist or Surrealist. Independence comes in different shapes, and there is critical merit in examining what or who, even while moving apace of an avant-garde, resists assimilation to it. Vorticism may have been primarily a boy's club, but some of its boys should warp our expectation and understanding of any attendant aesthetic.

Moreover there is every indication that some of the other *Blast* artists grasped this. As Pound put it in his memoir of the artist, 'Gaudier ... demonstrated the soundness of his instinct for the combination of organic with inorganic forms in such works as the "Stags" and "The Boy with a Coney." These and certain works have in them what Lewis has called "Brzeska's peculiar soft bluntness."'[37] Indeed, as Pound writes, Gaudier 'had planned an essay on "The Need of Organic Forms in Sculpture"' for the second issue of *Blast* (*AM*, 25–6).

Gaudier's final 'Vortex', 'Written from the Trenches' just prior to his death, illustrates the melding of disparate masculine rhetorics. On the one hand he would echo the Vorticist (and Futurist) Malthusian espousal of war as hygiene: 'The war is a great remedy. In the individual it kills arrogance, self-esteem, pride. It takes away from the masses numbers upon numbers of unimportant units, whose economic activities become noxious as the recent trade crises have shown us' (*B2*, 33). He goes on, however, to record stealing a German rifle in order to experiment with the reciprocal exchange between 'emotions' and 'surfaces', and the tone begins to shift. 'Its heavy unwieldy shape swamped me with a powerful image of brutality. I was in doubt for a long time whether it pleased or displeased me. I found that I did not like it. I broke the butt off and with my knife I carved in it a design, through which I tried to express a gentler order of feeling, which I preferred.' Even so, this design, with its 'gentler order', in Gaudier's final words, 'got its effect (just as the gun had) from a very simple composition of lines and planes' (*B2*, 34). The vortex here brings the aggressive tools at hand – both knife and gun – into immediate contact with a planar aesthetic that in its pleasing gentleness is at odds with the very mechanisation that motored it. Given the war, we will never know what would have come next in the artist's career, and, as Pound says, 'The essay on "The Need of Organic Forms" was left unwritten' (*AM*, 26).

This chapter has argued that a clearer-eyed view of Gaudier's work allows us to make strange what has been taken as the exhaustively masculinist aesthetic of Vorticism, as well as the aesthetics attendant upon the wider vocabulary of masculine primitivism, abstraction and the artistic twists of the period. At times virile, at times quiescent, and even, in Pound's word, snuggly, Gaudier's work exhibits a blend of what was otherwise understood as the mutual exclusivity of abstraction or empathy; representational or abstract; organic or geometric. Pound's description of the work as snuggly suggests how even from the start Gaudier's aesthetic both met with approbation and exceeded the terms with which approbation was typically accorded; neither the adjective nor the art entirely conformed to Pound's lexicon, even as the writer recognised the artist's power. Too frequently misunderstood as indicating a site of repudiation for Vorticist masculinist aesthetics, organicism in the hands of Gaudier mixes the ends of sculpture and sexual politics. Such mixing complicates any simple allocation of modernism to masculinism to abstraction, or even Vorticism as a simply – or simplistic – masculinist endeavour. It may be that, compared to Italian Futurism, '*Blast* was indeed a dull affair.' If so, this results from overemphasising a recapitulation of the technophilia that Italian Futurism so noisily, and successfully, and earlier, engaged. This chapter has instead argued that critical understandings of the masculine, and Vorticism, have been overly blunt-edged. Recognising Gaudier's importance in a particular genealogy of modernist organicism and whittling away at the complications beneath *Blast* reveal the artist's objects as breathtaking, vitally so, in their obdurateness to current critical narratives surrounding the work of gender and aesthetics.

Notes

1 Ezra Pound, 'Exhibition at the Goupil Gallery', *The Egoist*, 1:6 (16 March 1914): 109; hereafter abbreviated 'EGG'.
2 Namely 'The Vorticists: Rebel Artists in London and New York, 1914–1918' (2010–2011); and 'Wild Thing: Epstein, Gaudier-Brzeska, Gill' (2009–2010).
3 Lawrence Rainey, 'The Creation of the Avant-Garde', in his *Institutions of Modernism: Literary Elites and Public Culture* (New Haven, CT: Yale University Press, 1998), p. 38.
4 Miranda Hickman, *The Geometry of Modernism: The Vorticist Idiom in Lewis, Pound, H. D., and Yeats* (Austin: University of Texas Press), p. 7; hereafter abbreviated *GM*. Thanks are due to Rachel Blau DuPlessis for this source.
5 Ezra Pound, 'Translator's Postscript', in Remy de Gourmont, *The Natural Philosophy of Love*, trans. Pound (New York: Boni and Liveright, 1922), p. 206; hereafter abbreviated 'TP'.
6 Ezra Pound, 'The New Sculpture', *The Egoist*, 1:4 (16 February 1914): 67; hereafter abbreviated 'NS'.
7 Lisa Tickner, *Modern Life and Modern Subjects: British Art in the Early Twentieth Century* (New Haven, CT: Yale University Press, 2000), p. 206.

8 Evelyn Silber, with photographs by David Finn, *Gaudier-Brzeska: Life and Art* (New York: Thames and Hudson, 1996), p. 58; hereafter abbreviated *LA*.

9 Pound to Harriet Monroe, quoted in Hugh Kenner, *The Pound Era* (Berkeley: University of California Press, 1971), p. 174.

10 Ezra Pound, 'The Caressability of the Greeks', *The Egoist*, 1:6 (16 March 1914): 117.

11 *The Freewoman: A Weekly Feminist Review*, 1:17 (14 March 1912): 340; 1:18 (21 March 1912): 360; 1:19 (28 March 1912): 380; and, for Pound and Mansfield's besting, 1:20 (4 March 1912): 400.

12 Edward P. Comentale and Andrzej Gasiorek, 'On the Significance of a Hulmean Modernism', in Comentale and Gasiorek, eds., *T. E. Hulme and the Question of Modernism* (Burlington, VT: Ashgate Publishing, Ltd., 2006), p. 2.

13 Kate Lechmere, paraphrasing Hulme, quoted in Cork's interview with Lechmere; see Richard Cork, *Vorticism and Abstract Art in the First Machine Age*, 2 vols. (Berkeley: University of California Press, 1976), vol. 1, p. 160; hereafter abbreviated *V*. Silber pairs the quotation, sensibly, with *Knuckle-Duster* #88 (*LA*, 272).

14 Paul O'Keeffe, *Gaudier-Brzeska: An Absolute Case of Genius* (New York: Penguin, 2004), p. 229; hereafter abbreviated *ACG*. See also Robert Ferguson, *The Short, Sharp Life of T. E. Hulme* (New York: Penguin, 2002), and Alan Munton, 'Abstraction, Archaism and the Future: T. E. Hulme, Jacob Epstein and Wyndham Lewis', in Comentale and Gasiorek, eds., *T. E. Hulme and the Question of Modernism*, pp. 73–92.

15 Jacob Epstein, quoted in *ACG*, p. 229.

16 See *LA*, 272. This second knuckle-duster (#89), while identical in overall proportion to the first (#88), lacks a central hole, the one that Hulme associated with the vagina. This may explain a lot, but of what?

17 Jonathan Wood, 'Ornaments, Talismans and Toys: The Hand-held Sculptures of Henri Gaudier-Brzeska', in Jonathan Black, ed., *Blasting the Future!: Vorticism in Britain, 1910–1920* (London: Philip Wilson Publishers, 2004), p. 42; hereafter abbreviated 'O'.

18 See Michael H. Levenson, *A Genealogy of Modernism: A Study of English Literary Doctrine, 1908–1922* (New York: Cambridge University Press, 1984), pp. 94–96 and passim.

19 T. E. Hulme, 'Modern Art and its Philosophy', in Herbert Read, ed., *Speculations: Essays on Humanism and the Philosophy of Art* (1924; New York: Routledge and Kegan Paul Inc., 1987), p. 81.

20 Wilhelm Worringer, *Abstraction and Empathy: A Contribution to the Psychology of Style* (1908), trans. Michael Bullock (New York: International Universities Press, Inc., 1980), p. 15; hereafter abbreviated *AE*.

21 I elide Worringer's explanation of the respective cultural psychologies and their different approaches to space and, in the case of abstraction, topophobia. For more on the topic see my *Cold Modernism* (University Park: Pennsylvania State University Press, 2012).

22 See Lisa Tickner, 'Men's Work? Masculinity and Modernism', *Differences*, 4:3 (Fall 1992): 10, hereafter abbreviated 'MW'; and Geoffrey Wagner, *Wyndham Lewis: A Portrait of the Artist as the Enemy* (New Haven, CT: Yale University Press, 1957), pp. 110–111.

23 One exception is Jane Beckett and Deborah Cherry, 'Modern Women, Modern Spaces: Women, Metropolitan Culture and Vorticism', in Katy Deepwell, ed., *Women Artists and Modernism* (New York: Manchester University Press, 1998), pp. 36–54.

24 Janet Lyon, 'Militant Allies, Strange Bedfellows: Suffragettes and Vorticists before the War', in *Manifestoes: Provocations of the Modern* (Ithaca, NY: Cornell University Press, 1999), pp. 109, 110.

25 *Blast*, 1 (1 June 1914): 33, 30, 123–124; hereafter abbreviated *B1*.

26 See *ACG;* Ede's biography differs in casting their sexual relations as sparing.

27 Jacob Epstein, quoted in *ACG*, p. 132.

28 Quoted in William Wees, *Vorticism and the English Avant-Garde* (Buffalo, NY: University of Toronto Press, 1972), p. 133.

29 See *ACG*, p. 142.

30 *The Egoist*, 1:6 (16 March 1914): 117–118.

31 Mark Antliff, 'Sculptural Nominalism/Anarchist Vortex: Henri Gaudier-Brzeska, Dora Marsden, and Ezra Pound', in *The Vorticists: Rebel Artists in London and New York, 1914–1918* (Durham, NC: Nasher Museum of Art at Duke University, 2010), pp. 47–57; hereafter abbreviated 'SN'.

32 Susan Lanzoni, 'An Epistemology of the Clinic: Ludwig Binswanger's Phenomenology of the Other', *Critical Inquiry*, 30 (Autumn 2003): 164–165.

33 Wyndham Lewis, 'The London Group', *Blast*, 2 (July 1914), 78; hereafter abbreviated *B2*.

34 If anything is owed here, it belongs to Julian Murphet.

35 See Mark Antliff, '"Their Country": Henri Gaudier-Brzeska's Anarchist Anti-Militarism, 1910–1914', in *"We the Moderns": Gaudier-Brzeska and the Birth of Modern Sculpture* (Cambridge: Kettle's Yard, 2007), 75–87; and Antliff, 'Henri Gaudier-Brzeska's *Guerre sociale:* Art, Anarchism and Anti-Militarism in Paris and London, 1910–1915', *Modernism/modernity*, 17:1 (January 2010): 135–169; and Antliff, 'SN'.

36 Jon Wood, 'Henri Gaudier-Brzeska: Artistic Identity and the Place of Sculpture in the Omega Workshops', in Alexandra Gerstein, ed., *Beyond Bloomsbury: Designs of the Omega Workshops, 1913–1919* (London: Fontanka, 2009), pp. 35–36.

37 Ezra Pound, *Gaudier-Brzeska: A Memoir* (1916; New York: New Directions, 1970), p. 26; hereafter abbreviated *AM*.

CHAPTER 13

Bravura or Bravado? Reading Ezra Pound's Cantos

Peter Nicholls

Liking an elegance of which
the source is not bravado

Marianne Moore, 'The Steeple-Jack'

In some lines composed late in his life, Pound wrote emphatically of his enduring commitment to poetry as song:

> Poetry speaks phallic direction
> Song keeps the word forever
> Sound is moulded to mean this
> And the measure moulds the sound

Hugh Kenner quotes these lines in *The Pound Era*, describing them as Pound's attempt to improve on 'Fenollosa's glosses on an ancient gnome. It remains amid the scraps of an unwritten book, Ezra Pound's last apologie for poetry.'[1] This late 'apologie' – Kenner assigns it to 1958 – memorably reaffirms some familiar elements in Pound's thinking: most notably, it attributes to lyricism a 'phallic direction', summarising the poet's enduring conception of the roots of lyric in the expression of male desire.[2] This desire – synonymous, for Pound, with the force of will (the *directio voluntatis*, as he takes it from Dante[3]) – is what renders the truly great poem immutable; in fact, the ambiguous 'this' in the third line of the passage hints at an essential bond between phallus and immortality. What a song 'means', then, is inseparable from the performance of its own power of survival, a power that 'keeps the word forever' by 'moulding' it in a complex weave of sounds and 'measure'. 'Rhythm is a form cut into TIME, as a design is determined SPACE', Pound declared, this act of quasi-sculptural incision resisting time's relentless flow.[4]

The lines Kenner quotes may be a version of an ancient Chinese text, but they also irresistibly recall one of the poems of *Hugh Selwyn Mauberley* whose 'Envoi', written almost forty years before, contains this famous passage:

> ... I would bid them live
> As roses might, in magic amber laid,
> Red overwrought with orange and all made
> One substance and one colour
> Braving time.[5]

Poet Geoffrey Hill's comments on this passage suggest one way of understanding the connections Pound perpetually assumes between poetry and masculinity:

> What is 'braving time'? [asks Hill.] It is to challenge, to defy, with a tincture of 'bravura', the 'display of daring or defiance; brilliancy of execution', as in 'a passage or piece of music requiring great skill and spirit in its execution, written to task the artist's powers'.[6]

Drawing on the *Oxford English Dictionary*, Hill's gloss on Pound's notion of 'braving time' discovers in what is at first sight a highly conventional trope of transcendence (one critic has even dubbed it 'Palgravian') a new subtlety that activates the semantic field of 'bravery'/'bravura' and, I suggest, the cognate 'bravado'. Pound's 'Envoi' in fact artfully rewrites his source-poem, Edmund Waller's 'Goe lovely Rose', 'singing not beauty's early mutability but rather its transcendence,' as critic Carey Wolfe observes.[7] Hill similarly notes that Pound 'sets himself the task ... of transposing "bravery" from the domain of the merely "sincere" (which is ephemeral and solipsistic) into a form of "substance" and "colour" successfully detached from the ephemeral.'[8] This 'bravery', we might add, is to be valued not simply because it expresses art's capacity to outlast its historical moment but also because it bespeaks an active *defiance* of time. Pound's poem deliberately challenges both the mutability that Waller's verses lament and the pragmatic and poignant tone of acceptance with which the earlier poet acknowledges death as 'The common fate of all things rare'.[9]

The 'bravura' exhibited in Pound's 'Envoi' thus derives from a handling of artifice that, for Renaissance rhetoricians, had been itself a kind of 'braverie'. 'Braverie of speech,' wrote Abraham Fraunce, 'consisteth of tropes or turnings, and in figures or fashionings.'[10] For Pound in *Hugh Selwyn Mauberley*, it is precisely such 'fashionings' that constitute the means by which art might transcend the 'merely human'. Of Raymonde Collignon, the singer who is often thought to be the 'Luini in porcelain' of the 'Medallion' that closes the sequence, Pound wrote:

> No one has a more keen perception than she has of the difference between art and life; of the necessary scale and proportion required in the

presentation of a thing which is not the photograph and wax-cast, but a re-creation in different and proportional medium. As long as this diseuse was on stage she was non-human.[11]

In considering here Pound's relation to a poetics of masculinity, I shall be more concerned with the ambiguities of art's potential capacity for 'defiance' than with the poet's expression of particular attitudes toward the sexes. Those attitudes are well known and regrettable as much for their conventionality as for their often crass misogyny. This is the Pound who alleges in his early poem 'The Condolence' that 'the female is ductile' and then modifies that definition in a letter to Marianne Moore to conclude instead that '[t]he female is a chaos', a phrase that yields an extended passage in Canto XXIX/144 ('the female / Is an element, the female / Is a chaos / An octopus / A biological process', etc.).[12] This is the Pound who seizes on Remy de Gourmont's association of creative thought with ejaculation and who complains of the difficulty of 'driving any new idea into the great passive vulva of London.'[13] When Marianne Moore reviewed Pound's *A Draft of XXX Cantos* in 1931, she found herself having to confront again that barb about the female as chaos and was provoked to ask: 'is not the view of woman expressed by the Cantos older-fashioned than that of Siam and Abyssinia?'[14] The question was predictably on target, for it's not just that Pound's misogyny was thoroughly traditional, but that it was also in a perfectly conventional way twinned with a sentimental 'feminolatry', as Moore called it.

When it comes to questions of Pound and gender, then, we might seem to veer between the risk-taking 'bravura' Hill rightly admires in 'Envoi' and the embarrassing 'bravado' of 'the female / Is a chaos.' How, though, might we best define this particular kind of 'bravado?' The *OED* offers the following:

> Boastful or threatening behaviour; ostentatious display of courage or boldness; bold or daring action intended to intimidate or to express defiance; often an assumption of courage or hardihood to conceal felt timidity, or to carry one out of a doubtful or difficult position.

Comparing this definition with the *OED*'s entry on 'bravura' makes it clear that a fine line separates the two kinds of 'defiance' or 'challenge'. On the one hand, 'bravura' is a quality affirmed in the execution of the work, testifying to the artist's skill and to the deep intimacy with cultural tradition that this exemplifies.[15] The skilful meeting of a challenge or resistance is what is primarily at issue here.[16] 'Bravado,' on the other hand, entails a projection of features conventionally characterised as 'masculine,' but one whose excessive articulation has the paradoxical effect of revealing such features as merely vain display. Even more important in Pound's case is 'bravado' as a deliberate flying in the face of the facts, a cleaving to forms and values that for historical reasons have ceased to be tenable. In this second sense, 'bravado' enables a speaker to assert a continuing connection to something lost through sheer force of rhetoric and in that way to provide a 'strong' resistance to the overwhelming nostalgia that would otherwise result from the full acceptance of that loss.

Even to contrast the two terms in this abbreviated way is to see how close in implication they actually are, and perhaps inevitably so for a writer, like Pound, whose sense of aesthetic value hinges on the artwork's power to defy time (Horace's 'monumentum aere perennius' and Théophile Gautier's 'l'art robuste / Seul à l'éternité' are two of his favourite critical touchstones).[17] It is, in fact, a feature of Pound's poetry, and especially of *The Cantos*, that the 'braveries' of writing should be intimately bound up with an oscillation, at once formal and conceptual, between the registers of 'bravura' and 'bravado,' and that a 'masculine' poetics should be forged in the semantic orbit of these proximate but differently inflected terms. Certainly, Pound would exploit the ambiguities of their relation in the early stages of his long poem, investing almost from the first in a particular type of 'bravery' that associates masculine drive with aesthetic constructivity. Rejecting the 'Thin husks I had known as men' and their empty 'shell of speech', Pound casts his lot with 'The live man' who is 'more full of flames and voices'.[18] That man would dramatically appear in the Cantos that immediately follow: Sigismundo Malatesta, betrayer of allies, blasphemer, adulterer, likely a rapist and murderer ('there was the row about that German-Burgundian female' [IX/36]) but a man whose iniquities, as Pound's throwaway phrasing suggests, pale in significance before his achievement in constructing the Tempio Malatesta in Rimini ('*templum aedificavit*' [VIII/32]). Sigismundo's career is the very epitome of bravado, and Pound delights in the maelstrom of unscrupulous activities and alliances that defines his career. But this is a bravado that significantly masks an exceptional bravura whose achievement outlasts the messy detail of national rivalries. 'All that a single man could, Malatesta managed *against* the current of power,' Pound would later observe, and this act of defiance, 'the effect of the factive personality',[19] is, tellingly, figured in the internal decoration of the Tempio, a subtle intertwining of mythic motif ('pagan works', IX/41) and sexual passion of which Pound will deliberately show us little in the Malatesta Cantos. In this sequence, we are given the sound and the fury of 'an entire man', but the nuanced inner calm of the Tempio is largely withheld from the reader, left, as it were, to speak for itself.[20]

In these early Cantos, we may discern a structural tension that characterises the parts of the poem that precede the so-called Italian Cantos, first published in 1944 but not included in the complete *Cantos* until 1987. Before Cantos 72 and 73, the poem deploys its multifarious materials not only to 'set down part of / The Evidence' (XLVI/234) against the usurers and war-profiteers but also to secure moments Pound had earlier described as 'bust thru from quotidian'.[21] In often extended lyric passages, he seeks to capture precisely that nexus of values announced in the lines with which I began this essay, finding in the precisions of 'song' a 'measure' of right action and right thinking. In the visionary performances of Cantos such as XVII, XXXIX, and XLVII, the idiom is more self-consciously ornamental and the images more fragile and evanescent. Yet while there is 'Passion to breed a form in shimmer of rain-blur' (VII/27), the 'shimmering' effect is at the same time characteristically mitigated in the substantival and signature compound 'rain-blur'. Such passages feature, then, a superficially 'feminine' fragility and poise in contrast to the boisterous bravado of the Malatesta sequence, but Pound's real concern is with the expression of desire as *virtú*, and in that sense the erotic drive of these Cantos still asserts that this is a 'manly' writing (*vir-tú*).

Indeed, the challenge that Pound sets himself in the early Cantos hinges on his attempt to configure what he regarded as the 'phallic' implications of lyric as part of a tradition of *civic* virtue, a 'manly' language expressing not just sexual desire but also a will toward both social and spiritual order. So we may see that the 'ornateness' or bravura of Cavalcanti's *'Dona mi pregha'*, as recreated in Canto XXXVI and echoing Waller's poem in its conclusion ('Go, song … / For so art thou ornate') comes to resonate with 'the light of the doer' in Canto LI/251, a phrase celebrating the force of intelligence that might successfully counter the depredations of '*usura*'. The grass which is said here to be 'nowhere out of place' may recall the pastoral landscape of earlier Cantos such as XX/90, but the same phrase has already been deployed in Pound's account of the Sienese bank, the Monte dei Paschi, which derives its credit from 'the fruit of nature' (XLIII/219, 218). As Pound proposed in his essay on Cavalcanti, then, 'there is some proportion between the fine thing held in the mind, and the inferior thing ready for instant consumption'[22] – a 'proportion,' we might say, that reveals visionary and material worlds as intimately bound together in a dialectic tension that emphasises mutual relation rather than simple transcendence. When we arrive at the Chinese Cantos (LII-LXI), it is this 'proportion' that is seen to underlie the structural order of the Confucian state:

> Urbanity in externals, virtu in internals
> > some in a high style for the rites
> some in humble;

> for Emperors; for the people
> all things are here brought to precisions. (LIX/324)

Pound goes on to quote a phrase from Cavalcanti's Canzone ('*perpetuale effecto*') thus bringing the light imagery of that poem into relation with the '*lumen rationis*' of Confucianism, concluding that 'all order comes into such norm.' There is, for Pound, a kind of bravura in this conjunction of stylistic 'urbanity' with imperial *virtú*, an overcoming of divisive social difference in an allegedly 'enlightened' ideal of hierarchical order.

Yet the 'urbane' surface of the Chinese Cantos themselves, with its orderly Latin phrases and its images of transparent rationality, is constantly torn as Pound intermittently lashes out at the forces of *dis*order that he associates with Buddhism:

> MOU-TSONG drove out the taozers
>   But refused to wear mourning for HIEN his father
> The hen sang in MOU'S time, racin', jazz dancin'
> And play-actors, Tartars still raidin'
> MOU'S first son was strangled by eunuchs. (LV/291)

The demotic language of such passages, with their ominous singing hens and symptoms of cultural degeneration ('racin', jazz dancin''), unleashes a vindictive name-calling ('taozers', 'goddam bhuddists') that gives us an early taste of what happens when bravado parts company with bravura. The reader who is willing to accept Pound's praise of enlightened rulers now has also to cope with the celebration of emperor Yang-kien as 'rough, able, wrathy / flogged a few every day / and sacrificed on Mt Taï Chan' (LIV/284). To the extent that Pound's commendation of Yang-kien seems unequivocal, so he challenges the reader to accept this 'rough' violence as somehow related to the Confucian 'urbanity' lauded in Canto LIX. The pressure on the reader further increases a few lines later when emperor Yang Ti, of the same Soui dynasty, is praised for an even more extreme oppression of his people:

> 1600 leagues of canals 40ft wide for the
>   honour of YANG TI of SOUI
> the stream Kou-choui was linked to Hoang Ho the river
>   great works by oppression
>   by splendid oppression
> the Wall was from Yu-lin to Tsé-ho
> and a million men worked on that wall. (LIV/285)

Here we might feel that the stakes are being raised and that a distinctively new tone has entered the poem. It is a tone, also, that will not now leave it, as we see from the Pisan sequence, where Yang Ti's 'splendid oppression' is echoed in Stalin's 'canal work and gt / mortality / (which is as may be)' (LXXIV/461). Pound knows that all but a few of his readers will be shocked by this bit of bravado and its throwaway tone, but the effect is calculated and designed to sound impressively tough and politically savvy.

This partly explains a growing sense of strain in the Chinese Cantos, as Pound finds himself addressing an Anglo-American audience while at the same making a 'patriotic' investment in the fortunes of the Italian regime. A political manoeuvre of this kind was bound to be unsuccessful, as would be painfully clear from the poet's foray into pro-fascist journalism and his infamous broadcasts for Radio Roma.[23] Initially, though, as he became an increasingly enthusiastic supporter of Mussolini it was by an aesthetic route that he attempted a rapprochement with the regime. As Miranda Hickman has recently shown, the thirties saw Pound extolling the virtues of Futurism as Italy's genuinely modern aesthetic and making of this a kind of bridgehead to the installation of his and Wyndham Lewis's Vorticism as a related but ultimately more effective model for the development of the arts.[24] In his London years, of course, Pound had been highly critical of Marinetti's Futurism, describing it in *Blast* as merely 'accelerated impressionism,' and as 'the disgorging spray of a vortex with no drive behind it, DISPERSAL',[25] but now he was keen to cultivate the Italian impresario and war hero, whose links to the regime and to Mussolini himself he no doubt hoped to exploit. Ironically, then, by 1932 it was precisely Marinetti's manly 'drive', his bellicosity and patriotic fervor, that Pound would seek to emulate.[26] In Spring of that year he '[h]ad amiable jaw with Marinetti in Rome and [had] come bak loaded with futurist and fascist licherchoor'.[27] A genial relation now obtained between the two men and an exchange of letters ensued.[28] As Pound's biographer Humphrey Carpenter suggests, this renewed connection with Marinetti undoubtedly 'played some part in pushing him over the brink into active support of Mussolini'.[29]

There was a second powerful influence on Pound's move toward fascism: during another trip to Rome, in late 1932, he was able to visit the Exhibition of the Fascist Revolution (Mostra della Rivoluzione Fascista). This monumental installation, built to commemorate the ten-year anniversary of the March on Rome, celebrated both the political and aesthetic achievements of the 'revolution', exhibiting the work of modernists such as Giuseppe Terragni and Mario Sironi within a connected complex of rooms and central chambers narrating the history of Italy from 1914 to 1922. Two aspects of this highly successful exhibition must have impressed

Pound especially: first, the apparent hospitality the regime extended to modernist art,[30] and second, the centralising and heroic force of Mussolini himself. Room T of the Exhibition provided a reconstruction of the office used by Il Duce from 1914 to 1920, offering, as one historian puts it, 'a slice of fascism in its most radical phase: Mussolini's paper-covered desk strewn with hand-grenades and a carelessly placed revolver; behind the desk hung a black flag with skull and cross-bones.'[31] Pound would recall it briefly in Canto XLVI/231: 'Decennio exposition, reconstructed office of Il Popolo, / Waal, ours was like that, minus the Mills bomb an' the teapot.' Pound makes little of the Exhibition here, although that is in line with his habit of keeping fascism in the background of the middle Cantos, evoking its 'spiritual' dynamic indirectly, staging it in other times and other cultures and leaving it to the canny reader to grasp the analogy.[32]

Elsewhere, however, he remarked more directly that 'At the Esposizione I, as a scholar of history, learned things that I did not know as of the last number of this *Supplement*.'[33] Although he doesn't mention it specifically, Pound could not have been unreceptive to the heady mix of political history and the ritualised forms of 'faith' and observance on which fascism was coming increasingly to depend.[34] Furthermore, in the next issue of *Il Mare*, to which Pound also contributed, P. M. Bardi stressed how the Mostra, in 'a typically twentieth-century way', harnessed its political narrative to the new technologies of sound and cinema.[35] Pound was quick to grasp the Exhibition's modernist thrust: he had, in fact, already drafted a scenario for a film presenting the history of fascism for the decennial celebrations. According to bibliographer Donald Gallup, that draft contains fairly extensive notes on a sequence depicting the March on Rome. The whole scenario, to be titled *The 'Black Flames,'* (Le 'Fiamme Nere', a Blackshirt division) was printed as a scenario for private circulation in December 1932, although the film was never made.[36] Pound presented the draft as part of his petition for an audience with Mussolini that was granted one month later.[37] The poet was now increasingly impressed by the celebratory mood of the Exhibition and by the auratic presentation there of fascist masculinity. Indeed, an ideal of heroic manhood or, to use Pound's favourite word, *virtú*, was at the very centre of the Exhibition, expressing the notion popularised by, for example, journalist Giuseppe Bottai that '[t]he Fascist man is completely directed to the totality; he moves from the particularity of his being to the unity of the state; and in this ascent ... he gains self-knowledge and personal awareness.'[38]

Even before he saw the Exhibition, Pound was certain that Mussolini 'will end with Sigismondo and the men of order, not with the pus-sacks and destroyers'.[39] This amounted to something more than praise for Il Duce, reflecting Pound's growing sense of convergence between the aspirations of his own long poem and those of the regime. Critics have tended to view the poet's developing attachment to fascism as a corruption of his earlier modernism, as a swing from what was an initially open cultural eclecticism to one that was subsequently damaged and degraded by the closure of purely ideological thinking. But recent work on modernism and fascism has regarded the relation between them rather differently. Roger Griffin's *Modernism and Fascism*, for example, builds on accounts by Emilio Gentile and Claudio Fogu to define the culture of Italian fascism as, in Griffin's phrase, 'a political variant of modernism', while William Adamson similarly emphasises that it is to be regarded as 'the politicization of Italian modernism' and as 'an extension – or clarification – of the modernist project'.[40]

Mussolini's state might in this sense have been seen by Pound as a fateful embodiment of the many different strands of thought he had already tried to activate in *The Cantos*. At least by the end of the thirties, the fascist aesthetic had already laid the foundations for what Emilio Gentile in his classic account of Italian fascism calls 'the sacralization of politics', by which he means 'the search for a new form of secular or lay religion for modern Italy'.[41] This search, argues Gentile, had already been undertaken by the Italian avant-garde with its cult of action, its intolerance of dissent, its desire for the new and the youthful, and its violent break with tradition.[42] Forms of what Griffin calls 'liturgical nationalism' generated a newly decisive 'mythic thinking', which filled the vacuum left by the old religious orthodoxy, often inflecting elements of Catholicism in the direction of pagan topoi.[43] The idiom of fascist myth seemed, then, to draw on the same mythopoeia that had always been so crucial to Pound, albeit now formalised as a pattern of symbolic oppositions around which the poet's thought would similarly begin to revolve: state and 'anti-statal' values, European and 'Hebraic' cultures, valid mythologies and those based on 'blood-rites', grain and gold, agrarian and 'nomadic', totalitarian 'faith' and 'bestial superstition', and so on. In the rhetoric of the regime, the cults of *italianismo*, of *romanità*, of *mediterraneità* put Italy at the centre of what Pound, in an essay written in 1939 but not published, called the 'European paideuma', a cultural map which confirmed his thinking about the transmission and persistence of 'sacral' Mediterranean sites and practices:

> The Xtian [sic] Church was of very mixed elements. The valid elements European. That church went out of business about AD 1500, semitized

from two forces, one usury, and the other the revival of jewish texts (old testament). The only vigorous feasts of the Church are grafted onto European
roots, the sun, the grain, the harvest and Aphrodite.[44]

The simplicity of the 'Mediterranean imaginary' thus disposes of those
familiar threats to the fascist *mentalité* that historian Angelo Ventrone lists
as follows: 'deracination, the indeterminate, heterogeneity, confusion, bas-
tardization, and the complexes and afflictions that characterized bourgeois
modernity'.[45] In repudiation of this etiolated modernity, Pound celebrates
'vigour', strength, energy, vitality, the *virtú* that confirms Mussolini's place
alongside Sigismundo as a 'man of order'.

'Order', however, was by now a multivalent word in the Poundian
lexicon, and as it became more closely bound up with the paradigm of
Italian fascism, so it began to express a particular and *essential* kind of bravado. What, in the case of Sigismundo, had amounted to one man's stand
against 'the current of power' was now to be regarded as an heroic national
resistance to the foreign money-powers. Insofar as defiance was to become
the Italian posture, so bravado would define the tone of a 'sacralized' politics, its idiom of 'faith' and 'courage' coupled with the trademark response
to those 'outside': *me ne frego*, 'I don't give a damn.'[46] Nowhere, perhaps,
was this more fully articulated than in '[t]he fascist ritual of martyrdom,
in which martyrs' names were called and those present were to respond
'Presente!' to the names of dead'.[47] In the Exhibition's so-called Chapel of
Martyrs a 'metal cross stood on a "blood red" pedestal. As if in response
to the inscription on the cross, the walls repeated the word *presente*, referring to the living memory of the fallen. The fascist anthem "Giovanezza"
was quietly played in the room as a disembodied chorus of the dead.'[48]
This, in a sense, provides a key to Pound's Italian Canto LXXII, where
Marinetti utters a strong 'Presente!', thereby affirming that he lives after
death and giving that word, for the believer, a seemingly performative status.[49] Here bravado characteristically draws strength from its statement of
the impossible.

We realise now how inadequate was Hugh Kenner's view that the
absence of LXXII and LXXII from the collected *Cantos* registered simply 'a fault line, record of shifting masses,'[50] for the belligerent tone
so prominent here would linger on into the Pisan sequence, coloring
an apparent lyric stoicism with a peculiar bravado. In Canto LXXII,
Marinetti yearns

> ...to be reborn & thus become a panther
> & so know the second birth, & die a second time
> Not old in bed,

but die to sound of trumpets
& come to Paradise. (LXXII/432)

As Robert Casillo explains in his detailed account of the two Italian
Cantos, the buoyancy of mood here 'coincided with the resurgence of fascist hopes during the winter of 1944, when the Allies bogged down in the
Battle of the Appenines'.[51] The 'second birth' for which Marinetti pleads is
thus associated with this 'resurgence' and with hopes for the Repubblica
Sociale Italiana, the puppet-state in which Hitler had reinstalled Mussolini
as nominal dictator in September of the previous year. Canto LXXII
is full of exhortations, to 'drive out the foreigners' (*marocchini ed altra
immondizia*[52]) and, in Marinetti's words, to 'Go on! Go on!' (434). The
primary motif here is that of 'return': 'we will return', declares Marinetti
after Italy's defeat at El Alamein in 1942; 'I believe you,' Pound cries, and
the Canto ends by demanding that the reader 'Listen to me before I turn
back into the night / Where the skull sings; / The regiments and the ban-
ners will return' (437). This may be a blind expression of fascist 'faith', but
it is also bound up with a deliberately 'tough' assertion that ends justify
means, with the usurers depicted as 'groaning to you that Faranacci [sic]
/ Has rough hands, because he has seen thru the swindle' (435). Roberto
Farinacci, one of the most brutal of the early fascists and an ardent anti-
Semite, is honoured for his perception of the bankers' 'swindle' and for
losing one of his 'rough' hands in combat.

This embrace of violence carries over into Canto LXXIII, where Pound
uses Cavalcanti's stepped-down lines to recount the story of an heroic
'country girl' who led a group of Canadian soldiers to their death in a
mine-field. In her sacrifice we are meant to read the promise of a new
beginning:

> What a beautiful winter!
> In the north the fatherland is reborn.
> What a girl!
> what girls,
> what boys,
> wear the black![53]

As Casillo observes, Canto LXXII is 'much more straightforward [than
its predecessor] and often close to propaganda', although it is here that
Pound's attempt to identify Cavalcanti's formal bravura with the rhetoric
of fascist bravado comes decisively unstuck. Pound's 'Gloria della patria!'
jars grotesquely with the verbal precisions of Guido's Canzone, compelling
us to remark that Italy can never in any real sense be Pound's 'homeland'
and that his heroic rhetoric is clumsily out of joint with the time.

The disastrous failure of political 'vision' in the Italian Cantos would nonetheless be recruited as a kind of strength in the Pisan suite to come. The ideogram Hsin doesn't actually appear there (it is first inscribed in Canto XXXIV/171 and echoed much later in Canto LXXXVI/584) but its meaning begins now to underpin the writing at every point: 'Fidelity to the given word. The man here standing by his word.'[54] The ideogram stands for 'truth' and 'sincerity', with man seen pictographically in the Chinese character standing next to his 'word'. But in the context of the later Cantos, this graphic sign expresses less the truth of the word itself than the resoluteness with which a man may 'stand by' it. So, marooned in the debris of an 'Italia tradita' (LXXIV/450),[55] 'betrayed' on all fronts, by Marshall Badoglio and the returning King, by the external money-powers and by the persistent forces of disorder within the regime ('Jactancy, vanity, peculation to the ruin of 20 years' labour' (LXXVII/490), 'poison, veleno / in all the veins of the commonweal' [LXXIV/457]), Pound, facing a dangerously uncertain future in the death-cells at Pisa, will yet 'surrender neither the empire nor the temples' (LXXIV/454); he will continue 'to dream the Republic' (LXXVIII/498) precisely 'quia impossibile est' (LXXIV/462), 'because it is impossible'.

Incarcerated at Pisa, Pound seems to draw strength from his own intransigent commitment to the failed regime, and the reader may still be surprised by the directness with which (the Base Censor notwithstanding[56]) Pound manages to memorialise 'poor old Benito' (LXXX/515) and his achievements ('Put down the [Ethiopian] slave trade, made the desert to yield / and menaced the loan swine' [LXXVIII/499]). All this, however, is as little when compared to the opening lines of Canto LXXIV, added belatedly to the sequence, as Ronald Bush has shown.[57] No reader could have missed the elegiac quality of this lament for 'Ben and la Clara a Milano / by the heels at Milano' (LXXIV/445), and for Pound to have written this in the cage at Pisa bespeaks a singular bravado indeed. At the same time, however, he was, arguably, beginning to realise that the effect of not speaking directly could be equally powerful. In Canto LXXII, he had been able to list as a roll of honour the names of leading Fascist generals ('There are a lot of them', 435). At the end of The Pisan Cantos, however, the celebration of 'men full of humanitas (manhood)' (LXXXIV/559) gives only first names, thus partially eclipsing the identities of those honoured (all had been recently executed, a fact that may have made even Pound hesitate to name them directly).[58]

In the closing movements of The Cantos, this curious combination of bravado and reticence would be much in evidence. In Section: Rock-Drill

(1955) and *Thrones* (1959), Pound would continue to refer to the 'dream' of fascism and to remember Mussolini 'Dead in the Piazzale Loreto' (LXXXV/579). He would write, too, that 'It may depend on *one man*' (LXXXVI/583; my emphasis), a designation traditionally applied to Chinese emperors but here, of course, obliquely recalling the authority of Il Duce.[59] The specter of 'fascist man' flickers on through these pages, with frequent references to courage and tenacity ('men even in my time', XCV/664), but the 'bravery' celebrated here is less a quality of verbal artifice than of a language compelled to struggle against its own self-censorship even as it cleaves to the more familiar Poundian values of clarity and directness.[60] It is almost painful to observe Pound wrestling with a rebarbative idiom that will, quite definitely, *not* 'Get the meaning across and then quit' (LXXXVIII/595), as he takes the principle of 'discourse' from the Confucian *Analects*.[61] Indeed, surveying the 'historic black-out' (LXXXIX/615), Pound goes on to quote Lenin to illustrate his own predicament: 'Aesopian language (under censorship) / where I wrote "Japan" you may read "Russia"' (C/733).

Pound's internalisation of censorship after Pisa leads to a habit of deferral in the writing, to a holding back of grammatical elements that would make a statement immediately intelligible. To give a relatively trivial example – but one that recalls many others, almost as a signature: '"L'adoravano" said the sacristan, Bari / "come Santa Lucia" / So it, a stone cupid, had to be stored in the sacristy' (CV/767). If we are seeking traces of bravura in these late Cantos, then, we may now be expected to find them in those passages where the 'display of daring or defiance' resides in the partial saying of what should not be said and in the teasing presentation of what are regarded as 'dangerous' materials. But this is, of course, not really bravura at all but rather its trickier twin, bravado. In these late Cantos, readers will react with increasing suspicion to Pound's ellipses and omissions, especially when they recall that at St Elizabeth's he was writing partly for that small but dedicated group his daughter Mary called witheringly the 'disciples', the band of racist followers who visited the poet regularly at the hospital and catered to – indeed inflamed – his anti-Semitism and conservatism.[62] There were, then, some readers skilled in the arts of Pound's obscurantism; they, he knew, would quickly fill in the missing text and they, he also knew, would understand the 'tactical' reasons for such omissions.[63] Bravado might seem to press for full disclosure but ultimately, given the force of the 'historic black-out', it must content itself with dark insinuation. At the same time, however, Pound, with his customary pedagogical ambition, could never be completely satisfied with his restricted audience at St Elizabeth's. So we find that in Canto CVII/782 he cannot resist openly associating the Jews with cultural decline: 'Flaccus' translator wore the crown / The jew and the buggar dragged it down.' The reference to the 'jew' here may be specifically to Queen Elizabeth's doctor Rodrigo Lopez (often thought to be the model for Shakepeare's Shylock), just as the 'buggar' may allude, as it has previously, to James I, but as Massimo Bacigalupo notes, these terms also have a generic force, the particular reference thus partly occluding or tempering the more shockingly general one.[64]

The sense we may have here of conspiratorial powers at work, which compel the text toward a kind of self-censorship, is confirmed by some related lines from Canto CVIII, where a highly fragmented passage records Edward I's banning of usury:

> Was 15 000 three score.
>   Divers had banished
> But the usuries, no King before him.
>   Holl fol 285
>   Wals hypod
>   Florilegius Dunstable
> Angliae exeuntibus,
>   And Uncle Carlo
>   And, from Taufers, Margherita. (CVIII/779)

Critic David Gordon, anxious about charges of anti-Semitism, writes: 'As Coke points out many had decisively banished the Jews and discriminated against them racially, but Edward I saw the injustice of this and merely made a law against usury.'[65] Carrol F. Terrell's *Companion to The Cantos* follows Gordon's gloss, noting that Edward 'guaranteed safe-conduct to Jews if they wanted to leave the country'.[66] But look more closely at Pound's lines: 'was 15 000 three score'. The reference is to the number of Jews who left England at this time and this is followed by some significant omissions which Bacigalupo restores: 'Divers [kings] had banished [the jews, and yet they returned] but the[ir] usuries, no King before him.'[67] Unlike Gordon, then, Pound himself acknowledges that the Jews were not bidding a voluntary farewell to England but that they had been *banished* (they would not formally return until 1655). This is, after all, the whole point of the reference and Gordon has to work hard to conceal it. Edward's ruling, enlightened in Pound's eyes for its prohibition of usury, is known, in fact, as 'The Edict of Expulsion' of 1290. Pound was certainly aware that the Jews were removed from England under threat of execution for non-compliance, although he

deliberately buried this knowledge in the bland phrase 'Angliae exeunti-
bus', 'to these leaving England'.

And if all this did not uncomfortably recall more recent political
excesses, Pound proceeds for good measure to name a hero of Italian fascism, 'Uncle Carlo'. The nickname conceals Carlo Delcroix, the fascist
deputy who had been blinded and mutilated in the First World War and
who was subsequently acclaimed for his work with the Association of War
Wounded and Invalids.[68] *Time* magazine in December 1924 had described
Delcroix as 'Italy's living symbol of the war and all the horrors and glories
it represented', comparing him with Mussolini and D'Annunzio, and in
these late Cantos, Delcroix does indeed become a sort of paradigmatic
hero, his mutilation evoking both the disfiguring of the fascist dream
and the personal agony that now begins to grip the poem (allusions to
Herakles's death in the poisoned robe abound after Pound's translation of
Sophocles' *Trachiniae*). At the same time, however, personal pain is coun-
terbalanced by the pleasure Pound seems to take in punishments meted out
for monetary crimes. In his redaction of the *Eparch's Book*, for example, we
are told repeatedly that offenders were to be 'shaved whipped and chucked
out' (XCVI/685), 'flogged, shaved and exiled' (XCVI/687) and that such
crimes 'shall cost 'em a hand' (XCVI/687), and these instances of brutal
'justice' now express the impotent anger that colours much of *Thrones*. Yet
curiously there is a kind of pathos in this empty vindictiveness. Pound will
continue to assert the claims of the phallus ('man's phallic heart is from
heaven / a clear spring of rightness' [XCIX/717]), but the sense of 'measure' with which it has been associated is now inflected by a painful sense
of debility and personal finitude.

'Shall audacity last into fortitude?' he asks in Canto XCIII/652, hoping
that there is some point of stability beyond the courageous and soldierly
push that 'Risked the smoke to go forward' (LXXXV/579). If there is, it
will be once more a matter of man standing by his word, and we now see
the profound circularity attaching to Pound's figuring of masculinity as the
poem's fundamental ground: for a man who does not stand by his word is
simply not a man and must be called something else, hence the taunting
and name-calling that frequently disfigure these late Cantos ('that slob-
bering buggar Jim First / bitched our heritage,' 'Noll cut down Charlie',
etc.).[69] The bravado in such passages reveals, as ever, an impotence masked
by aggression; this is a violence that in fact recoils upon the writer, exposing his rhetorical excesses as signs of merely personal frustration.

In the final sequence of *The Cantos*, however, the inchoate *Drafts and
Fragments*, the old hand would recover its cunning, but only by dispensing

with the willful fantasies of a 'second birth' and by accepting instead the imminent realities of 'a tomb, an end' (800). The sequence begins with these lines in which bravura is brilliantly reaffirmed:

> Thy quiet house
> The crozier's curve runs in the wall,
> The harl, feather-white, as a dolphin on sea-brink
>
> I am all for Verkehr without tyranny
>   —wave exultant
>   in caracole
> Hast'ou seen boat's wake on sea-wall
>   how crests it?
> What panache?
>   paw-flap, wave-tap,
>   that is gaiety,
> Toba Soja,
>   toward limpidity,
>   that is exultance,
>   here the crest runs on wall
> che paion' si al vent'
>   ²Hăr-²la-¹llü ³k'ö
>   of the wind sway... (CX/797)

The lines open with a complex sense of immemorial time. The Madonna's 'house', the Basilica of Torcello, is 'quiet', but carries the mark, or 'curve', of the Bishop's staff. This image is then connected with the Middle English word 'harl', meaning fibers, filaments, the crest of a bird, perhaps – an association Pound develops in 'feather-white'. This in turn is like foam on a wave, leading us sinuously to the dolphin, a classical symbol of immortality, here glimpsed on 'sea-brink'. Or on 'wave exultant': like the reference in an earlier Canto ('Circa 1941') to the black cat with its tail 'exalted' (820), Pound's phrase exploits etymology to catch the sense of both literal elevation and joy. Then we have 'caracole', an unusual word with a range of meanings: 'shell', 'winding stair', but the most relevant is its technical meaning as a term from dressage, 'a horseman's half-turn to the left or right' (*OED*). This might seem a strange intrusion into the seascape of the Lagoon, but after another allusion to 'crest', in turn recalling the feathers of the 'harl', Pound pursues it further, giving us 'panache', another word with rich etymological associations: literally, the plume of a helmet, but also, metaphorically, style and arrogance. With 'paw-flap' and 'wave-tap', familiar rhythmic figures are echoed from the earliest Cantos, further connecting the water's movement with metamorphosis and the motion of animals. The salute to Toba Sojo, a Buddhist painter whose 'limpidity' of style Pound admires, both gives the network of allusions a specific cultural signature and connects the mood of jubilation with technical 'panache' (Ernest Fenollosa tells us that Toba Sojo's work 'was dashed off in almost pure line, but with a racy vigour and sweep of motion that make it live'[70]). The 'wind-sway' of the Na Khi rites of Western China rhymes here with Dante's story of Paolo and Francesca 'who seem so light upon the wind'. But the 'lightness' is also that of Pound's lines themselves, where this dazzling word-play meets the challenge of the light and motion of the Venetian Lagoon and finds there a way of speaking at once of gaiety and death. This was the true 'bravery', perhaps, epitomised in the beautiful 'exultance' of this late Canto where bravura's 'brilliance of execution' would finally lay to rest all temptations to bravado.

Notes

1 Hugh Kenner, *The Pound Era* (Berkeley and Los Angeles, 1971), p. 104.
2 See Pound, 'Psychology and Troubadours' (1912), in *the Spirit of Romance*, reprinted in *The Spirit of Romance* (New York: New Directions, 1968), pp. 87–100.
3 See Dante, *De Vulgari Eloquentia*, II.2, on 'the right direction of the will'. The phrase appears several times in *The Cantos*: see LXXVII/487, LXXXVII/592, 596. Pound uses it to define one of the key ideograms in the *Ta Hsio*; see *Confucius* (New York: New Directions, 1951), p. 22: 'the will, the direction of the will, *directio voluntatis*, the officer standing over the heart.'
4 Pound, 'Treatise on Metre,' in *ABC of Reading* (1934; London: Faber and Faber Ltd., 1961), p. 198. Cf. Pound, "This monument will outlast' / from Horace', in Richard Sieburth, ed., *Ezra Pound: Poems and Translations* (New York: Library of America, 2003), p. 1146: 'Impotent / The flow of the years to break it, however many.'
5 Pound, *Collected Shorter Poems* (London; Faber and Faber, 1962), p. 215.
6 Geoffrey Hill, 'Envoi (1919)', in *Collected Critical Writings*, ed. Kenneth Haynes (Oxford: Oxford University Press, 2008), p. 253.
7 Carey Wolfe, *The Limits of American Literary Identity in Pound and Emerson* (Cambridge: Cambridge University Press, 1993), p. 129. The epithet 'Palgravian' is Wolfe's.
8 Hill, 'Envoi (1919)', p. 259.
9 Waller, 'Goe lovely rose', quoted in full in Hill, *Collected Critical Writings*, p. 662.
10 Quoted from Abraham Fraunce, *The Arcadian Rhetoric* (1588), in Donald Lemen Clark, *Rhetoric and Poetry in the Renaissance* (New York: Columbia Press, 1922), p. 59. For a modern usage of the term in this sense, see Donald Davie, 'Notes on George Oppen's *Seascape: Needle's Eye*', in Burton Hatlen,

ed., *George Oppen: Man and Poet* (Orono, ME: National Poetry Foundation Inc., 1981), p. 411: 'This writing denies itself certain traditional braveries (rhyme, assonance, determinable auditory rhythm) precisely because they would testify in the poet to a bravery that we cannot afford.'

11 'Music. By William Atheling,' *New Age*, 26, 24 (15 April 1920), reprinted In R. Murray Schafer, ed., *Ezra Pound and Music: The Complete Criticism* (London: Faber & Faber, 1978), p. 225. Elsewhere Pound spoke in a letter to Eva Hesse of 'Luini: Raymonde Collignon, diseuse, very Luini, type not prevalent in Britain' (see Eva Hesse, 'Raymonde Collignon, or (Apropos *Paideuma*, 7–1 & 2, pp. 345– 346: The Duck That Got Away)', *Paideuma*, 10, 3 (Winter 1981): 584. See also Jo Brantley Berryman, '"Medallion": Pound's Poem,' *Paideuma*, 10, 3 (Winter 1973): 391–398, and my '"A Consciousness Disjunct": Sex and the Writer in Pound's *Hugh Selwyn Mauberley*,' *Journal of American Studies*, 28, 1 (1994): 61–75.

12 Pound, 'Condolence', *Collected Shorter Poems*, p. 92. For the full letter to Moore, see Ronald Bush, 'The Doggerel Section of Letter to Marianne Moore', in Bonnie Kime Scott, ed., *The Gender of Modernism: A Critical Anthology* (Bloomington and Indianapolis, 1990), pp. 362–365. Pound does note that 'the male // is a fixed point of stupidity', but also that 'the male // is more expansive / and demands other and varied contacts' (362). The same dialogue was played out in the fifties between Diane Di Prima and Gary Snyder whose 1957 poem 'Praise for Sick Women' ('The female is fertile, and discipline / (contra naturam) only confuses her') triggered Di Prima's 1958 'The Practice of Magical Evolution' ('easy to say / this: the female is ductile / and / (stroke after stroke) / built for masochistic / calm.'

13 Pound, 'Translator's Postscript' to Remy de Gourmont, *The Natural Philosophy of Love*, trans. Ezra Pound (1922; New York: Collier Books, 1976), p. 150. Compare the lines (also in Canto XXIX/144): '"Nel ventre tuo, o nella mente mia, / "Yes, Milady, precisely, if you wd. / have anything properly made."'

14 *The Complete Prose of Marianne Moore*, ed. and introd. Patricia C. Willis (New York: Viking, 1986), p. 272.

15 See my *Ezra Pound: Politics, Economics and Writing* (London: Macmillan, 1984), pp. 88–89.

16 See also Hill, 'Envoi (1919)', p. 246: 'The world's obtuseness, imperviousness, its active or passive hostility to valour and vision, is not only the object of his denunciation; it is also the necessary circumstance, the context in which and against which valour and vision define themselves: "In the gloom, the gold gathers the light against it."' Compare, for example, Pound on Wyndham Lewis's 'Timon' series: 'For me his designs are a creation on the same *motif*. That *motif* is the fury of intelligence baffled and shut in by circumjacent stupidity' (*Gaudier-Brzeska: A Memoir* [1916; Hessle: The Marvell Press, 1960], p. 93).

17 *The Odes of Horace*, trans. James Michie (Harmondsworth: Penguin Books, 1967), p. 216; Théophile Gautier, 'L'Art,' in Douglas Parmée, *Twelve French Poets, 1820–1900* (London: Longmans, 1957), p. 180.

18 *The Cantos of Ezra Pound* (New York: New Directions, 1996), VII/26, 27. Further references in this format will be given in the text.

19 Pound, *Guide to Kulchur* (1938; London: Peter Owen Ltd., 1966), p. 159 (his emphasis), 194.

20 See Lawrence S. Rainey, *Ezra Pound and the Monument of Culture: Text, History, and the Malatesta Cantos* (Chicago and London: University of Chicago Press, 1991), p. 184, on Pound's deliberate excision of lyric associations with the Tempio from earlier drafts (e.g., 'but here Rimini, the voice, the stone' and the Tempio as 'a song caught in the stone').

21 *The Selected Letters of Ezra Pound, 1907–1941*, ed. D. D. Paige (London: Faber and Faber, 1971), p. 210: 'The "magic moment" or moment of metamorphosis, bust thru from quotidian into "divine or permanent world." Gods, etc.'

22 Pound, 'Cavalcanti', *Literary Essays of Ezra Pound*, ed., T. S. Eliot (London: Faber and Faber Ltd., 1968), p. 151.

23 See my 'Ezra Pound's Lost Book: *Orientamenti*', *Modernist Cultures* (forthcoming, 2014).

24 See Miranda Hickman, *The Geometry of Modernism: The Vorticist Idiom in Lewis, Pound, H. D., and Yeats* (Austin: University of Texas Press, 2005), p. 95ff.

25 Pound, 'Vorticism' (1914), in *Gaudier-Brzeska*, p. 92; 'Vortex. Pound,' *Blast*, I (1914), p. 33.

26 The point is also made in Robert Casillo, 'Fascists of the Final Hour: Pound's Italian *Cantos*', in *Fascism, Aesthetics, and Culture*, ed., Richard J. Golsan (Hanover, NH and London: University Press of New England, 1992), pp. 103–104.

27 Letter to Louis Zukofsky, quoted in Charles Norman, *Ezra Pound: A Biography* (rev. ed., London: Macdonald, 1969), pp. 309–310.

28 See Hickman, *The Geometry*, p. 104: '[I]n 1932 they were corresponding; Pound traveled to see Marinetti in Roma; and a card from Marinetti to Pound from that year indicates Marinetti's intention to return the visit.'

29 Humphrey Carpenter, *A Serious Character: The Life of Ezra Pound* (London and Boston: Faber and Faber, 1988), p. 489.

30 Marla Stone, 'Staging Fascism: The Exhibition of the Fascist Revolution', *Journal of Contemporary History*, 28, 2 (April 1993): 228: 'With its visible patronage of modernism, the Mussolini dictatorship became one of the first national governments to offer official sanction, commissions and space to avant-garde artists and architects.' Stone also observes, however, that 'Given the compromise over control, modernism lost the critical edge it had developed as an international movement and became a container for the regime's varied and contradictory messages.' See also Emily Braun, *Mario Sironi and Italian Modernism* (Cambridge: Cambridge University Press, 2000), p. 2. Braun (155) describes the Exhibition as 'an evanescent moment of equilibrium between the internationalism of modernism and the nationalism of Fascist ideology'.

31 Marla Stone, 'Staging Fascism,' p. 225.

32 The so-called Middle Cantos are remarkably restrained in their reference to Italian politics, with only occasional and highly abbreviated mention made of, for example, a speech about German-Italian unity by Rudolf Hess (LI/251),

the economic sanctions placed on Italy (LII /257), and a German submarine manoeuvre (LIV/279–80).

33 'Ave Roma', *Il Mare* (1933), translated in Hickman, *The Geometry*, p. 280 n.57.

34 So Margherita Sarfatti, biographer and lover of Mussolini, wrote in the year of the Exhibition's opening that 'For the first time in the modern period, a fact of contemporary history is embodied in the fervent atmosphere of religious attraction and ritual' (quoted in Braun, *Mario Sironi*, p. 147).

35 P. M. Bardi, 'Esposizioni', *Il Mare*, 12 (January 1933), reprinted in *Il Mare Supplemento Letterario* (Commune di Rapallo: Rapallo, 1999), p. 236.

36 See Donald Gallup, *Ezra Pound: A Bibliography* (rev. ed., Charlottesville: University Press of Virginia, 1983), p. 156.

37 See Carpenter, *A Serious Character*, pp. 489–490; Hickman, *The Geometry*, p. 101.

38 Bottai, quoted in Braun, *Mario Sironi*, p. 267.

39 Pound, *Selected Letters*, p. 239.

40 Roger Griffin, *Modernism and Fascism: The Sense of a Beginning under Mussolini and Hitler* (London: Palgrave Macmillan, 2007), p. 6; William Adamson, 'Modernism and Fascism: The politics of Culture in Italy, 1903–1922', *The American Historical Review*, 95. 2 (April 1990): 360, 390. See also Emilio Gentile, *The Sacralization of Politics in Fascist Italy*, trans. Keith Botsford (Cambridge, MA: Harvard University Press, 1996); Claudio Fogu, *The Historic Imaginary: Politics of History in Fascist Italy* (Toronto, Buffalo, London: University of Toronto Press, 2003).

41 Emilio Gentile, 'The Conquest of Modernity: From Modern Nationalism to Fascism', *Modernism/Modernity*, 1, 3 (September 1994): 58.

42 Ibid., p. 56.

43 Griffin, *Modernism and Fascism*, p. 175.

44 Pound, 'European Paideuma' (1939), ed., Massimo Bacigalupo, in William Pratt, ed., *Ezra Pound: Nature and Myth* (New York: AMS Press, 2002), p. 11.

45 Quoted in Griffin, *Modernism and Fascism*, p. 221.

46 See Jeffrey T. Schnapp, 'Epic Demonstrations: Fascist Modernity and the 1932 Exhibition of the Fascist Revolution', in Richard J. Golsan, ed., *Fascism, Aesthetics, and Culture* (Hanover, NH and London: University Press of New England, 1992), p. 32.

47 Barbara Spackman, *Fascist Virilities: Rhetoric, Identity, and Social Fantasy in Italy* (Minneapolis: University of Minnesota Press, 1996), p. 127.

48 Marla Stone, 'Staging Fascism', p. 226

49 See Ronald Bush, 'Modernism, Fascism, and the Composition of Ezra Pound's *Pisan Cantos*', *Modernism/Modernity*, 2. 3 (1995): 73; Robert Casillo, 'Fascists of the Final Hour,' p. 102. That moment is recalled in Canto LXXVIII/499: 'those words still stand uncancelled, / "Presente!".'

50 Kenner, *The Pound Era*, p. 469. Kenner is also wrong in assuming that the two Cantos were 'never published' – see Gallup, *Ezra Pound*, C1697b and C1699a.

51 Casillo, 'Fascists of the Final Hour', p. 99.

52 Casillo (ibid., p. 123) translates: 'Moroccans and other garbage.' Interestingly, Pound omits this line from his own translation (LXXII/434).

53 Casillo, ibid., p. 127. The reference to the fatherland reborn in the north is of course to the short-lived Salò Republic. For an account of the story of 'L'Eroina di Rimini' and its contemporary impact, see Antonio Pantano, *Ezra Pound e la Repubblica Sociale Italiana* (I Libri del Borghese: Roma, 2011), pp. 92–93. Pantano is able to give an especially spirited account of Pound's fascist investments because he fully shares them.

54 See Pound, *Confucius* (New York: New Directions, 1969), p. 22. *Mathews' Chinese-English Dictionary* (Cambridge, MA: Harvard University Press, 1960), M2748 gives 'To believe in; to trust. Truth, sincerity, confidence. A pledge or token.'

55 Interestingly, in his own translation of Canto LXXII, Pound renders 'Dopo il tradimento' as 'In the time of the collapse'. Elsewhere, he moves between the two meanings, talking either of 'the great betrayal' or 'the crash' – see *'I Cease Not to Yowl': Ezra Pound's Letters to Olivia Rossetti Agresti*, ed. Demetres P. Tryphonopoulos and Leon Surette (Urbana and Chicago: University of Illinois Press, 1998), pp. 80, 104.

56 Pound's response to queries from the Base Censor about whether he was writing in 'code' is reproduced in *Ezra and Dorothy Pound: Letters in Captivity, 1945–1946* (New York: Oxford University Press, 1999), p. 177.

57 Ronald Bush, '"Quiet, Not Scornful"? The Composition of *The Pisan Cantos*', in Lawrence Rainey, ed., *A Poem Containing History: Textual Studies in* The Cantos (Ann Arbor: University of Michigan Press, 1997), pp. 199–206.

58 In Canto LXXXIV/559, Pound names Alessandro [Pavolini], Party secretary of the Salò Republic, Fernando [Mezzasoma], Minister of Popular Culture for Salò, Pierre [Laval], premier of the Vichy government, Vidkun [Quisling], the Norwegian collaborator, and [Pierre] Henriot, radio broadcaster for Vichy.

59 See my *Ezra Pound*, p. 253 n.40.

60 As for example in the very last pages of the poem: '"A pity that poets have used symbol and metaphor / and no man learned anything from them / for their speaking in figures"' ('Addendum for C'/819).

61 Pound, *Confucius*, p. 269.

62 Mary de Rachewiltz, *Discretions: A Memoir by Ezra Pound's Daughter* (London: Faber & Faber, 1971), p. 295. De Rachewiltz notes that these 'disciples' would tease Pound's visitors from the Catholic University 'about their political and racial non-commitment'.

63 See, for example, Canto XCI/635: 'They who are skilled in fire / shall read [ideogram] tan, the dawn.'

64 Massimo Bacigalupo, *The Forméd Trace: The Later Poetry of Ezra Pound* (New York: Columbia University Press, 1980), p. 451. Compare Judith Butler, *Excitable Speech: A Politics of the Performative* (New York and London: Routledge, 1997), p. 29: 'Whether the name is shared by others, the name, as a convention, has a generality and a historicity that is in no sense radically

singular, even though it is understood to exercise the power of conferring singularity.'

65 David Gordon, 'Edward Coke: The Azalia is Grown,' *Paideuma*, 4, 2 & 3 (Fall and Winter 1975): 280. Gordon also argues, implausibly, that 'Pound had been outspoken in not associating usury with the Jewish people in his writings at least since 1935.'

66 Carroll F. Terrell, *A Companion to The Cantos of Ezra Pound* (Berkeley, Los Angeles and London: University of California Press, p. 706.

67 Bacigalupo, *The Forméd Trace*, p. 451.

68 Delcroix and Pound were well acquainted, and Pound sought him out in 1959 after his return to Italy (see Giano Acame, *Carlo Delcroix* [conference publication for Il Circolo di Cultura ed Educazione Politica REX, 1988]. Delcroix has already been named and quoted six times in *The Cantos* before he appears in Canto CVIII. See LXXXVIII/601, XCII/640, 641, XCV/663, XCVII/698, CI/746.

69 See also the discussion of the Confucian practice known as the 'rectification of names' in my *Ezra Pound*, p. 173.

70 Ernest Fenollosa, *Epochs of Chinese and Japanese Art* (1912; Berkeley, CA: Stone Bridge Press, 2007), 239. See Massimo Bacigalupo, *The Forméd Trace*, 464 for an alternative source.

Index